DEATH OF A
TEN POUND POM

by

MARY BAKER

A CIP catalogue record of this book
can be obtained from the British Library

Published in Great Britain by
Cam Publications

Cover Design by Anthony Thompson

To

Adventurers and Argonauts

Also by Mary Baker

Light Airs

Seventh Child

The Dummy Run

A Purposed Overthrow

The Live Ringer

The Purpose of Playing

Dentist Imperial

General Revenge

On a misty winter's morning in central London, only one person walking along Portland Place seemed to notice the day's golden potential, and as the crowd trudged its way to work, Veronica Thornthwaite longed to tell everybody where she was headed and why. Then, heart thudding with anticipation, she stood outside the BBC's Broadcasting House, an edifice that resembled a white ship's prow rising above the rotund darkness of All Souls Church, and ships always meant adventure.

In her mid-thirties, brown-haired and plain, unnoticed by anyone, yet feeling rather like the celebrity she knew that she would never be, Veronica Thornthwaite was ready for success. She had travelled across the world twice, but that drizzly and cold London morning seemed to be part of an even more exciting journey.

"Don't get too carried away, Vron. You're just the kid from a Nissen hut," she reminded herself.

****

Lieutenant-Colonel Peter Nissen DSO of the Royal Engineers was the man to blame, but as he had already taken his leave from earthly existence, the only hope of revenge was an afterlife in which he might be condemned to an eternity of hellish heat trapped inside one of his own huts.

"I thought that I'd left Nissen and his fiendish invention behind me forever when I got demobbed from the RAF," said Jeff. "I was given the impression that Australia would mean a whole new life, full of opportunities to throw boomerangs and wear a hat with corks dangling from its brim."

Thirty miles south of Melbourne, Victoria's Watson Valley Migrant Hostel made more Englishmen than Jeffrey Thornthwaite recall their days in uniform, when they had marked time during World War Two or National Service. In British military camps, the rows of tunnel-shaped Nissen huts had acted as ice-boxes, but in Australia those arcs of corrugated iron absorbed every ray of sun and turned six partitioned rooms into six stifling ovens. It was the early 1960s, and the Thornthwaite family had never heard of saunas, but they were living inside one. Daughter Veronica, plain and gawky despite owing a couple of her names to movie stars Veronica Lake and Olivia de Havilland, was young enough at ten years old to accept whatever happened as normal life, but parents Jeff and Elaine had thought more about escaping from their bleak London home in Acton, an area of high unemployment and low expectation, than how they would start the new life in a country that both blithely assumed would be the nearest they could get to living in a Hollywood film of prosperity and glamour, where hard work instantly bought them luxuries while the sun shone. And how that sun could shine: unbelievably, miraculously, continually.

The Migrant Hostel was a lively and youthful world, full of adventurous young families prepared to gamble on helping dreams become reality. They were the Ten Pound Poms, transported across the globe on ocean liners, a whole month of ease and leisure spent visiting exotic ports, fed the sort of food that they would have been unable to afford in Britain, cared for by attentive crews, at liberty to lounge on deck by day and dance through the evening, all for the cost of ten pounds per migrant

6

(children free) courtesy of the Australian Government and its scheme to bring workers to a country short of labour. The wonderful voyage had been the first time that the Thornthwaites felt like the idle rich, and it would also be the last.

Brown-haired, stocky, plain, opinionatedly overconfident Jeff saw himself as the head of the family, a benevolent dictator prepared to explain decisions already taken, and he even imagined that Jeffrey Leonard Thornthwaite had been the one who decided they would emigrate to the other side of the world and chance their luck, while the real culprit was his wife with her mentor Hollywood as co-conspirator.

Pretty, slim, dark-haired Elaine had once trailed in the wake of her mother and grandmother, following the conventional pattern of their cautious lives unquestioningly, which meant as fleeting a stay in school as possible, dead-end job until the husband appeared, and then domesticity in a backstreet terrace. Elaine easily attracted the husband, moved into the house, and gave birth to the compulsory child, before realizing that she had reached another dead-end. The remainder of her days were going to be an identical twin of the one she was living through without hope of wealth or adventure, and Elaine felt cheated, even though nobody had promised that her fate would be any different from her mother's. Elaine had been taught by example to choose the safest option, which meant snaring a reliable man able to support a family, and to a seventeen-year-old shop assistant, factory-worker Jeffrey Thornthwaite had seemed positively rich. He was ten years her senior, and generously willing to spend; however, presents and outings became unaffordable after marriage, the provider's money gobbled up by rent, food and then the expense

7

of a rapidly-growing child. Scrimping along on Jeff's low wages while she cooked and cleaned became a trap that Elaine had to escape, and movies showed visions of elegant clothes, hotels, mansions, flower-filled gardens, and cars bigger than the kitchen that imprisoned her. In the cinema, Elaine could visit a world where gorgeous stars pretended to be everyday people who chanced to possess the wardrobe of fashion models and had adventures on the way to their happy ending, after which Elaine would go out to the darkness of a cold night, knowing that if life were allowed to drift on monotonously, she would never have an adventure and never get anything more than she already had. California was unattainably out of reach, but Australia wanted British families, white British families with white British children. Australia wanted her, the price a mere ten pounds, and the only condition was that each migrant stayed for two years. Elaine filled out a newspaper coupon, and then strategically placed emigration brochures and booklets around the house for Jeff to find when he was particularly frustrated with the boredom of his job, and he often felt bored because Jeffrey Thornthwaite was no ordinary factory hand; Jeffrey Thornthwaite read books.

"The foreman's a half-wit, an idiot. I know exactly how our section could be run with a quarter of the effort, but he just said that if I didn't want to do a proper day's work, plenty of others did. For two pins, I'd tell him where he can stick his job. I've had enough."

"Look what came in the post," said Elaine, so ingenuously innocent that Jeff should have been suspicious.

Sunlit beaches, sparkling sea, wide desert skies, mountain gullies, sophisticated cities, prosperous suburbs, kangaroos, koalas, kookaburras, and not a foreman in sight. The brochures did their work, and Jeff never did think to ask why Australia House should have targeted the Thornthwaite family.

A medical and an interview came next, to make sure that no weakling or non-white managed to slip into the trawling-net, and good health and fair skin were rewarded with several short films of the new Technicolor life available to the chosen. Australians resided in spacious bungalows with vast gardens, spent their time at the beach smiling at blue sea, or in the bush smiling at gum trees, or on hilltops smiling at nothing in particular. Australians smiled in cities and Australians smiled in the outback. The message was clear; Australia smiled.

Then the Thornthwaites were smiling as well, smiling on board an ocean liner, the old life a fading memory, the new one making a magnificent start. Nobody asked Veronica's opinion of the decision to emigrate, and she had not wanted to leave her home or her schoolfriends, but the world beyond Acton turned out to be an astounding place, full of excitement and surprises. Now that she realized what could be on offer, Veronica felt that she had woken up properly after being half-asleep for ten years, and her parents were different people too. The photographs taken during the voyage were black and white, but Veronica would always remember them in colour. Elbows on deck rail, Jeff posed in blue shirt and grey trousers, brown hair ruffled by the sea breeze, while Elaine bit her lower lip as she tried to select an ideal instant to press the camera switch. Dark curls bobbing under the wide-brimmed straw hat that suited her better than any other she ever wore, Elaine looked her best in a pink frock, and Veronica was proud to have so pretty a mother, although it never occurred

9

to a child that an adult might appreciate hearing the compliment spoken out loud. It felt like being awarded a school merit badge when she was recognized as Elaine's daughter, and more than made up for Veronica's own lack of prettiness. She knew that Elaine was baffled to have produced a plain offspring, and that the only consolation was long fair hair, which condemned Veronica to hours spent having its length untangled, but Elaine's approval of Nordic plaits was ample reward for the tedium.

"Now I know what I want from life," Jeff announced.

"You want to travel?" asked Elaine.

"I want to be rich."

They were rich, and very lucky, but had no idea of it, because Jeff and Elaine compared their lives to those of film stars rather than the beggars who clustered around them in Port Said and Aden. The Thornthwaites also took health and each other for granted as well, not realizing that they were living through the best time they would have together. Being human, they wanted even more.

"Anyway, we'd better make the most of this before we're atomized to extinction."

White liner between blue sky and blue sea, yet Jeff had to spoil everything. He probably assumed that Veronica was too young to understand, but she knew precisely what his words meant. They meant that the United States and Russia cared nothing for Veronica Olivia Thornthwaite, and the world was about to explode around her. Frowning grown-ups would gather by the notice-board outside the purser's office each morning to read the latest details in the ship's newsletter of the Cuba missile crisis, but once they were reassured that nuclear bombs had not been detonated overnight, the adults attempted to shrug off the thought of annihilation, and devoted themselves to deck tennis and quizzes instead because there was nothing that they could do to avert fate. The nearness of World War Three was taken for granted by everybody, and Veronica went cold at each reminder. Back in England, her morbidly-superstitious grandmother might have said that someone was walking over Veronica's grave, only there would be no graves; there would be nothing.

Veronica had once believed that she knew exactly what to do when the nuclear bomb exploded. All the pupils in her Acton school had been instructed to turn their backs to the blast in case the flash hurt their eyes, but it appeared that the survival strategy of cold-shouldering the bomb might not work as well as expected because Jeff had laughed heartily when Veronica repeated the information to him. She knew he reckoned that, if they outlived the latest emergency, the earth was still not going to get past 1970, so they had at most six or seven years before the inevitable nuclear destruction, and although Veronica regarded anybody over the age of fifteen as a fully-fledged adult confidently able to tackle any situation, she was terrified by the coming war, despite rivalling Methuselah on the day when Jeff's timetable ran out. It was unfair, it was wrong, it was cruel, but it was going to happen. Sooner or later, it was going to happen.

"Every hour gets us nearer Melbourne," Jeff reminded Elaine. They both thought that Veronica had moved out of earshot as she retreated along the deck, but they were wrong. "Australia's the safest place in the world to be, when those atoms start splitting, and Melbourne's in the safest part of Australia. Nowhere on earth will be further away from the fall-out. It's a scientific fact."

Australia not only represented a golden land of promise, it seemed that Australia also meant the chance of Veronica Olivia Thornthwaite's life continuing after mankind had destroyed most of the planet. Australia was her only possible future.

****

The migrants were sorted into hostel groups after they disembarked at Port Melbourne, and began their new lives in a new country surrounded by hand-luggage in a large room with dozens of strangers who were not really strangers because all the families smiled, recognizing themselves in the other adventurers, as they waited for buses that would offer the first sight of Victoria beyond its docks.

Tall buildings in wide streets, trundling trams, big cars, and then willow trees beside dusty roads, townships with detached one-storey houses encircled by gardens of gum trees and wattle, yellowing paddocks and space, so much space and light and warmth.

"Oh look! There's an army camp," said Elaine, seeing rows of Nissen huts as the bus rounded a corner after passing some shops and a railway station. "All those children! There are hundreds of them. Australian soldiers must have enormous families."

Then their bus was driven into the army camp, came to a stop among the huts, and the Thornthwaites realized that they had arrived at Watson Valley Migrant Hostel, where they were greeted like relatives full of the latest family news. The people living there had come across the world by boat, with more than a month's travel between them and home, making the decision to emigrate

12

feel irrevocable. The only telephone on the hostel was in the manager's office, and attempting an international call from the phone box by the station was unthinkable because of the expense. Aerogramme letters took more than a week to reach their destination, and Britain became the far distant land that Australia had once been.

"Oh well, at least we won't feel so bad about being wiped out if either Kennedy or Khrushchev decides to press the nuclear button tonight," remarked Jeff, after surveying the Thornthwaite family's new domain, two rooms inside a six-room Nissen hut: plastic-covered sofa that flattened into a double bed beside a large chest-of-drawers for parents in one room, single bed and small chest-of-drawers for child in the other.

The glossy brochures had fleetingly mentioned temporary accommodation provided for migrants on arrival in Australia, the details of that accommodation sensibly left vague, and Elaine had pictured a modern block of flats, but their two rooms were a flat that simply chanced to be inside a Nissen hut, and temporary still meant temporary. "Remember what the man in Australia House told us? They're so short of workers out here that anyone can get a job in no time at all, and the wages are incredible. We'll soon earn enough money to move into a house."

"Assuming that we don't find ourselves obliterated by morning."

Jeff was still convinced that Veronica remained unaware of humanity's imminent extinction, but she heard his words, knew their meaning, and was shivery with fear.

****

13

Clive Leyton had no need to panic about whatever fate lurked ahead for mankind because he was in direct contact with God, and God had told him to go to Australia.

"You mean that you got the idea to emigrate while you were in church?" asked Elaine.

"No, it wasn't my idea. God spoke to me, and said that I had to go to Australia." Clive Leyton was small and thin, but he still managed to look pompously dogmatic, as became a recipient of the Almighty's personal attention. Ex-Pay Corps, dark hair slicked back with oil, narrow-eyed and tight-lipped, forty-year-old Clive was the insurance assessor who suspected everybody of fraud or the office clerk who believed that his private supply of biscuits had been raided by nefarious co-workers, and the thought of a deity selecting Clive Leyton to receive special instructions made Jeff Thornthwaite laugh.

"I didn't know that God helped out at Australia House, recruiting migrants."

Clive sighed at the flippancy, and Veronica hoped that God was not listening. Mrs Staunton, the omniscient teacher of Grade 4, maintained that non-believers went straight to hell but, if Veronica tried to warn her father again, Jeff would laugh even more at what he sacrilegiously termed the *Gospel According To Mrs Staunton*.

Despite wide-open doors and windows, it was still unbearably hot inside the Nissen hut. Jeff and Elaine had brought canvas chairs outside, and Veronica sat on the wooden steps between her parents while they waited for cooler evening air, the only thing that made sleeping in the hut a possibility on those December nights. Cicadas sang all around, a constant sound that

14

mingled with the shouts of children as well as a record of Beethoven's *Primavera* from the next room, while the pink walls of the hostel canteen across the road turned dark-blue with the abruptness that surprised anybody accustomed to lingering English twilights. Dulcie Leyton was out trying to locate her daughters, and Clive had followed his wife, apparently considering Dulcie incapable of accomplishing the task without his supervision.

"Clive sent off for some booklets, and we decided to emigrate after reading them," said Dulcie, uncomfortably aware of Jeff's mockery.

"God made the decision," Clive pointed out. "He told me that I had to come here."

Fair-haired, plump and cheerful Dulcie merely nodded, well-used to smiling at the people Clive alienated with his pedantic self-importance. "Veronica, do you know where Audrey is? She seems to have completely disappeared."

"What sort of voice does God have?" enquired Jeff. "Bass, baritone or tenor? Are you quite sure it wasn't *vox humana* on the church organ that you heard a-singing in praise of glorious colonial life?"

"It didn't happen in a church," said Clive. "God spoke to me when I was in the bathroom back home in Wolverhampton."

"I felt certain that Audrey would be here with you, Veronica." Dulcie went on smiling, but even a ten-year-old could tell that Mrs Leyton wanted the subject changed. "I can't think where she and the others have vanished to."

"The bathroom!" exclaimed Jeff, laughing again. "How very embarrassing, not to mention inconvenient. Why would God make

15

a personal appearance in a bathroom of all places? I thought he went in for burning bushes and mountaintops."

"God can be with us at any time, Jeff, in a bathroom or a church or outside a Nissen hut. I happened to be shaving when I suddenly heard God say, 'Clive, you've got to go to Australia.' I waited for a few minutes in case there were any further instructions, then I went downstairs and told Dulcie that we were emigrating as soon as possible." Clive spoke with the smugness of a man convinced that he alone knew the secrets of the universe, and to be on first name terms with the Creator would certainly reinforce anybody's confidence.

"Why would God want you in Australia?" asked Jeff.

"I don't know yet. I'm just following his will, and he said Australia."

"Was it Australia in general, or did God later specify Victoria rather than Queensland or New South Wales?"

"We're here because that's how things worked out," said Clive. "I didn't choose any of it, and never once thought about emigrating anywhere before God told me that I had to. He didn't give me a reason, but perhaps he intends my family to avoid nuclear war in Europe."

"Nobody on earth will be able to avoid that particular fate," declared Jeff.

"Then perhaps I have to bear witness to God's living presence in the world and convert atheists like you, Jeff, while there's still time. I don't know why I was sent to Australia, but I expect the bigger picture's going to be revealed to me any day now."

"How did you know that it was God on the line?" asked Jeff.

Clive raised his eyebrows at so absurd a question, and he sighed again. "Who else could it have been?"

"What about the devil? You believe in him, don't you?"

"Audrey was here until a few minutes ago," said Elaine, frowning at Jeff. "I thought that she'd gone back to you."

"Clive, it'll be dark as pitch soon," urged Dulcie. "We've got to find the girls."

"Ask God where they are," suggested Jeff.

"The little things we can do for ourselves," said Clive as he and Dulcie walked away. No amount of ridicule could shake his certainty, and he was very certain indeed that God had selected him to receive an individual briefing.

"Jeff, you shouldn't laugh at Clive," said Elaine.

"Why not?" Jeff demanded. "The man's a conceited fool. As if God would drop into a Wolverhampton bathroom for a chat with him!"

"I think you hurt Clive's feelings."

"The man's too stupid to have feelings." But everybody in the world was stupid, according to Jeff, and although he would never realize it, his scorn of others was more arrogant than Clive Leyton's belief that a voice in his head placed him among the prophets.

As a boy, Jeff won a scholarship to what had been called a good school. It was undoubtedly an expensive school, and might have been a good one for the boys whose parents paid fees, but it turned out to be a miserable experience as far as Jeff was concerned when he found himself ridiculed and despised. The other pupils jeered at his charity status and, despite being top in every class and every subject, Jeff was unable to cope with the constant mockery, and at fourteen he abandoned education for a factory job. His father had died when he was a baby, and extra family income stopped his mother from making any serious objection to so clever a child throwing away the chance of a more interesting future with a wider range of choice. It was wartime, and survival seemed due to luck rather than qualifications. Jeff would be in the forces if he lived to reach his eighteenth birthday, and only the present mattered because it was the one certainty: an outlook that stayed with Jeff. He rarely talked of the rejected opportunities to Veronica, merely saying that he had hated everything about the school, although Jeff kept the many prizes won there as proof of the academic potential he never fulfilled. The intelligence remained, but had its only outlet in mocking other people the way that Jeff had once been mocked himself, and Clive Leyton bore the brunt during those first weeks at Watson Valley Migrant Hostel.

****

The Thornthwaites occupied two of the rooms in Hut 34, the Leyton family had three, and a young man from Vienna with a passion for Beethoven lived in the remaining one, a record-player often the only reminder of his presence. Each room had its own front door, its own front door with a Yale Lock, something that made Veronica feel very adult, and those doors were a useful means of escape for the three Leyton girls. Even after their father confiscated the keys, they could still come and go as they pleased, because anybody was able to unlock any hut simply by pressing one of the glass slats to open the louvre window beside each door, and then putting a hand through the gap between panes to turn

18

the catch. Clive disapproved of the other hostel children, and tried to keep his family away from such frivolous company, but his daughters had other ideas.

Thelma, the eldest at thirteen, could have insisted on the glory of possessing her own room, but she and eleven-year-old Wendy got on well, while Audrey frequently squabbled with her sisters, and had unpleasant behaviour rewarded with the privilege and privacy of a single room. Audrey was six weeks and three days older than Veronica Thornthwaite, although it seemed a lot more because of Audrey's confidence, but all three Leyton girls were self-assured, attractively plump and fair-haired like their mother, with nothing of Clive's solemnity. If anything, his daughters veered a little too far in the opposite direction, and Mrs Staunton considered Audrey Leyton a bad influence on Grade 4. Few others dared to question Mrs Staunton's pronouncements, and querying a teacher came dangerously near to high treason in those days.

Mrs Staunton was tall and thin, dark-haired and sallow: a leathery-lean toughness after years of battling with a garden wilted under Australian sunlight. Plants were her passion, an unrequited love as they repaid Mrs Staunton's devotion by withering away to dust. Even the classroom geraniums, tended erratically by the children during term-time, only expired after Mrs Staunton took the flowerpots home for the holidays, and she was inclined to give botany lessons with the wistfulness of the broken-hearted reading a Shakespeare sonnet; however, the rest of Mrs Staunton was pure logic and efficiency.

"Five noughts make nothing, Audrey. What do five noughts make?"

"Five," declared Audrey, stubbornly and decidedly, looking at the five circles that their teacher had chalked on the blackboard. She knew exactly what Mrs Staunton meant, but Audrey relished the attention. She wanted to be a film star, and was already an accomplished actress.

"No. Five noughts can never be five. You can't have five of nothing," argued Mrs Staunton just as obstinately. "It doesn't matter how many noughts you have, they still make nothing, and nothing can't possibly be counted or divided or multiplied because it doesn't exist. Even if you had a million noughts, they'd still make nothing. So what do five noughts make? Think, Audrey, think."

Audrey thought, frowning to show the intensity of her deliberations. "Five," she said at last. "There are five noughts on the blackboard."

"Yes, Audrey's right, Mrs Staunton. There *are* five noughts on the blackboard." Ruby Farrell, a sandy-haired rival trouble-maker, had decided to join in.

Ignoring Ruby's interruption, Mrs Staunton obliterated the five circles with a sweep of the blackboard duster, and then she turned to tackle Audrey again. "Nothing is nothing. It doesn't exist, and so can't be divided or multiplied or added up. That's impossible because you can never have five of something that isn't there: never."

"But if you can't have five noughts, Mrs Staunton, why were there five drawn on the blackboard?" asked Audrey, innocence incarnate.

"The nought's merely a symbol of nothing. You know what a symbol is, don't you?"

"Yes. There were five of them on the blackboard just now, five noughts," Audrey pointed out, aware that she was coming very close to the end of Mrs Staunton's tolerance, but it simply meant that Audrey looked forward to the drama of punishment and posing as a martyr.

Mrs Staunton was a good teacher of those who wanted to learn, but she had no idea how to deal with the troublesome, the lazy, the bored and the downright baffled. She offered them educational riches, and they spurned her wealth. "Audrey, think of nothing, nothing at all. How could you possibly have five of that nothingness?"

"But there *were* five noughts on the blackboard."

"There were five nought symbols," Mrs Staunton conceded, "but nought itself is nothing, no matter how many symbols you might see. So what do five noughts make?"

"Five. I counted five of them," said Audrey, unable to resist having the last word even when *en route* to her starring rôle in a corner of the room and what teachers considered disgrace.

******

Grade 4 in a humid December, and Christmas was supposed to be on its way, but children sagged behind desks, overcome by lethargy in summer heat. Veronica's first Australian Christmas could be no real Christmas to a child who associated the season with frost and ice, and even the cards that they made in handicrafts for their parents were part of the pretence, as antipodean children, who had never seen a snowflake, drew traditionally Nordic pictures of reindeer, sleighs and skaters on frozen ponds.

Boys on one side of the room, girls on the other, and from the window shutters, pencil lines of gleaming sunlight travelled across the fair and light-brown heads of apathetic children. How could anyone possibly believe that it was nearly Christmas?

****

Veronica stared across the road, then raced around Hut 34, and spotted Audrey sitting in shade on the wooden steps that led up to an open door. "Come and look," cried Veronica. "Mrs Webb's taking boxes of Christmas decorations into the Rec, and she's already hung a million flags over its door."

"A million?" Perched on the sofa inside the hut, Clive looked up from the Bible held ostentatiously with both hands. "You counted each flag on the Recreation Hut, Veronica, and the total was one million?"

"No, I didn't count them," admitted Veronica.

"Then why did you tell Audrey that there were precisely one million flags?" Clive enquired.

"I meant that there are a lot of flags over the Rec door," muttered Veronica.

"And how many flags add up to a lot?"

"I don't know."

"Ten? Fifty? A hundred? A thousand?"

"I don't know." It was like being in school after flouting one of the rules that Veronica had never known existed until a teacher started to scold.

"A thousand flags would probably cover the entire Recreation Hut," persisted Clive. "Is the Hut now completely hidden from view?"

Veronica shook her head, and hated Clive for his cold literalism.

"Then what exactly did you see?"

"There's a string of flags over the Rec door."

"And how many flags are on this string, Veronica?"

"I don't know."

"If the string's over the door, it can't be longer than a couple of yards, but the number of flags hanging from it would depend on the size of each flag." Clive put the Bible down beside him, held his arms out wide and then brought his hands together in a demonstration of dimensions. "Are the flags large or small?"

"Clive, it doesn't matter," said Dulcie, folding sun-bleached dresses into a blue plastic laundry-box.

"Yes, it does matter," insisted Clive. "Truth's the most important matter of all, and Veronica told a lie when she claimed to have seen a million flags."

"She was just exaggerating."

"Exaggeration's the same thing as a lie, Dulcie. I've clearly established that there can't be a million flags on the Recreation Hut, yet that's what Veronica told us, and so she lied."

"There *are* a million flags," declared Audrey.

"Don't be ridiculous," snapped Clive.

"But there are. Mrs Webb said that she was going to put a million flags on the Rec for Christmas, and I want to see them. Let's go, Vron."

"I heard Mrs Webb say a million flags too." Wendy emerged from the room that she shared with Thelma, and glared at Clive, her belligerence out of all proportion to his niggling pedantry. "Don't you want to see the million flags, Thel?"

"Of course I do," declared Thelma, hurrying after Wendy, but family solidarity was a weapon against another member of that family as the three Leyton girls abandoned the hut, ignoring Clive's protest.

"There aren't a million flags," Veronica called, running after the sisters.

"Yes, there are," maintained Audrey. "We'll all see a million flags hanging on the Rec, and I'll have counted a million flags as well, one by one."

"But your father will know how many there really are, when he goes over to the canteen."

"Is it our fault that Mrs Webb took some of the flags down before he got a chance to see them?" asked Wendy.

****

Five shelves of books in the Recreation Hut comprised Watson Valley Migrant Hostel Library, a library rigidly divided into three sections: one shelf for history and general knowledge, two shelves of stories intended for boys and two shelves for girls. As the boys living on the hostel seemed to consider reading books the shameful brand of a sissy, all five shelves were available to Wendy Leyton and Veronica Thornthwaite, opening up a second new world for both of them. Audrey sneered at the library because there was no drama section and actresses only read plays, Thelma was too busy languishing as a star-crossed lover to have any interest in other people's make-believe, but Wendy and Veronica educated themselves at the Chalet School, flew with Biggles, and found buried treasure alongside the Famous Five. Wendy dismissed less modern books as too old-fashioned for her, after she had been hoodwinked by the title of *The Fifth Form at St Dominic's*, but Veronica happily tackled *Seven Little Australians*, *The Family at Misrule*, *Anne of Green Gables*, *Little Women*, *Tom Brown's Schooldays* and *Tom Brown at Oxford*. However, all faded to insignificance beside that book of books: *The Swish of the Curtain*.

"You've simply got to read it," Veronica urged Audrey. "It's the most brilliant book that I've ever read in the whole of my life, all about some children who write plays and then act them in an old building that they turn into their own theatre: the Blue Door Theatre."

"Well, perhaps I'll have a look at the first chapter, and see what it's like," Audrey conceded magnanimously, not realizing that she too was about to become a Blue Door devotee.

In Hut 34's wooden side, the front door that opened directly into Veronica's room was painted dark blue, and it seemed a sign, even a promise, that destiny would one day open the other Blue Door for her, and lead Veronica Olivia Thornthwaite to a magical world of achievement far from the factory that her parents worked in. On the hostel, there were netball teams for girls, football teams for boys, while the adults were offered Norman Wisdom films that Jeff said reminded him why he had left England, but the nearest Veronica could get to her own theatre company was writing one-scene plays that she and Audrey continually rehearsed without ever finding an audience interested enough to attend a first performance.

"I'm going to be so famous one day that people will have to pay to get into a cinema and watch me act. And then Sandra Portman will be sorry that she said she'd rather go to the station, and have a look what's happening there, than see our play. Nothing ever happens at the station. A train comes in, half-a-dozen people get on or off, and that's it. The end." Audrey had an odd way of jerking her head to one side as she spoke, and combined with her round eyes and peaked nose, she often reminded Veronica of a bird, and it seemed to guarantee that Audrey's dream of soaring skywards to join the stars would come true. "Just let Sandra Portman wait until I'm world-famous in Watson Valley."

"Do they make films in Australia, or will you have to go back to England?" asked Veronica.

"I'm going to Hollywood, but we could start a Blue Door Theatre in Melbourne before I leave. You write the plays, and I'll star in them. If you come to Hollywood with me, you can write my films as well."

"OK," said Veronica. "I'll begin by writing for the wireless."

"The wireless!" scoffed Audrey. "There won't be any radio soon. Everyone's going to have a television."

"Yes, I know, but if I'm an ABC Argonaut in the meantime, they might read out my letters and stories on air. They're called contributions, and the whole of Australia hears what you've written. The programme comes from Sydney, and it's on every day at five o'clock. You should listen because they do plays too."

"Can I act in them?"

"No, they don't let the Argonauts act. It's usually just Mac and Jimmy and Robyn and Earl: the people in the studio."

"No point in me being an ABC Argonaut then," declared Audrey. "But you can join, and start to become a famous play writer."

"Nobody would know that I'd written a word. Argonauts are rowers in different ships, and contributions get read out with just your ship's name and whatever number rower you are. Your real name isn't mentioned even once."

Audrey looked scornful at the idea of anybody prepared to work anonymously, because the entire world was going to celebrate the name of Audrey Leyton one day, but she accepted that lesser mortals might have to make compromises. "I suppose it'll be good practice for when you write my films," she acknowledged.

****

Wendy Leyton also had future plans, but they centred on being a Head Girl or Games Captain. She devoured every boarding-school story on the five shelves of the hostel's library and yearned to live in a world of midnight feasts, team spirit and playing the game, although it was hardly playing the game to hide her borrowed books in Veronica Thornthwaite's room. Clive Leyton regarded all fiction as printed lies, but the illicitness merely added glamour to the tales, and Wendy studied earnestly in school, hoping to become clever enough to blossom as a scholarship girl like the heroines in so many of the stories that she read over and over again.

"But Dad told her that no daughter of his was leaving home until she got married," said Audrey.

"My Dad won a scholarship to boarding school, and hated every single minute that he was there," reported Veronica. "He couldn't wait to leave. Why would anybody want to live at school?"

"Don't ask me, but Wendy's hopping mad because Dad won't even find out if there are boarding schools with scholarships in Australia. And she says that she can't bear her name and wants to be called Rosamund from now on, and Dad told Wendy that she'll keep the name God gave her, but God didn't choose it. Mum did."

"You ought to be allowed to pick your own name because I absolutely hate being called Veronica Thornthwaite. It's so very long, and just about everybody says Vron anyway. That's even worse, and sounds exactly like a motorbike starting up. It's awful."

"You should stop answering to your name then. It's what Wendy's doing. She told us that she's Rosamund or nobody from now on, and even Dad can't make her hear when he says Wendy."

If Clive Leyton thought that he had problems with one academically-aspiring child longing to escape from home, another daughter was about to appal him.

Thelma had acquired a boyfriend, and the ambition of her life was fulfilled. She found Alan Yoxall rather dull and monosyllabic, but that was unimportant because at last she could walk proud and tall in the knowledge that Thelma Deanna Leyton was now able to anguish with other teenage girls about the heartbreak of love. Even better, her father had forbidden Thelma to see Alan again which was the perfect finishing touch to a glorious situation, and made the short and skinny Alan seem considerably more alluring than he actually was. If she could have kept her romantic status without ever speaking to Alan again, Thelma's happiness might have been complete, but unfortunately the necessary proof of her standing involved being seen with a Romeo from time to time, and as Alan Yoxall was the only boy who showed interest in the would-be Juliet, he had to be endured. Luckily, Alan was second reserve goalkeeper for the Watson Valley Hostel football team and spent his Saturdays watching matches against other Hostels and his evenings at practice, which gave Thelma so little time in Alan's company that the romance flourished.

"Dad says that Thelma's too young to have a boyfriend," Audrey reported.

"Too young!" marvelled Veronica. "But she's thirteen."

"Dad says that no girl should go out with a boy unless they're able to get married, and that if he catches her alone with Alan again, he'll lock Thelma in her room."

"But she wasn't alone with Alan," Veronica pointed out. "We were outside the shop too, and dozens of other kids as well."

"Yes, but Dad only saw Thelma and Alan. And they were eating ice-cream, and we're not allowed ice-cream except on Sundays. There was a terrible row, and Wendy told me that Thelma cried half the night. It might even have been the whole night, but Wendy fell asleep."

According to Elaine, Clive Leyton had such a filthy mind that he would never need to watch a blue movie. He saw sin and corruption everywhere, and undersized Alan as Watson Valley's answer to Casanova, seducing Thelma with sophisticated worldly guile and licentious dollops of vanilla ice-cream. The scene Clive made outside the Nissen hut that housed the hostel shop had been very dramatic and very public, with a grimly outraged father apparently under the impression that he had caught his thirteen-year-old daughter in *flagrante delicto*, while Thelma wept noisily and Alan squirmed, red-faced with embarrassment. The story promptly sped through every hut on the hostel, gathering zesty detail along the way, until Clive was portrayed as a raving madman who threatened to kill both Alan and the supposedly-pregnant Thelma. Nobody doubted a word of the sensational tale, although imagination was the only part of Clive Leyton known to run wild, and in his head, illicit ice-cream led straight onto debauchery and an illegitimate grandchild, but behind his back, Dulcie Leyton laughed with Elaine.

"Thelma's thrilled to bits, picturing herself as the star of a Hollywood weepie."

"But the co-star's no Hollywood hunk," said Elaine. "Thelma could flatten that puny Alan Yoxall with one punch, if he tried anything."

"Yes, and Clive wasn't quite so virtuous when we were courting. I do wish God had spoken to somebody else. It's ruining life for the girls. They get hardly any fun these days, and poor Wendy's been forbidden to play on the netball team next Saturday afternoon because they're off to Fisherman's Bend Hostel, and Clive's convinced himself that she'll somehow be led astray at half-time."

"He'll get over it."

"You don't know Clive, and nor do I now." Dulcie thought that she talked only to Elaine, but Veronica was next door in her bedroom and could hear every syllable. There were few secrets when families shared huts with thin partition walls. "I didn't want to leave Wolverhampton and come to Australia. The girls were doing really well: Thelma in a grammar school, Wendy about to take her Eleven-Plus exam, and I'd just got Audrey to go to Brownie meetings. Clive was in the wage office at Viking Cycles, and my mother and sister lived up the road from us. It was all so nice."

Until God intervened. Dulcie left the words unspoken, but she knew where the blame lay, and there was no chance of convincing Clive that he might have been mistaken about the voice, because nobody had ever persuaded Clive Leyton to doubt anything that he chose to believe.

"You'll get another house before long," said Elaine, but aware that with only one wage coming in and three daughters, the Leytons were unlikely to leave Watson Valley and move out to Australia proper for some considerable time. The hostel rent was high, but Clive disapproved of working mothers, and Dulcie did not seem the type to rebel.

"We had such a lovely house, carpeted throughout," Dulcie recalled, sighing with rare self-pity. "It was big enough for the girls to have their own bedrooms, and I'd just found the perfect sofa-cover: one that cleaned up like new, even after Audrey spilt cocoa all over it."

"How nice." Elaine made an attempt to sound sympathetic, but housework had never been of interest to her, whether as a chore or a topic of conversation. "I couldn't wait to get on the boat and come here. We lived in a poky dark house in a poky dark backstreet where nothing ever happened, and I didn't want that to be the rest of my life. In Australia, I've got the chance of a much more exciting future."

"But don't you miss your family?"

"Yes, of course," Elaine replied automatically before she laughed and conceded, "Putting thirteen thousand miles between me and Mum is actually a plus, because she's always criticized everything I do and she hates Jeff like poison. There's also the advantage that she doesn't realize I'm now living in less than half of a Nissen hut."

"I haven't revealed the true picture to my mother either," admitted Dulcie. "I've deliberately let her think that we're in a three-bedroomed flat, and I'm glad she doesn't know the whole story, but the girls miss their grandmother, particularly Audrey."

For a second time, Elaine tried to sound sympathetic, even though she could hardly describe the despised grandchild, condemned from birth as 'Thornthwaite's daughter,' and the dictatorial grandmother being devoted to each other. "It's very difficult at times," she said as a compromise.

Veronica saw no difficulties. Life just happened, things just happened, and that was that.

2

Detective Senior Constable Gilda Garfield had only viewed migrant hostels from a distance before she went to Watson Valley. Fourth generation Australian, third generation police, Gilda was Melbourne born and bred, inclined to assume that nothing much had happened in the city's hinterland since the days of the Kelly Gang. People who lived in small towns got up, went to work in factories, came home, and then listened to the radio or watched television until it was time to go back to sleep. Life was in Melbourne; the rest of Victoria slumbered.

One of the few women police officers in the State, Gilda at thirty-two had lately become even more unusual by joining the Detective Branch, but she possessed an important advantage that separated her from the other females in the force: Gilda was plain and as thin as a fence post. At work, no feminine curves distracted the men, and with light-brown hair scraped back in a knot, she was practically one of the blokes because an unattractive woman did not count as a woman at all, except in very special circumstances, and those circumstances were cases that involved children. Detective Sergeant Lance Palmer was the father of two daughters, but when his job meant dealing with kids, he remembered that child-free Detective Senior Constable Gilda Garfield was female and therefore automatically expert in talking to anybody under the age of twelve.

"A migrant hostel's bound to be overrun with kids, and there are three Leyton girls. You'd better come along in case we need statements from them. They'll talk to you more easily."

"More easily than to a certain Detective Sergeant who presumably talks to his daughters every day?" enquired Gilda.

"That's different," claimed Lance.

Gilda was tempted to ask why, but too many questions about Palmer home life were off-limits, and she had no wish to find herself demoted and sent to deal with belligerent drunks when the bars closed after the six o'clock swill. The late Inspector Vincent Garfield would have been pleased that she refrained from rocking the boat too much because, in the absence of a son, he had expected his daughter to blaze a trail to the top in true Garfield family tradition, and Gilda was still uncertain whether she had freely chosen to join the police or merely done so after years of brainwashing.

Vincent had loved his job, loved the authority it gave him, and loved the sense of purpose he felt. Anarchy reigned unless society was firmly policed, and there were only two kinds of people, according to Vincent: the law-abiding and the lawless, as unconnected as different continents. He protected the worthy and thwarted the worthless, never doubting his own judgment as to who went into which category. Vincent's daughter grew up on her father's tales of action-packed cases and the ultimate triumph of right over wrong, until Gilda had been convinced that any other job was too dreary to contemplate, despite being fully aware that Vincent could have taught Government departments a lesson or two about propaganda.

And there she was, her father's daughter, the last of the Garfields, a detective travelling over miles of dusty road to Watson Valley, a township that could boast an ice-cream factory and a railway station with a cluster of small shops around it. Once the highway had passed through the stagnant commercial district, a side road led around a corner, and Gilda saw the rows of Nissen huts. No doubt a former military camp, the hostel was situated at the lowest point of the valley, the bottom of a basin, before the road continued uphill towards a line of identical one-storey detached houses, each in the centre of a square patch of garden. Except for that unmistakeable Australian heat, the migrants could have been living in almost any suburbia in the world, and the trackless bush land of kangaroos and koalas seemed even further away than Melbourne.

Unwilling to be seen chauffeured by a woman, Lance Palmer had chosen to drive, and he parked in the road behind a police car, then glanced around in the hope of spotting uniformed lackeys prepared to jump to attention at the sight of his tall, dark-haired handsomeness, but there was nobody to notice so exalted a presence. "Where is everyone?" demanded Lance, as though invitations had previously been sent out specifying an exact time.

"Not possessing psychic powers, I'll have to investigate," replied Gilda, climbing out of the car into air that smelt of road tar. A heat haze shimmered on the horizon, but the hostel had no respite, and the red clay surrounding each Nissen hut was cracked under the sun's ferocity. Even the cicadas were silent, and Gilda felt like a foreigner in her own country.

On the opposite side of the road, facing the huts, there was a large one-storey wooden building painted a sun-blistered pink, and separated from it by wide stretches of red clay, a long shed had a hand-written notice on one of its two doors proclaiming *Manager*, but when Gilda knocked, that was the only sound to break the silence. She tried the door handle but the office was locked, and Lance sighed, impatient with events he could do nothing to alter. Rumour maintained that his marriage was on the rocks, and Gilda could well believe the gossip she had heard. Lance Palmer would scarcely be the most easy-going of husbands when a mere empty office had him muttering in exasperation. A pointless display of annoyance, luckily, because a short middle-aged man with neat brown hair was trotting across the road towards them, and although shirt sleeves were rolled up as a concession to the day's heat, he wore a tie, and his tailored trousers cried out for a matching jacket. The man so obviously belonged inside an office that Gilda hardly needed to ask if he were the hostel's manager.

"We've never had anything like this before," he protested, apparently contradicting an unspoken accusation. "A man died a few months ago, but that was his heart, and yet he'd passed the emigration medical back home at the end of last year. Then a teenage boy was killed in a motorbike accident on his way to work, but this — never!"

The accent was English, with only a faint trace of Australian infiltration, reinforcing Gilda's sense of having entered foreign territory with its own laws, but Lance was looking even more irritated, and she tried to stem the flow of useless information. "We're police —"

"Yes, I know," the man agreed. "Constable Dexter told me. He's outside Hut 34 now, and said to bring you straight there, because you'll want to go in and look around before they move the — before they take Mr Leyton away."

It was most definitely not a case of wanting to see the body, but Gilda nodded. "And your name is —?"

"Hubert Webb. When Mrs Leyton ran into the office, and asked me to phone for a doctor because her husband was unconscious, I thought, 'Oh, no, not another heart attack.' I never for one second imagined —"

"I'm sure you didn't," snapped Lance. "Where's this Hut 34?"

"The end one there," replied Hubert, pointing rather unnecessarily to the collection of Nissen huts across the road. He was too bewildered by events to notice the abruptness of Lance's tone, but Gilda felt compelled to overcompensate by smiling at Hubert. Her father had been a self-important man with no time for anybody he considered a nonentity, and Lance occasionally reminded her of Vincent.

"Where are the migrants?" asked Gilda. "The hostel seems deserted."

"The children are at school, the babies and toddlers in the kindergarten on the other side of the huts, and the adults at work," Hubert explained as he hurried off, leaving Lance and Gilda to scurry over the road in his wake. "You hardly ever see anyone around here most weekdays, apart from a few mothers with very young babies, and Mrs Leyton of course. She doesn't go out to work. My wife's with her now in 32, but that hut's meant for a family arriving tomorrow and if the Leytons are still there, I'll have to try and get the Orvilles placed in another hostel. The school holidays start tomorrow as well."

"Who looks after the school kids then, if their mothers go out to work?"

"The children look after themselves mostly, but my wife and I are always here, and a few parents on night-shift as well. The

37

kids have meals in the canteen and there are organized games. Oh, it seems to sort itself out. We've never had a problem at Watson Valley."

"A kid's paradise."

Hubert smiled, accepting a compliment that Gilda had not intended to offer. "I like to think this is a happy hostel. Not everything's perfect, but on the whole, we all get along, and there's plenty for the children to do, especially with the football tournament. The wrong time of year, I know, but the boys prefer that game to cricket, and so I —"

"Did you know Clive Leyton well?" asked Lance, to end the advertisement for Watson Valley's happy Migrant Hostel.

The smile hastily vanished from Hubert's face as he recalled the sombre reason behind a police visit. "I only ever spoke to Mr Leyton when he came into the office to pay his rent or pick up letters, and I've usually got quite a crowd in the room. There are nearly a hundred huts here, and almost double that number of families, as well as a few single migrants."

"The families don't get a hut each?" Gilda said in surprise.

"It's only temporary accommodation, and nobody expects luxury. We come to this country prepared to work for our futures." Hubert reacted as though the police suspected him of cramming as many migrants as possible into each room while pocketing their rent, and he added with stern self-righteousness, "We don't look for handouts or an easy ride. We believe in standing on our own feet."

"Where did Mr Leyton work?" asked Gilda, before Lance could voice the resentment crossing his face at a lecture on independence and effort delivered by a Pom.

38

"I'd seen him around at lunchtimes, so he probably worked in the ice-cream factory," replied Hubert. "This is where he — this is Hut 34."

They had crossed the road, walked along the first row of huts, and were now in front of the end one, but instead of taking them up to the blue-painted door cut in the middle of the arched corrugated iron, Hubert led Lance and Gilda down a stony path, past two further blue doors in the hut's wooden sidewall, to the back where Constable Dexter stood near yet another blue door. Police hat in hand, his arms waved frantically like someone sending out an urgent message in semaphore, and Gilda's heart sank. The flies had arrived in a black swirling cloud.

Constable Harvey Dexter was red-faced after the endeavour to repel so many flies, and his fair hair had darkened with sweat. He was too young to have much experience with sudden death, and visibly relieved to see somebody who would give him orders. "No one's been inside since the doctor left. He had to rush off to an appointment, but I've got his phone number in case you want to talk to him."

"I'll want to talk to him." Lance climbed the four wooden steps in front of the door, pushed it open and went inside the hut, accompanied by a rush of flies. Gilda followed, and had to force herself not to recoil at the heat in case anyone thought the sight of a body made her squeamish. She was accustomed to a hot climate, but under the corrugated iron roof, the room temperature soared far beyond anything she had previously known.

"Ask that Constable if a photographer's been in here yet," said Lance, and Gilda retreated to the steps, glad to be freed from such intense heat even for a few seconds.

"The photographer?" she queried, and never had fresh air smelt so good.

"I don't know where he is, but Sergeant Kirkham's gone to hurry things up a bit," reported Harvey, and he was so pleased at being able to deflect any blame away from himself for the inefficiency that he showed no sign of resenting a female officer, even though she outranked him. "The doctor said it was important to get Mr Leyton moved out of the hut as soon as possible."

"Before the children are back from school, I hope." Hubert looked appalled at the idea of so public an ending to a private tragedy on his happy hostel, and the thought of such police indelicacy even stopped him noticing the number of flies that were settling on his white shirt. "We can't let the children witness any of this."

"We'll get the area blocked off if necessary," said Gilda. Reinforcements should already have been there doing just that, but it was the absent Sergeant Kirkham's headache, and Gilda took a deep breath to prepare herself for going back inside the hut. Now that Lance had moved away from the door, she could see Clive Leyton sprawled on the black-and-white plastic cover of a sofa, one hand touching the dark-brown oilcloth on the floor, a thick book close by as if he had dropped it.

"No sign of a struggle," commented Lance, waving away flies. "No sign of a gun either. I hope the doctor didn't move him too much. It looks like someone could have stood on the top step and shot him while he was reading — reading the Bible," Lance added, after bending down for a closer inspection.

****

40

The square of the hypotenuse of a right-angled triangle equals the sum of the squares of the two adjacent sides. Gilda suddenly realized why her mind had drifted back to school geometry. She and Lance were sitting on canvas-backed chairs inside a right-angled triangle. The middle partition wall dividing the hut was straight, the floor impeccably level, but the other wall had been formed by the wavy curve of a corrugated iron roof, and inside her triangle, despite the airless heat, Dulcie Leyton was polishing a room that seemed to be newly-painted and entirely dust-free, but she obviously needed to do something, anything, to try and keep her thoughts fixed on trivia. Gilda wished the questioning could have waited, although she knew that answers were more likely to be useful before Dulcie had time to tidy up details in her mind and re-arrange them, whether unconsciously or not.

"How do you bear the heat inside these huts?" asked Gilda.

"I suppose you get accustomed to it, but we can't stay here now. I want to go to another hostel. And the girls will be back from school in a little while. They won't know where I am." Dulcie polished the black metal bars of a bed frame as she spoke, wielding a duster produced from the bulging pocket in her yellow apron: a duster apparently carried at all times ready for instant use. Gilda knew that she herself would never be able to reach such heights of domesticity, and it seemed yet another reason to turn down Jerome Henderson's marriage proposal.

"I'll drive you to the school," offered Gilda, but Dulcie shook her head, at last able to be decisive.

"I want the girls to have as long as possible before they're forced to deal with — I'll go over to the Rec and meet them there."

41

"The wreck?" queried Lance, picturing a mangled car.

"Yes, the Rec. There are two ways that the girls can take to get back here from school, and I don't know which one they'll use this afternoon, but if I stand by the Rec, I'll see them whether they come down the hill or over the fields to the railway crossing. Yes, I can stand by the Rec." Dulcie sounded relieved to have a plan, presumably because it meant that something in the chaos of the day was under her control.

"Did your husband have a gun?" asked Lance, and Gilda was taken aback by the abruptness of his question, but nothing could make matters worse for Dulcie, who seemed unaware of Lance's offhand manner.

"Oh, no, Clive never had a gun. He was a pacifist. Well, not always. Clive fought during the war, of course. Not that fighting people was ever a part of his Pay Corps duties, but he became a strict pacifist after God spoke to him."

"Would you say that name again, please? I missed it," said Gilda, looking up from the notes she was writing. "Who spoke to your husband?"

"God. He told Clive to emigrate to Australia."

"*God* told him?" Lance tried to sound casual, but failed utterly. God had never ordered him about, and so there could only be a single explanation of that talkative deity. "You mean, your husband heard voices in his head?"

"Just one voice: God's. Back home, in the bathroom."

"Did your husband have a long history of mental illness?"

"He didn't have any history of mental illness at all. I don't think that they'd have let us emigrate to Australia if he had." Dulcie looked surprised at a question with so obvious an answer,

42

and she knelt down on the chocolate-brown lino to dust under the bed, her right arm moving in wide arcs. "Every migrant has to pass a medical, even the children, and the doctor asked us all about our health."

But presumably that doctor had neglected to enquire if any family member had heard God's voice issuing orders lately, thought Gilda. "Was your husband from a very religious background?"

"Oh, no. Clive never bothered with church or the Bible or anything like that before God spoke to him. He did try going to the chapel down our road for a while afterwards, but then he stopped. No point, Clive said; God wasn't there." Dulcie hauled herself upright using the bed frame for support, and added, "Clive wondered if God intended him to start a brand-new religion in Australia."

Had Dulcie wanted to establish her husband as a raving madman in Lance's eyes, she could hardly have done a better job. God had never spoken to any member of the Palmer family, and should he start chatting, medical help would immediately be summoned to silence him. Amazed at the carelessness of migrant selection in Britain, Lance demanded, "How often did your husband hear this voice?"

"Only that one time, but Clive was expecting a second message to tell him why we had to come to Australia and what he ought to do here."

"Why did he think that it was God speaking to him?" asked Gilda, unsure whether Dulcie could really be as trustingly guileless as she appeared. "Did your husband simply assume that the voice belonged to God?"

"Perhaps God introduced himself. Clive was very certain it was God, anyway." Dulcie glanced around the room in search of something else to dust, and began vigorously polishing a narrow chest-of-drawers.

"Did you believe your husband?" Lance's own scepticism was all too apparent, and he made no attempt to disguise it.

"Clive never told a lie, even before God spoke to him, so I knew that he'd definitely heard a voice."

"But do you really think that it belonged to God?"

"I don't know. I didn't hear the voice. But Clive had no doubts." Dulcie went over to the window and started to dust slats of glass, despite a view of the long concrete block that housed toilets and showers hardly being worth her efforts.

"Did you mind leaving England?" asked Gilda.

"Oh, yes. I hated having to say goodbye to my mother and sister, and selling the house too. We lost a lot of money on the sale because there was so much mortgage still to repay, but Clive said that we had to get rid of the place as quickly as possible, and he accepted the very first offer that came along, and of course we had to leave the furniture behind as well. It was all so sad."

"So you had arguments about emigrating," Lance stated, his experience of married life behind every word.

"Oh, no. Clive and I never argued," said Dulcie. "Besides, God might not have liked it, if Clive didn't do exactly what he'd been told."

Dulcie had to be a fake, thought Gilda. No woman on earth could possibly manage such compliance when a husband's whim went against everything that she knew and valued in life. The submissiveness had to be an act. It had to be. There was no other explanation. "Did you tell your husband that you wanted to stay in England?"

"Yes, but he said that what we wanted to do wasn't important any more, and I suppose it isn't when God's got a special plan for you."

The supposedly divine plan had turned out to be a decidedly catastrophic one for Clive Leyton, and Dulcie was either very cunning or very stupid. Lance had already made up his mind which theory he supported, and Gilda was inclined to agree with him, knowing that her father would have regarded the case as closed. A resentful wife, stranded far from home in a Nissen hut under an unrelenting sun with a mentally-ill husband, had a moment of madness herself. But where did Dulcie get the gun?

"You must feel threatened, being in a new country and surrounded by strangers," remarked Gilda. "These huts don't appear very secure."

"They're not, but practically everyone who lives here comes from Britain, so it's not like being in a foreign land at all, and sometimes I can't believe I'm on the other side of the world." Yet, that day, Dulcie must have been conscious of every mile and every country between the hostel and the place that would always be home. She had to stay strong for her daughters, but there was nobody to support Dulcie.

"Other people don't feel safe in these huts," said Lance. "Somebody around here's got a gun."

"I suppose so." Dulcie pushed the thought away by furiously polishing the window for a second time. Whatever she had or had not done, all at once she appeared genuinely upset and bewildered. "If I can't go back into Hut 34, we only have the clothes I left on the washing-line and what we're wearing now. The bank account's in Clive's name and I haven't got enough cash to buy anything more for the girls or to pay next week's rent. I must get a job. Yes, I must get a job. If we have to stay in Watson Valley, I'll go to the ice-cream factory and ask about vacancies."

It seemed obvious to Gilda that Dulcie was still unable to grasp the fact that Clive no longer existed. Life had changed forever, and Dulcie could say the words, talk about him in the past tense, know why she was being questioned, but the reality of her new situation had yet to sink in. No matter who caused Clive's death or why it had happened, Dulcie was moving through a bad dream that she half-imagined would end at dawn the next morning, but she was never going to wake up from that particular nightmare. "Did your husband work in the ice-cream factory?"

"Yes, Clive got a job there in the wage office." It sounded an inappropriate occupation for a man awaiting instruction direct from God, but Dulcie remained unaware of the oddity, and she ploughed on. "I'm sure they'll be able to find me something at the factory, even if I just clean for them. That's one thing I know about: cleaning."

"Where did the gun come from?" Lance demanded, in an attempt to startle Dulcie into blurting out a few incriminating words, but she merely shook her head.

"I don't know. I've never heard anything about guns, except that the police have them over here. Can I talk to you later instead of now? I'll have to go and meet the girls soon. I've got to tell them —" Dulcie froze for a few seconds, and then forced herself back to the pettiness of detail. "Audrey will have to share a room with me if we stay in this hut, and she won't like that at all."

"What happened between you and your husband after the kids left for school?" Lance was trying his would-be shock tactics once more, but Dulcie apparently failed to notice.

"I took the washing down to the laundry-room, and then hung it on the line outside the hut. I went in —" Dulcie shook her head again, dazed by the drama that had blundered into a mundane summer morning. "I thought he'd had a heart attack like poor Mr Fergal."

"But what happened after the kids left and before you went out to do the washing?"

"Nothing. I gathered the laundry together, and Clive was reading. I thought he'd have gone to work by the time I got back."

"You were both completely silent?" scoffed Lance. "You didn't talk about anything?"

"Not that I can remember. Clive never bothered with breakfast, but it's always a rush for me in the mornings, getting the girls out of bed, down to the shower block, over the road to the canteen, and then finding everything they'll need at school that day. After the girls leave, it's nice to have a few moments of peace and quiet, and I like to listen to Oskar's music anyway."

"Whose music?"

"Oskar's. He lives in the end room on the Thornthwaite side of Hut 34 and his record-player's as good as being at a concert. Clive complained it was so loud, he couldn't think straight, but Oskar just laughed and said that was the best thing about music. He's a nice boy."

Nice boy or not, loud music made Lance instantly picture a teenage rebel. "So your husband objected to being forced to listen to hour after hour of rock 'n' roll."

"Beethoven."

"Beethoven?" queried Lance, taken aback.

"Mostly Beethoven, but Schumann wrote one piece that I asked about. I never knew I liked classical music until I came to live on the hostel. I thought that symphonies and things were only for clever people, but all you have to do is listen, as Oskar said."

"However, your husband didn't share your appreciation?"

"Not really, but the girls and I —" Dulcie's voice faltered, although she was able to pull herself together more quickly than Gilda would have believed possible, and Dulcie perhaps sensed the doubt because she added, "I've got to keep calm for the girls, but I feel as if somebody's hit me over the head with a ton weight."

"Did your husband have trouble with anyone else?" asked Gilda, to remind herself that she was supposed to be an impartial gatherer of evidence, not a courtroom judge about to announce Mrs Leyton's sentence for killing Mr Leyton.

"Trouble? Well, not trouble exactly, but Clive didn't like Jeff Thornthwaite much, especially when Jeff made fun of him. And Jeff's daughter Veronica is a dreadful little liar, and Clive worried about her being a bad influence on Audrey. Veronica makes up stories in her head, then tells them so convincingly, you'd think they actually happened, and I suppose that she believes they did. You can't expect anything else from an atheist family, but her mother's quite nice, even if she does allow Veronica to run wild. It's Jeff's fault really, and Elaine ought to stand up for herself more and not let him rule the roost."

Advice that Dulcie might have profitably given herself. Gilda could picture the whole scene: a pointless argument flared up over an insignificant detail, but years of suppressed resentment surged through Dulcie as she snatched up the gun in an uncontrollable rage that cared nothing for consequences. A neat theory with but one loose end. Where did the gun come from for the infuriated wife to snatch up? "Anyone else your husband didn't get on with?"

"The Yoxalls in Hut 33, but nobody likes them. They drink and shout at each other and swear: not very nice people at all. I avoid them as much as possible, although it's difficult sometimes if a family's in the next hut to you. Clive asked Mr Webb to move them, but nobody wants the Yoxalls as neighbours."

"When you went out to do the laundry, did you see anyone hanging around?" asked Gilda.

"No. The children had gone to school, and everybody else would be at work or over in the canteen, I suppose."

"Did you have a chat with anybody while you were doing the laundry?"

"No one was around, as I said. There never is anybody in the laundry-room at that time. It's the reason I always do the washing then, otherwise I have to waste hours waiting for a free sink. But I can't talk to you any longer," decided Dulcie, to reclaim a little more control over the day. "I've got to meet the girls. Their school's closing early as it's the end of term."

"Shall I come along?" Gilda felt duty-bound to make the offer, but the idea of being an intrusive spectator of family grief appalled her. In a sudden blast of painful memory, she was seven years old again, climbing wooden steps to the veranda, just home from school on a day no different to any other, except that through the wire-mesh door protecting the house from flies, she could see her restlessly-active Dad, who never sat still, sitting quite still in the front room. Even odder, there was no music playing. The wireless that Mum listened to from morning until night had been switched off.

"This is something I have to do by myself," said Dulcie, with a sigh that shook her whole body. "And when I've told the girls what's happened, nothing will ever seem difficult again."

Dulcie was right. Some days changed life forever, separating you from the past as well as the rest of humanity, and there could be no going back. Three young girls were about to have their world shattered, and Gilda was glad not to be a witness.

****

Still wearing her apron as though prepared to dust anything that she encountered on the way, Dulcie hurried across the road towards the Recreation Hut, and Lance began to explore the hostel with Gilda. They walked down the stony path leading to a long concrete building that contained toilets and showers, according to the notice on its door, and Lance paused to look around the area. Constable Dexter was the only person in sight and beyond him, on the far side of Hut 34, stretched an expanse of red clay with two swings, a climbing frame and a slide close to the road. Hostel land ended with a white picket fence next to a strip of grass in front of a brick house on the hill slope: grass sparse and yellow, offering no quick hiding-place for a gun. In the other direction, there was a line of Nissen huts raised above ground level by wooden posts, the bare earth underneath too hard and too visible for anybody intent on secreting a piece of inconvenient evidence. "She shot her husband and got the gun out of the hut easily enough by wrapping it up in the laundry. But which way did Dulcie go then?"

"She could have put the gun inside one of the cisterns," said Gilda, going into the toilet block.

"Too obvious and too easy for us to find." Lance was right, as the cisterns were the only possible hiding-place in the building, despite the many cubicles. "Presumably the gun can be linked to her husband or Dulcie wouldn't have removed it."

"Unless she just panicked," suggested Gilda.

"I suppose there's a chance she might have. Tell that Constable to take a look inside the cisterns, if we ever get some organization around here."

They skirted the toilet block, went past row after row of silent Nissen huts until they reached the back of the hostel and found the laundry-room: another concrete building that forced them to stand in its doorway to give their eyes time to adjust after the glare of sunlight on metal roofs. Eventually they could see fifteen deep sinks lining the cool darkness of the room, each basin with a water tap above it, and they knew that no gun could be hidden in the simplicity of that room.

"So she left the washing in a sink, and then went out again," decided Lance, crossing the room to a second door that opened to reveal a wide hollow of wasteland leading down to a creek. The highway was on the left, well above head height, and the steep slope going up to it was bordered by a few straggly bushes that petered out close to the road bridge over the creek. On the right, there was another area of red clay, and more swings with metal chains that would certainly blister any hand grasping them after so many hours in such unremittingly fierce sunshine.

51

"She ducked behind those bushes in case anybody was watching her from one of the huts," continued Lance. "Then she went down to the creek, and threw the gun in the water under the bridge. No, that's too obvious. She dug a hole —"

"What with? The heat's baked the clay to brick. Dulcie would have needed a pickaxe."

"Perhaps she pulled up a bush, and hid the gun under its roots."

Squinting in the sunlight as she emerged from the laundry-room, Gilda walked over to the nearest shrub, and tried to yank it out of the ground. "No. I don't think Dulcie managed to uproot one of these: not if she valued the skin on her hands."

"Then the gun's got to be in the creek or under the bridge," Lance concluded. "After all, she wouldn't have much time in case anyone went into the laundry-room and could later tell us that Dulcie wasn't there."

Wafting away clouds of flies, they ambled down to the creek, crossing bare clay that was iron-hard with cracks zigzagging out in every direction like a giant's road map, and Gilda realized that they were walking on what would be the creek-bed when the rains eventually came. Summer heat had left a mere trickle of sluggish water to meander around rocks before it disappeared under the highway, and on the opposite bank, there was more red clay, and then a few scraggy bushes that only began to grow thicker as the hill slope reached a far distant plateau.

"Dulcie would have to be one of those Olympic javelin throwers to pitch the gun up there," remarked Lance.

"Perhaps she once was an athlete. We don't know much about these people."

"We don't know anything about them. Yet."

Gilda ducked her head and walked underneath the highway bridge, cool shade a welcome respite from sticky heat. Concrete arches rose above the creek in a smooth semi-circle oddly reminiscent of a cathedral, and on the tunnel's other side, there was more red clay and then the unexpected sight of what appeared to be a golf course stretching out to the horizon. A sudden scurry of movement under an arch made her suspect the presence of rats, or even snakes and red-back spiders, and Gilda prudently retreated.

"The gun isn't here," said Lance. "Of course, Dulcie could have lied about going to the laundry-room, but she'd be gambling that nobody was in there at the time or would see her somewhere else. Dulcie hung dry clothes on the washing-line, and then went running to the manager's office. Or perhaps she did do some laundry, and hid the gun on her way to get Hubert Webb to phone for a doctor. Or she might have given the gun to an accomplice who disposed of it for her."

"Or she's innocent, and everything happened exactly as Dulcie said it did." However, Gilda knew that she sounded as unconvinced as the expression crossing Lance's face, and she added, "There might be a boyfriend, but one who waited until he saw Dulcie leave the hut with the washing, and then boyfriend shot inconvenient husband."

"She's in a new country and doesn't go out to work. If Dulcie's acquired a boyfriend, he lives on this hostel."

They looked back across the red clay to the huts, silver tunnels, identical, characterless and anonymous in the sunshine: a foreign land for everyone, including Lance and Gilda.

3

The hostel might have been designed with the impossibility of hiding a gun as the prime purpose of construction, and Lance had become thoroughly annoyed at Dulcie's sleight of hand by the time they reached the manager's office, where Hubert Webb was sitting at his desk behind a counter that ran the full length of the room, an electric fan whirring hot air to a breeze only marginally cooler than its original temperature. His wife was sorting out letters by hut number and placing them in pigeonholes that covered the back wall, and even the arrival of two police detectives was not enough to make her look around until she had finished the task. A few of the letters were in white or brown envelopes, but blue aerogrammes formed the vast majority with news a week old inside them, the migrants' only contact with home, and Mavis Webb knew the importance of her job. She was a small and thin perfectionist with a determined expression, rigidly controlled fair hair and a horror of mistakes.

"The other people in Hut 34," began Lance. "Who are they?"

"The Thornthwaite family have two rooms, and a young man called Oskar Hauser has the remaining one," replied Hubert. "All very nice people."

"What do you know about them?"

"They pay their rent on time. The Thornthwaites are from England: Londoners. A quiet family, and very nice, as I said."

"And Hauser?"

"He's from Vienna. A very nice, polite and —"

"Yes, yes," Lance said impatiently. "Who's in the next hut?"

"Hut 33?" Hubert hesitated, then stood up and slid open a drawer in one of the metal cabinets behind the desk to consult a file. He had not thought to refresh his memory about the occupants of neighbouring huts, and was flustered at being caught out. "Yes, of course. The Kendricks. They have four rooms. Very nice people. And the Yoxalls."

"Not so nice?" prompted Gilda, recalling Dulcie Leyton's less than enthusiastic mention of the family.

"Mrs Yoxall works in the hostel canteen, and I've had to warn her about bad language, but there's been no real trouble: not what you could call trouble."

"We never have trouble here," added Mavis. She turned to face them, and the crisp voice reminded Gilda of schoolteachers she would prefer to forget.

"How old are the Leyton girls?" asked Lance.

"Thirteen, eleven and ten," replied Mavis. "I ordered Christmas presents for them only yesterday, poor things. You never know what life's got hidden up its sleeve."

"We have a children's party every year, and I dress up as Santa Claus," Hubert said, proud to offer evidence of his happy hostel. "It's great fun, and really makes Christmas special for the kids."

"The eldest Leyton daughter's thirteen?" queried Lance. "Any boyfriend bother?"

"You can't use a term like boyfriend when a girl's only thirteen," decreed Mavis. "Thelma's a child."

Gilda could remember being hopelessly in love at the age of thirteen with a devastatingly handsome boy. Unfortunately, she had been at least ten inches taller than Duncan Anderson, but the eldest Leyton girl might be less doomed by height. "Then does Thelma have a friend who's a boy?"

"Well, I did hear a rumour about her and Alan Yoxall," Mavis conceded. "But it means nothing at Thelma's age."

Mrs Webb was forgetting both Romeo and Juliet, thought Gilda. "What did you hear?"

"Oh, just idle gossip, and Clive Leyton was quite right in my opinion. Thelma's far too young to go around with a boy."

"Mr Leyton objected to the friendship?"

"Yes, of course," said Mavis. "What parent wouldn't, when a girl's only thirteen?"

"How old is Alan Yoxall?" demanded Lance.

"Around the same as Thelma: possibly fourteen now."

Lance looked disappointed, having hoped for a burly eighteen-year-old and a quick result to the case, but he persevered. "What sort of boy is this Alan Yoxall?"

"Very quiet," replied Hubert. "He's not at all like his parents. Alan's a football team reserve, and might be a useful goalkeeper if he grows a bit."

"Did the relationship cause trouble between the Leyton and Yoxall families?"

"You can't call it a relationship," protested Mavis. "They're children."

Lance frowned, and Gilda reckoned that he was picturing one of his own daughters seduced by a brawny sportsman, even though Thelma's footballer was already established as an undersized reserve. "How did you come to hear about all this?"

"Gossip," replied Mavis, waving a hand to show how airily she dismissed hearsay. "It's not worth mentioning."

"Why would anyone bother gossiping about a couple of kids?" asked Gilda.

"None of it probably happened anyway," said Hubert.

"But what's the 'it' that probably didn't happen?"

"There was talk of Mr Leyton getting rather upset when he found Thelma with Alan one evening, but you know what gossip's like."

"Where did Leyton catch them together?" Lance demanded, paternal imagination on overdrive.

"It depends on who's telling you the story," said Mavis. "But they're children, just children."

"Yes," agreed Gilda, as she underlined the name Alan Yoxall in her notebook.

"We'll need somewhere to work from: a place for interviews and so on," Lance remarked, with a proprietorial glance around the manager's office.

"The room next door isn't in use," said Hubert, speaking quickly to avoid any chance of eviction from his headquarters. "Well, I keep some files in there, but only ones concerning people who've moved off the hostel, and nobody ever looks at the old records so you won't be disturbed."

"Why keep files that you don't need?" asked Gilda, amused at the bureaucracy.

"In case somebody wants to check them one day," replied Hubert, surprised at having to explain himself. "I'll get a table and a few chairs, and give you a key to the room. I'm sure you'll find it adequate, although it's not much bigger than a wardrobe and the light switch doesn't always work. That can be a bit of a nuisance at times as there's no window, but you're very welcome to the place for as long as you like. Oh, and I wouldn't open the cupboard by the door, if I were you, because I once found a rat inside, a live rat, but they don't usually wander this far from the creek."

"That's reassuring," said Lance. "I'm certain that Inspector Fairfax will make a point of thanking you for your hospitality the moment he shows up."

Hubert smiled his appreciation, and Gilda hoped that he was not counting on effusive gratitude.

****

"I can't work in an oven," Detective Inspector Fairfax announced from the doorway.

"Wait until you've been inside one of the Nissen huts," said Lance. "The migrants are parboiled."

Whatever others might have to endure was of no interest to Wilbur Fairfax, and Gilda accepted her rôle as fetcher and carrier. "I'll go and ask the hostel manager if we can borrow the electric fan in his office."

"Why wasn't one provided in the first place?" Wilbur Fairfax expected to live in a permanent state of room service, and he also expected circumstances to adapt to him without any sort of compromise on his part. He was tall and fair-haired, with a face that bore a slight resemblance to the film actor James Cagney, and when a very young Constable, Wilbur had been known to do imitations of his *Public Enemy* twin, as well as attempting stiff-legged tap-dances at the merrier of Christmas gatherings, but such light-hearted times were long gone. Detective Inspector Fairfax now took himself very seriously indeed, and work could not commence until Gilda returned trailing wire as she lugged an electric fan into the room.

"The manager's being very helpful."

"I should hope so," said Wilbur, condescending to sit down as though the mere sight of a fan made the room cooler. "Well, what have we got here? Suicide?"

"Unlikely," replied Lance. "Clive Leyton was shot in the chest, not the head, and the gun's vanished."

"Is there a wife, and did she find the body?"

"Yes to both."

"Then simply look for a suicide clause in the life insurance policy." Wilbur sat back in his chair, case solved, the formalities over and Dulcie Leyton practically convicted. "The wife got rid of the gun. It's obvious what's going on here."

"Clive Leyton was religious," said Gilda. "He even believed that God spoke directly to him, and that he was meant to launch a new sect in Australia."

"Who told you that? The wife?"

"Yes," conceded Gilda.

"There you are then," decided Wilbur. "She wants to establish him as far too much of a holy Joe even to think about suicide."

"She's established Clive Leyton as crazy in my mind," said Lance. "Only a madman would hear God talking to him in a bathroom."

"A bathroom? If the wife expected you to believe that, then there must be a few rotten apples in her own barrel as well," decreed Wilbur. "What clown selected people like this lot as suitable migrants? We've already got enough maniacs in Australia without importing more of them, especially when they might have a killer wife in tow."

"The family would have looked good on paper," commented Gilda. "Pay-clerk father with three daughters."

"Three kids who are probably as crazed as their parents," said Wilbur. "It's definitely suicide or the wife killed him, given the sound of this crackpot family. After all, it can't be connected to a robbery. These migrants have arrived here with nothing, or they wouldn't be forced to live in Nissen huts."

"Dulcie Leyton might have a boyfriend," Gilda suggested.

"You've picked up rumours?"

"No, but it's a possibility."

"Everything's a possibility," declared Wilbur. "But if there's a boyfriend involved, the wife will have persuaded him to kill her husband. It's the usual way."

Lance nodded, and Gilda tried to image Dulcie as a slinkily seductive vamp, but the apron and dusters rather spoilt the picture. Yet Dulcie had been alone hour after hour in a Nissen hut on an apparently empty hostel, and must have passed the time somehow.

The whirring fan made little difference to the temperature inside the room, and Wilbur had had enough. He stood up and headed for the door, eager to get back to the comforts of civilization. "I'll leave you to gather the details, but it all seems very straightforward. Put pressure on the wife until she cracks. Is she English? Good. She won't be used to armed police."

"It would seem that there's a chance Dulcie Leyton might be armed herself at the moment," remarked Gilda, and Wilbur laughed.

"If it comes to a shoot-out, just make sure that you don't hit one of her kids. The newspapers can get so very sanctimonious about incidents like that. Well, going by what I've heard, I don't reckon this investigation should present even one problem, so I'll expect you to wind everything up in a couple of days at the most. Any questions?"

"Yes. Who shot Clive Leyton and why was he killed?" enquired Lance, and the Inspector laughed again as he strolled out of the room. "That's the case solved then, but I forgot to ask Wilbur if we pistol-whip Dulcie or merely hold a gun to her head."

"A daughter's head might be more effective," said Gilda, "as long as we remember not to press the trigger in case a newspaper editor disapproves of us killing a child."

"There wouldn't be all these restrictions if Dulcie had timed her husband's murder to coincide with the Melbourne Cup. No death wouldn't get a mention in any of the papers on that day. She ought to have had more consideration."

Clive Leyton's daughters had perhaps just heard that their father was dead, and Gilda felt ashamed of forgetting the fact even for a few seconds. "Do you think it might have been some sort of accident?" she asked, hoping that the three girls would have at least one parent left at home to help them get to adulthood.

"An accident?" repeated Lance, sighing at Gilda's naivety. "You reckon that Clive Leyton was cleaning a pistol while reading the Bible?"

"Dulcie might have planted the Bible before she got rid of the gun. Surely all that hogwash about voices and bathrooms has to be phoney."

"If there really had been an accident, why would Dulcie bother planting Bibles or inventing crazy tales of God in a bathroom?"

"Panic?" But the idea sounded feeble even to Gilda, and she opened her notebook in search of a better theory. "Clive Leyton didn't get on with his neighbours."

"And I reckon those neighbours weren't all that fond of Clive Leyton. The man was clearly insane, if we can believe the Dulcie version of him," said Lance. "But whatever happened, she's the most likely person to have disposed of the gun."

"Unless there's a lover who did everything, with or without her knowledge."

"In that case, Dulcie must be the type who drives all men to insanity, not just her husband."

"I can't imagine Dulcie Leyton as a *femme fatale*. She doesn't appear that devious or complicated." To Gilda, Dulcie had seemed a mother first and foremost. She would cope with the death of a husband because children needed her, but the death of a child might destroy Dulcie's whole world. "If there's a boyfriend so desperate to be with her full-time that he's prepared to kill, he'd have to accept the kids and be good to them. I don't think Dulcie's the sort to put her children second."

"Your own kids are difficult enough at times. No boyfriend's going to saddle himself with another man's three brats," declared Lance, but he was speaking about himself. Gilda had never been married, yet she believed that Lance was ridiculously cynical because the childhood loss of her mother had always inclined Gilda to idealize family life. The real Dulcie Leyton still remained unknown to both of them.

****

Hubert Webb had never once thought that the job of a hostel manager could involve anything but the most minor of domestic crises. He had assumed that it would be a more interesting career than the usual office monotony, with greater opportunities for escaping the rut of routine, and he saw himself as a genial host welcoming people on the brink of new and exciting lives. Hubert often said that he aimed at a family-like atmosphere of support and helping hands, but Hubert grew up an only child, and therefore had no idea what he was talking about when he used the expression family-like.

"I don't think that anybody on the hostel considered Mr Leyton a friend." Mavis Webb tried to be as idealistic as her husband, but she had left three sisters behind in England, and should she never see any of them again, grief would not overwhelm her. "If you ask me, the man was completely and utterly unbearable."

"I didn't take to him myself, but nobody on our hostel would shoot anyone," declared Hubert. "They're all such nice and tolerant people."

"The Yoxalls?"

"Well, perhaps the Yoxalls aren't among my favourite families, but I'm sure they wouldn't kill anybody."

"Are you?" Mavis thought of belligerent David and foul-mouthed Irma, and was easily able to imagine them killing each other. The only hope seemed to be that no outsider would get caught in the crossfire. "Mr Leyton never stopped complaining about the Yoxalls."

63

"And I don't blame him. But he complained about everybody, and couldn't seriously have expected me to uproot the Thronthwaites because they're atheists."

"You should have told Mr Leyton that you're an atheist as well. He might have moved his family from our ungodly hostel and be alive now."

"I'm far too English. I don't discuss religion or the lack of it. I'm also a coward, and there was something unnerving about Mr Leyton," admitted Hubert, but he smiled at the idea of an ex-soldier, who had survived a world war, being intimidated by a factory clerk.

The Webbs were in the manager's office, and very conscious of a police presence in the next room. Although Hubert and Mavis had lived in Australia for over twelve years with no intention of ever going back to Britain, that day both of them felt foreign in an alien land simply because none of the police in the vicinity were English.

"Mrs Leyton seemed more agitated than grief-stricken," said Mavis, "but that might have been the shock."

"What else could it be?" asked Hubert.

Terror of getting found out and arrested for murder, thought Mavis. Her husband was an atheist and she had grown up in a strictly Methodist God-fearing home, but Hubert appeared to have the supposed-Christian charity that constantly eluded her. "It must have been an attempted robbery," said Mavis, hoping to dismiss all suspicion of Dulcie Leyton from her mind. "Yes, a robbery's the most likely explanation."

"Then it definitely wasn't anybody from our hostel who squeezed that trigger," declared Hubert. "Everyone's too busy saving for a house or the fare home to waste money on anything that would interest a thief."

A stupid thief in collision with a man who continually made trifling complaints. Whatever the reason for Clive Leyton's death, it was certain to be a petty one, because there had been nothing tragic or great about the supercilious wage clerk who was convinced that the hostel should be run according to his demands. "I still think David Yoxall stole that rent money."

Mavis's remark was apparently a random one, but Hubert could follow the direction that her mind had taken. "There's no evidence. And there's no evidence that Mr Kendrick put any money on the counter, although I believe him."

"So do I. He did put the money there, I'm sure of it, and I'm equally sure that David Yoxall pocketed the lot. He was in the office, and then he was gone, just like the cash."

"It doesn't mean that he went out to steal from the Leytons this morning, armed with a gun."

No, because Dulcie Leyton had somehow acquired the gun. Then Mavis felt ashamed of having allowed her imagination to convict a wife and mother of cold-blooded murder, or even hot-blooded manslaughter. It was safer to think the worst of an unpleasant and stupid drunk. "I wish the Yoxalls would leave the hostel. They simply don't belong here among the other families. Alan's a nice enough boy, but I certainly don't know how he managed it with those parents. I'm not surprised that Mr Leyton was so against his daughter having anything to do with the Yoxalls."

"Just a clash of personalities," said Hubert, unwilling to believe in a melodrama of revenge killings on his impeccably-run hostel. "Even the Kendricks have never grumbled about living next to David Yoxall, and they've got every right to protest after that rent money business. The Thornthwaites don't complain either. There have to be a few concessions made to allow for differences when families live in close proximity, but Mr Leyton had such inflexibly high standards."

It was a polite way to describe Clive's regular gripes at being forced to live in the midst of lesser beings, and Mavis pitied Dulcie. "I don't know why the police are so eager to talk to the Thornthwaites and Oskar Hauser. If they or anyone had heard gunfire this morning, they'd have reported it to us before going to work, and Mrs Leyton wouldn't have shot her husband while the children were around anyway."

"I thought David Yoxall was your chief suspect," Hubert reminded Mavis, smiling.

"Well, if somebody's got to be arrested, I certainly hope it's him. It'd make life a lot easier for us." Mavis sighed for the might-have-been, picturing David Yoxall sneaking into the Leyton rooms in search of any cash left lying about, but unexpectedly encountering Clive instead. It would be the solution to many problems, and a solution that neatly removed the two most objectionable residents from the hostel. Then Mavis sighed again, knowing that she was far more likely to see Dulcie Leyton led away in handcuffs than David Yoxall.

****

"That's Mr Thornthwaite," said Mavis. She stood in the store-room's open doorway, pointing at the road, and then called Jeff's name, beckoning to him.

Gilda looked up from the notes that she was re-reading, and Lance jumped to his feet, hurriedly crossing the room as though he expected to see Jeffrey Thornthwaite attempt to run off. A plain, thickset, brown-haired man in his mid-thirties, wearing a suit with the jacket folded on one arm, sauntered over the gravelly clay towards Mavis, and he was the first relaxed person Gilda had seen for hours.

"Mr Thornthwaite, the police want to talk to you," cried Mavis, unable to keep such startling news to herself for the few seconds it would take him to reach the office.

"The police?" Jeff looked bewildered, and then demanded, "Vron? Is she hurt? Has there been an accident? Elaine?"

"No, no, it's got nothing at all to do with Veronica or Mrs Thornthwaite," Mavis assured Jeff. "You won't believe it, but Mr Leyton was shot this morning."

"Shot? Clive Leyton? You're right; I don't believe it."

Gilda expected Lance to intervene, and ask Mrs Webb to go away so that he could talk to Jeffrey Thornthwaite in private, but Lance was watching the reaction to Mavis Webb's revelation. Dulcie Leyton might already be declared guilty in his mind, but that was no reason to stop looking for a possible accomplice, and if Dulcie had found herself a lover, the man who lived in the other side of the hut was very conveniently located.

"It's true, Mr Thornthwaite, quite true," said Hubert, bustling out of his office to join in the excitement. "The police are here right now."

"How on earth did Clive Leyton manage to get himself shot in an ice-cream factory of all places?" asked Jeff, seeming more amused than shocked. "Did somebody try to make a getaway with the wage office cash, and God told Clive not to hand over the key to the safe?"

"Mr Leyton's dead," said Mavis, as reprovingly as a headmistress catching a pupil joking in the middle of assembly.

Jeff shook his head decisively. "He can't be dead, not Clive Leyton."

"I said that you wouldn't believe me," Mavis commented.

"And Mr Leyton wasn't shot at work," added Hubert. "It happened right here on the hostel."

"Poor Mrs Leyton found him when she went back to the hut after doing some laundry, and —"

"The hut!" gasped Jeff. "Where's Vron?"

"Don't worry," said Mavis. "Veronica's still at school. All the children are."

"But Vron didn't go to school this morning. She was ill, and Dulcie Leyton said that she'd look after her."

"Mrs Leyton never mentioned Veronica," cried Hubert in alarm. "We assumed that your rooms were empty. No one even bothered to check —"

Jeff swung around and started running towards the road. Gilda leapt up, pushed her way past the Webbs and dashed after him, with Lance pounding several paces behind her. She caught up with Jeff as he reached Hut 34, and Gilda tried to grab his arm, but he shook off her grasp, jumped onto the steps, thrust his hand through the open window beside the door, turned the lock and ran inside the hut, shouting Veronica's name. Dreading what she might see, Gilda followed him and hurried past a sofa identical to the one that Clive Leyton had died on only a few feet away, the other side of a partition wall. She stopped at the internal

68

door that led into a second room, and saw Jeffrey Thornthwaite shaking the shoulder of a fair-haired child in a white nightdress who was lying on top of a single bed.

"Vron! Wake up! Vron!"

For a split-second, Gilda thought the worst, but then the girl opened her eyes, looking half-dazed to be shaken out of whatever dream had been reality a moment earlier.

"Vron, are you all right?" demanded Jeff.

Veronica nodded, eyes widening in surprise to see a strange woman in the room. The girl looked so very young and vulnerable, lying on top of the bed in her nightdress, that Gilda felt only a miracle could have kept any child safe that day in a room so close to Clive Leyton's body.

Jeff sank down on the bed, his legs abruptly buckling beneath him, and he laughed unsteadily. "Now I know why Leyton tried to keep his kids locked up."

"Veronica, did all the noise frighten you this morning?" asked Gilda.

The girl sat up, long plaits falling over her shoulders, and she glanced doubtfully at Gilda before turning to Jeff for an explanation.

"I don't know who she is either, Vron," he said. "Are you sure you're all right? No one came in here?"

Veronica shook her head, but moved closer to Jeff as Lance rushed into the hut, demanding breathlessly, "What happened? Is she OK?"

"Yes, everything appears to be fine," replied Gilda. "I was just asking Veronica if she'd been frightened by any noises this morning."

"And was she?" Lance seemed to think that a translation service was required when dealing with children, and he looked at Gilda, rather than Veronica, as he spoke.

"Nothing frightened you, did it, Vron?" asked Jeff, but he wanted the reassurance for himself. His young daughter had been left alone inside a Nissen hut with doors anyone could unlock, and Jeff guessed that the police considered him a feckless parent, especially as excuses were all he could offer by way of defence. "Dulcie Leyton said that she'd watch Vron until I got back, and my wife would have taken the morning off work if Dulcie hadn't promised us that she'd look after Vron."

"Yes, yes," said Lance, eager to hustle the investigation along. "What did she hear?"

"Veronica, was there any noise earlier on? Any sort of noises at all?" Gilda had little hope of a child talking freely in front of strangers, but to make matters worse, the Webbs chose that moment to hurry inside the hut.

"Is Veronica OK?" Mavis called, as she and Hubert tried to see whatever Lance was blocking from their view.

"Everything's fine," said Lance, turning around and attempting to usher the Webbs out. "Nothing happened in here."

"Oh, that's such wonderful news!" There was genuine relief in Mavis's voice and Hubert actually laughed aloud, forgetting that the sound would travel through partition walls into a mirror-image room where Clive Leyton's body had lain on the plastic cover of a sofa.

"I didn't think that there could be any good news today," declared Hubert, rejoicing in his happy hostel's reprieve, "but this is the very best news I could hear."

"It makes all the difference," agreed Mavis, apparently now able to dismiss Clive Leyton's death as a minor event, but Gilda knew exactly what Mavis meant. A young girl was alive, and the fact seemed enough to cancel out the rest of the morning.

As Lance escorted the Webbs out of the hut, Gilda turned back to Veronica who had the stubbornly blank expression of a child about to face a scolding, and any information would have to be prised out of her because school had taught Veronica that she was in the wrong, no matter what the circumstances. Gilda understood, having once adopted the same blank look whenever a teacher asked a question, but Lance expected the kid to talk in response to that magic instinct he assumed all women must have, and Gilda forced a smile before recognizing her salvation in the shape of a small metal badge on top of a chest-of-drawers next to the bed: a badge of a ship with billowing sails, and the name *Argo* underneath. She had spotted a link, a conversation-opener.

"Good rowing, Argonaut," said Gilda, and Veronica glanced up, blue eyes round with surprise. "I was Hesperides 25. What's your ship and number?"

"Herodotus 19." Veronica was no longer deliberately blank, but intrigued. She had never met a fellow Argonaut.

"I was thirteen when I joined, so only managed to get as far as Dragon's Tooth, but you've got plenty of time to reach the Golden Fleece. Have you had any contributions read out yet?"

"Just one."

"That's quite an achievement at your age," Gilda commented. "What did you write about?"

"Coming to Australia, and the ports that the ship visited on the way."

"I wish I'd heard it. You must be very clever."

"No, not really." Veronica squirmed, both pleased and embarrassed by the compliment.

"I've never been on board a ship, but you had a genuine Argonaut journey to get here. Which places did you see?"

"Malta and Egypt and Aden and —"

"What's Aden got to do with it?" asked Lance, back in the room and impatient for Gilda to extract some useful information from the kid. "What are you talking about?"

"Greek mythology on the whole, and you'd be amazed how much Veronica could tell you about Jason and his voyages," replied Gilda, noting that the child had immediately readopted her blank expression at Lance's abruptness. "Neither of your daughters can be an Argonaut, I reckon, if you don't know the badge when you see it."

"It's a bit like a Masonic Lodge for kids," said Jeff, still trembling slightly, yet unable to resist an opportunity to air his heavy-handed humour in an effort to pretend that everything was normal and that there had never been any threat to his daughter's safety. "Vron's being indoctrinated via the wireless by your ABC *Children's Hour*, and her mother and I aren't allowed to speak a word between five and six o'clock each evening."

"Oh," said Lance, unimpressed.

"The Argonauts send in letters and stories, and if your contribution's read out on air, you get points that take you further on your journey to reach the Golden Fleece," Gilda explained.

"Oh."

Lance appeared unable to see the necessity of getting past the child's wariness, but a minor part of Gilda's life, a club she once joined because a schoolfriend had, indicated a possible way forward. "There are songs and plays too, and talks on art and books — well, it's a lot more fun than I'm making it sound, isn't it Veronica?"

"I'm sure it's fascinating," retorted Lance. "But we've got a job to do."

And Gilda was trying to do it. "Tell me about this morning, Veronica."

"She was disappointed to miss the end of term," said Jeff. "It's a gala day apparently, with film shows and ice-cream, but when even the thought of those attractions couldn't cure her, we knew that Vron was a genuine invalid. Probably something to do with the heat, because we're not used to these temperatures yet, but Vron seems to have slept off whatever ailed her."

"Was she asleep when you left?" asked Lance, pleased to gather evidence without having to acknowledge the presence of a child.

"No, but she'd gone back to bed. And Dulcie Leyton promised to look after her."

"Yes, you told us earlier," said Lance, to cut short another round of Jeff's excuses for leaving his sick daughter on her own.

Gilda wished that Lance would either go away or keep quiet, but she persevered. "Did you sleep right through the morning until your Dad came in just now, Veronica?"

"No one could possibly sleep inside this hut today," decreed Lance. "The heat's ridiculous. It's too hot to breathe in here."

"We manage," said Jeff, pleased to feel superior and imply that Lance was a weakling. "Obviously the famed Dunkirk spirit has kicked in."

"If she's been asleep in these temperatures all morning, it's a wonder that she isn't completely dehydrated by now."

"Then a miracle's happened, and Vron can now take up her bed and walk over to the canteen for lunch," said Jeff. "There's no point in asking Vron any more questions. I know she won't be able to help you because nothing wakes her once she's asleep. Vron's been like that since she was a baby. Head on the pillow and she's out like a light. They say it's the result of a clear conscience."

"Did you wake up, Veronica?" asked Gilda. "Do you remember any noise? A loud noise?"

Veronica shook her head, and Gilda was torn between relief that a child had been spared hearing any part of Clive Leyton's death, and frustration at not being able to glean the slightest information from someone so close to the crime scene. However, it was unlikely that anybody on the other side of a thin partition wall, no matter how sound a sleeper that person might be, would remain undisturbed by violent arguments and gunshot, so presumably there had been no screams, no shouts and a silencer on the gun. Negative testimony, assumed but not confirmed.

"Veronica, you're quite sure that you didn't wake up?" pleaded Gilda. "Not even for a moment, say, after a really bad dream?"

Veronica shook her head again, and Lance turned to Jeff. "What time did you go out?"

"Just after eight. I had to catch a train at eight-ten."

"Was your wife still here?"

"No, her shift started at eight, so she left about ten to. Elaine works at the ice-cream factory by the station."

"Where do you work?"

"The same place, but this morning I was going to a job interview at Hardy Spicer's. If Dulcie Leyton hadn't promised to look after Vron —"

"Yes, yes, I know," said Lance. "Did you hear anything from the Leyton side of the hut before you went out?"

"No, but Oskar was playing his records, and you're only aware of Beethoven when the volume's turned up full blast. We like the music, although Clive Leyton kicked up a fuss about it most days, but complaining was his hobby when he wasn't glued to the Bible."

"Would you describe him as a religious man?"

"I'd describe Clive Leyton as a deluded man," Jeff replied. "How would you describe someone who claimed that God chatted to him in bathrooms?"

"Do you mean that Clive Leyton claimed it in person, or did his wife tell you about those hallucinations?" asked Lance, seizing the opportunity to strengthen a prosecution case against Dulcie.

"Clive told everybody who'd listen that he and God were on first name terms," said Jeff, scornful at the memory of human conceit. "He even maintained that it was God who ordered him to emigrate, and I think he genuinely believed —"

"Jeff! Jeff, the Webbs told me —" A dark-haired woman in her mid-twenties ran into the hut, stopping abruptly at the sight of Lance Palmer. Looking fresh enough to have just taken a shower, Elaine Thornthwaite in pale-blue dress, high heels and skilfully applied make-up appeared the least likely person to have recently finished a factory shift.

"Vron's OK," called Jeff. "She's been asleep all morning. Didn't hear a thing."

"Yes, the Webbs said that she was OK. I can't believe any of this. It's like being in the middle of a film. Awful for Dulcie."

No one said awful for Clive, Gilda noted. In fact, no one had said a word that made Clive Leyton sound much of a loss to humanity, and the picture forming in her mind showed a self-centred man whose rationality was in short supply. Had Clive lived, he might even have persuaded himself that he was Christ reincarnated as he slid further towards insanity, and his death had perhaps removed many future problems.

"I saw the whole Leyton family this morning, and not for one second did I think that something so dreadful was about to happen," Elaine marvelled, despite her having no history of clairvoyant abilities. "It was just an ordinary morning: Dulcie getting the girls ready for school, and Clive sitting on the sofa reading his Bible. I asked Dulcie to look after Vron, and she promised me that —"

"Yes, we know," said Lance. "What time did you see the Leytons?"

"Twenty to eight? A quarter to?" Elaine looked at Jeff for confirmation, and he nodded.

"It would have been around then because you left for work about ten to eight, didn't you? You'd gone when I got back."

"Back from where?" asked Lance.

"The toilet block. All mod cons on this hostel."

"Vron was in bed, and so I left. I didn't want to be late." Elaine sounded awkward, and was compelled to add, "But if Dulcie Leyton hadn't promised me —"

76

"Yes, yes," said Lance. "So you didn't notice anything unusual about the Leyton family this morning?"

"No, nothing at all. Not a thing." Elaine shook her head at such a lack of intuition, and looked helplessly at Lance.

"How long did you talk to Mrs Leyton?"

"Only for a few minutes. I explained about Vron, and Dulcie promised to keep an eye on her. If she hadn't promised —"

"Did Mrs Leyton seem agitated or upset?" Lance hated the way witnesses strayed off in all directions when he wanted concise information, and somebody who had seen the family on the last occasion that they would all be together ought not to dwell on herself.

"It was just an ordinary morning," Elaine said again. "The children were about to leave for school, Clive was on the sofa holding a Bible up in front of his face, and I stood on the steps and chatted to Dulcie for a couple of minutes. That was it. Just the start of another hostel day."

"Did you notice anyone hanging around?"

"Hanging around? Everyone was rushing around," Elaine replied. "The children have to get breakfast and pick up their lunchtime crib bags in the canteen, and the ice-cream factory's day shift starts at eight, so everybody's in a hurry at that time. Apart from Clive. He didn't have to be in the office until nine, so he was sitting still. I can't believe that he's dead; I simply can't."

"So you didn't notice anything different?"

Elaine thought, gazing at Lance as if she imagined the sight of his handsome face would produce the answers he wanted. "I'm sorry, but I didn't notice a thing, but that might have been because I was thinking — thinking about Vron and not being late

77

— oh, just thinking. Perhaps that's why I didn't pick up the slightest sense of something awful about to happen."

"You never do notice other people," declared Jeff. "You don't look further than their clothes. If Dulcie had been standing with a gun pressed to the side of Clive's head, you'd just remember that she was wearing black shoes."

"Brown sandals this morning," said Elaine, trying to smile. "Pale-green dress and yellow apron."

The hut was getting increasingly stuffy, its oppressive heat as uncomfortable as a damp coat, and Lance mentally wrote off the Thornthwaite family, so close to the death of Clive Leyton and yet so useless. "We'll take formal statements when there's a bit more time, and you can read them through before signing them."

"But there's nothing worth a signature," said Jeff. "Vron didn't hear a sound and, unless you want a fashion report, Elaine might as well have talked to Dulcie with eyes shut."

"Your wife saw Clive Leyton alive at around twenty to eight. That could be important evidence."

"Lots of people would have seen Clive reading," said Elaine, flattered by Lance's attention and the words that she took as a compliment, although an English upbringing forced her to seem modest. "The hut door was wide open."

"But you actually spoke to the family."

"Only to Dulcie, not the girls or Clive. I knew how much he hated being disturbed when he was reading his Bible, so I didn't say hello to him, or goodbye. No, I didn't even say goodbye." Elaine sighed, because it felt right to appear regretful at such a time, but her thoughts were with Dulcie and the widow's newfound freedom.

78

"If you remember anything more, anyone acting oddly, let us know," said Gilda, as she and Lance went out of the hut.

"Yes, of course. I'll tell you at once." But Elaine was speaking to Lance.

****

"Is Mr Leyton really dead?" asked Veronica. "Dead forever?"

"Don't think about him," said Jeff. "He's in the past, and the past doesn't exist any more. It's gone."

"Gone forever?"

"Forever," declared Jeff.

4

The children were back from school, and the silent hostel sprang into life. High-pitched voices shouted and laughed in celebration of the long summer holidays, as running footsteps pounded on the stony paths between huts.

"Time to track down teenage idol Alan Yoxall," said Lance.

****

Hut 33 was a precise replica of both Huts 32 and 34, outside and inside. A blue door opened to reveal more cream paint on the walls of a right-angled room that contained an identical sofa-bed covered in black and white plastic, while the same airless heat baked the hut's inhabitants.

"I suppose you thought that Alan would be on his own at this time of day, and you could put words in his mouth," Dave Yoxall snarled.

"Your son's own words are the ones I want to hear," retorted Lance.

Dave Yoxall snorted derisively at the attempt to dupe him. He was a bulky man from Sheffield, red-faced and plain, automatically hostile to any form of authority, and with a fixed belief that bad manners equalled independence of mind. "Alan didn't get her pregnant, so we're not forking out for any brat whatever they think."

Lance had taken a few steps inside the room, but Gilda stood in the doorway and she noticed that groups of children were drawing gradually closer to the hut, fascinated by the sound of Dave's belligerence and the sight of strangers. "We could talk more privately in the store-room next to the manager's office," Gilda suggested, indicating the children, but Dave bristled at the idea of being silenced.

"I've got nothing to say that can't be said openly in front of anyone. Alan didn't get the Leyton girl pregnant, and that's the end of the matter, like it or lump it."

"Did Clive Leyton accuse your son of getting one of his daughters pregnant?" asked Lance, already wearying of Dave's pig-headedness.

"Everybody on the hostel thinks that Alan got the little tart pregnant, but he didn't, and I don't care what you say. You can't prove a thing."

"I asked a question that you chose not to answer, Mr Yoxall. Did Clive Leyton accuse your son of getting one of his daughters pregnant? Yes or no?"

"I suppose now you're going to charge Alan with killing the nutter. Well, he didn't do that either. He was at school this morning, all morning, and we can prove it." Dave smirked in triumph, convinced that he had just foiled a police scheme to haul Alan away in handcuffs.

"Your son's not accused of anything," said Gilda, hoping to shield Lance from the temptation to arrest Dave for obstructing the inquiry. "We have to talk to everybody who knew Mr Leyton to build up a picture of the sort of man he was."

"A nutcase," declared Dave. "That's the sort he was. And before you start accusing me of anything, I was at work this morning. You can check at the factory all you like, because I was on the eight o'clock shift. It's the ice-cream factory by the station, and you can ask anybody and they'll all tell you that Dave Yoxall was there the whole morning."

"I'm sure they will," agreed Gilda, certain that no one in the vicinity of loud-mouthed and heavy-footed David Yoxall could remain unaware of the fact. "Is your son here?"

"Alan!" bellowed Dave, evidently imagining that his shout needed to reach the other end of the hostel, and an undersized fourteen-year-old boy appeared in the doorway of the next room. "Tell them it's not your brat, whatever those Leytons claim."

"I didn't get Thelma pregnant, honest I didn't," mumbled Alan, too embarrassed to look up. "We never — Thelma and me, we never — you know — not once. Honest."

"So how can it be Alan's kid?" demanded Dave. "And we're not paying a penny, not a single penny, so you can put that in your pipe and smoke it."

"Have the Leytons asked for money?"

"It wouldn't do them any good if they did."

"So they haven't?"

"You can tell them from me that they're not getting a farthing," declared Dave, brooding on his wrongs. "I work all the hours God sends, and I know my rights. I'm not stupid. I could have been a professional footballer, if that door hadn't done my knee in, and Walter Winterbottom himself said to me, 'Dave,' he said, 'Dave, if only I could have you in the England team, we'd win every match we played.' Those were Walter Winterbottom's very words, and nobody's going to trick me into parting with money."

"Do you have a gun?" asked Lance, and Gilda half-expected to witness a spectacular display of spontaneous combustion as David Yoxall exploded.

"I haven't held a gun since the war, and I wouldn't be fool enough to tell you if I had one now. Do you think I'm stupid?"

"Thank you for your co-operation," said Gilda, trusting that Dave's question had been a rhetorical one.

The crowd of children was growing with every minute, but Dave apparently had no objection to private matters turning into public knowledge, because he followed Lance and Gilda out of the hut onto the steps, and shouted after them, "You're not fitting me up to take the rap, and my wife works in the canteen with most of the hostel as alibis, so don't even think of trying to accuse her of murdering Leyton."

"That's one migrant I hope goes back where he came from," remarked Gilda, conscious that the flock of children had started to trail after her and Lance.

"England would pretend Yoxall's passport was a fake, and return him on the very next boat," said Lance. "Interesting bit of information all the same. I wonder who did get the Leyton girl pregnant."

"Probably Alan. Would you admit the truth to that father?"

"Have a quiet word with the girl," ordered Lance, glad to delegate the responsibility of dealing with a bereaved and pregnant thirteen-year-old.

"God help Alan if the baby's his," said Gilda.

****

The worst jobs were easiest when tackled at once, before there was time to dread them. Gilda forced herself up the steps of Hut 32 and knocked on the open door, even though she could see the Leyton girls sitting in a row on the sofa. They were fair-haired, pretty copies of Dulcie, and all three looked warily at Gilda who was relieved that there were no tears.

There had been no tears when Vincent Garfield tried to tell his seven-year-old daughter that Mum was now in heaven with the angels. Gilda covered her ears and refused to listen, because once the words were spoken aloud, life would become the howling wilderness: an expression that troubled her, despite not knowing what it meant. Yet the howling was already inside her as she screamed and screamed without a sound being heard by the people who told Gilda how brave she was.

"Oh, it's you," said Dulcie, glancing around. "Mr Webb's got us some rooms in another hostel, and he can drive us there straightaway. That'll be all right, won't it?"

"Yes, I'm sure it's OK. Could I talk to Thelma, just for a moment?"

"Oh, you're not going to ask her if she's pregnant, are you?" said Dulcie, with a weary sigh. "When I heard that repulsive Yoxall man shouting, I should have known the very next thing would be you turning up on the doorstep with questions. Everybody's so understanding and sympathetic, and there's no need for either. It was that nasty-minded Veronica Thornthwaite who spread the story. She's such a liar, and I'll be glad to get my daughters away from her. You can't trust a thing that girl says, and yet Veronica's totally convincing when she spins one of her yarns. Clive got really worried by the rumours, and actually took Thelma to see a doctor, and it was all Veronica's fault, although she'll deny saying a word."

So the holier than holy Clive Leyton had required medical proof, rather than believe what his daughter would undoubtedly have told him. Thelma was listening impassively, the middle girl gazed at the floor, but the youngest stared antagonistically at Gilda, challenging the outsider who thought that she had the right to blunder into their private world on such a harrowing day.

"I'll see that the rest of your things are sent on as soon as possible," said Gilda. "And there's an organization that helps migrants get through difficult times. I could contact them and explain the circumstan—"

"We don't need charity," declared Dulcie.

"You can repay any loan when the insurance policies —" Gilda tactfully left the rest of her sentence to hang in air, hoping that the kids had no idea what she was talking about.

Dulcie moved into the doorway, making Gilda retreat down the steps. "There aren't any policies. After God spoke to him, Clive cancelled all our insurance."

"How come?" asked Gilda, surprised at such recklessness in a wage clerk. "Was it something else the voice told him to do?"

"No, but Clive decided that taking out insurance showed lack of trust, as well as lack of faith. God had a plan when he created us, so whatever happens is his will, and we have to accept it unconditionally. At least, that's what Clive said."

A pity that sainted Clive had ignored the quotation about the Lord helping those who helped themselves, but Dulcie would probably blame her husband enough in the coming months and years without Gilda joining in the criticism. "If there's anything I can do, don't hesitate to ask."

"We'll be all right," said Dulcie, but more for the children's benefit than because she believed her own words. She turned back into the hut, dismissing Gilda like a fly that had been wafted away from sight and mind, but Dulcie would be unable to fool herself for long. The family needed help, whether or not Dulcie's pride got hurt.

It was impossible to wish the Leytons luck at such a time, and so Gilda merely said goodbye. The crowd of hostel kids must have decided that a policeman was more interesting than a policewoman, and they had continued to follow Lance, but Gilda skirted around the stragglers, and caught up with him outside the manager's office, where he was listening to Hubert Webb.

"There's no reason why the Leytons can't leave for Nunnawading today, is there?"

"Not that I can think of," replied Lance. "I'll mention it to Inspector Fairfax, but you can drive them there now, if you like."

"Good," said Hubert, smiling with relief. "Mrs Leyton wants to get away from here as soon as possible, and I think she's right. It'll be the best thing for the girls. A completely new place will be a distraction."

The Leytons would need more than a change of address to help them forget what had happened, but Hubert looked as though he had discovered a magic wand that could make anything vanish, and Gilda hoped he would also be able to access more mundane assistance for the Leyton family.

"Mr Webb, there's an organization that helps migrants in financial difficulties. I can't remember the name —"

"I've already contacted them, and explained all the circumstances. Everything's arranged," said Hubert, proud of his efficiency. Children were jostling each other to hear him, and he waved an arm in an attempt at crowd dispersal. "There'll be games in the Rec starting in five minutes: games with lots and lots of prizes. Let's find Mrs Webb, and get everything organized. Come on."

The children accepted Hubert's bribe, and began to drift off in his wake, a few of the younger ones walking backwards to make certain that they were not being cheated out of witnessing a dramatic demonstration of police action, and Lance breathed freely again. "If only the kids had done something, I could have ordered them to go away," he complained. "But all they did was follow me. Well, is lover-boy Alan the culprit?"

"No, the baby was fathered entirely by gossip. Thelma's not pregnant, but apparently her word wasn't good enough for Clive Leyton. When he heard the rumours, the poor kid got dragged off to visit a doctor."

"Oh well, Leyton did us a favour. At least we can be sure that something didn't happen."

"My father would have believed me," said Gilda.

"And I'd believe my daughters," claimed Lance, to link himself with Vincent Garfield's high paternal standard. "I reckon this probably means that we can forget about Alan Yoxall."

"But perhaps we ought to remember his aggressive father," Gilda suggested.

"If he was inside an ice-cream factory when Clive Leyton was shot, it doesn't matter how stupid or resentful the non-expectant grandfather is."

"There's something not right about David Yoxall though. I think it wouldn't take much to turn that man violent."

"Half-witted thugs and madmen hearing the voice of God in bathrooms," sighed Lance. "Who the hell's selecting these migrants?"

Gilda had imagined that a young Viennese would be blond and sturdy: an athlete who regarded running up an alp or two as no more than the daily stroll that prepared him to waltz through the evening. However, Oskar Hauser was thin and brown-haired, and even when ushered into the store-room to face police questioning, he had a great deal of composure for a man in his early twenties who only a few months previously had arrived alone in a new country.

"Yes, I heard in the shop, the delicatessen where I work, that Mr Leyton was dead, but failed to realize it meant I would be stopped by the police and then have to answer questions before I could return to the hut," said Oskar, his careful English a tribute to the European system of education. "Have you searched my room?"

"Would you object?" Lance was guided by routine into a show of investigating every possibility, but he had no real interest in Oskar Hauser as a suspect.

"You think that I might have shot Mr Leyton?" Oskar looked astonished, and then shook his head in a disbelief that was mingled with amusement. "Why would I do so bizarre a deed?"

"I've heard that Clive Leyton complained about you playing loud music."

"You seem to be confusing me with Beethoven, who would certainly have been tempted to shoot Mr Leyton after such a complaint. But perhaps you think that I shoot anyone who fails to appreciate music? The world might be a better place if I did, but the action would have disagreeable consequences for me."

Lance was used to belligerence and defensiveness when he asked questions, but quiet confidence made him suspect that a mighty detective sergeant was being mocked, and he demanded, "What happened this morning?"

"I got out of bed, went to the shower block, went to the canteen for breakfast, and then went to work." Oskar shrugged, resigned to the eventlessness of his routine, and added, "It was a morning like any other for me."

"So you'd have no objection to your room being searched?"

"Do what you must, but if I had shot Mr Leyton, I would be most unlikely to leave a gun in my room for the police to find."

Lance stiffened, aware that he had been snubbed by a shop assistant. "Did you hear the argument?" he snapped.

"I heard something of it, but turned up the volume on my record-player."

"There *was* an argument!" Lance said in triumph, looking at Gilda to make sure that she noted the way his skilful interrogation technique had finally uncovered the truth. "When did you hear them arguing?"

"It was after breakfast, but long before I went to work: in fact, it was during the second movement of the Ninth Symphony, and I had time to listen to the finale, so the argument must have been close to eight o'clock. Does the exact hour matter?"

"I'll be the judge of that. Did you hear what they were arguing about?"

"I only heard the child cry out, and Mr Thornthwaite shout."

"Thornthwaite?" gasped Lance.

"Yes, and then nothing but my music. I turned up the volume, as I said."

"You're sure it was Jeffrey Thornthwaite you heard, not Clive Leyton?"

"The noise came from the Thornthwaite rooms."

"But you can't be sure of that, can you?" pleaded Lance. "You had music playing, so it could have been the Leytons?"

"At the time it seemed to me that all sounds came from the Thornthwaite side of the hut."

"But you can't be absolutely certain about that."

"I occasionally pretend to be a philosopher, therefore is anything in this life certain?" Oskar shrugged again, evidently regarding himself as a passive audience member rather than an active participant in the life of the hostel. "I thought that the noises came from the Thornthwaite rooms, and I apologise for any mistake."

"Did you hear a woman's voice too?"

"No, just the child and Mr Thornthwaite."

Oskar Hauser was going to make a good witness in the future trial, decided Gilda: a very good witness indeed. Dulcie's lawyer would point out that there had been no proof found of a Leyton argument, and Oskar's quiet coolness was unlikely to be shaken. "Did you recognize Mr Thornthwaite's voice?" asked Gilda.

"I heard a man," Oskar replied, after a moment's consideration. "And which other man but Mr Thornthwaite would be in that side of the hut with Veronica?"

"What's he like?" Gilda's brain raced ahead of the evidence, and she was fairly sure that the same theory had leapt fully-fledged into Lance's mind as well. "Does Jeffrey Thornthwaite often get cross with his daughter?"

"No. I was surprised. A very quiet family. But Mr Thornthwaite told me that they all like to hear my music, so of course I approve of him."

"And Mr Leyton?"

"Mr Leyton," repeated Oskar, grimacing. "Mr Leyton failed to make earth a happier place because of his existence."

"What are you talking about?" asked Lance. "Do you mean the way he treated his family — his daughters?"

"He made things more disagreeable than they need be."

"More disagreeable for who? His daughters?"

"Yes, certainly," agreed Oskar, without hesitation.

"In what way?"

"He tried to keep his children in a prison. He wanted to stop them talking to people."

"Stop them talking about what?" Lance leaned forward, frowning his censure of the Leyton pervert's conduct even before an answer had been given.

"Stop them talking and making friends," replied Oskar. "I heard him say that the other children living on the hostel were running wild like animals, but he was probably frightened that they would teach his daughters to laugh and be happy."

"His daughters weren't happy then? Did you hear him shout at the girls?"

"Constantly. Laughter ended when Mr Leyton was there."

"Did he often upset his daughters?" Lance was trying not to put words into a witness's mouth, but Gilda knew precisely what he expected to be told. "Did you ever hear the girls crying?"

"I've heard the eldest girl cry. Thelma was friendly with a boy, and Mr Leyton disapproved, of course."

"How come?"

"Mr Leyton wished to control every aspect of family life."

"But how come you think that?"

"Because he was a dictator, with wife and daughters as his only subjects."

"So, in your opinion, he wanted power over the girls?"

"A fact, not an opinion," declared Oskar. "Perhaps he ruled under divine instruction. Mr Leyton thought that he was religious, but the God he invented made the world a very bleak place."

"Did the other daughters cry?"

"I played my music loud for a reason," said Oskar. "I preferred not to hear the Leyton family."

"How come?"

"Because they depressed me."

"What exactly did you find depressing about the Leyton family?"

"Dictatorships are always depressing," replied Oskar, surprised that Lance had failed to grasp the point for himself.

"Would you say that Clive Leyton ill-treated his daughters?" urged Lance, eager to steer Oskar from political philosophy and back into the area of evidence.

"Mr Leyton refused to let the girls be themselves: be children."

"What do you mean?" Lance demanded. "How did he refuse to let them be children?"

"They had no freedom, no happiness. The lives of children are often far from ideal, but there was no war or poverty in this case. There was only Mr Leyton."

"Did he argue with his wife?"

"Dictators scorn argument."

"Then what else did you hear?"

"Beethoven, and sometimes Schubert or Schumann," said Oskar. "I turned up the volume of my music to avoid being reminded of the Leyton family."

****

"It's always the self-styled religious ones, always. Either Clive Leyton's daughters weren't enough for him or Dulcie managed to protect them," declared Lance.

"That's not precisely what Oskar said," Gilda pointed out, but Lance had made up his mind.

"Jeffrey Thornthwaite found his little girl hysterical inside the hut, got the story out of her, and then went and shot Clive Leyton. I'd do exactly the same if that pervert had attacked one of my daughters."

"Where did the gun come from?" asked Gilda.

"Jeffrey Thornthwaite was either in the war or did his National Service afterwards, so he'll have had access to all sorts of guns, and know how to use them. I'd take a gun to a new country as well, to protect my kids. Those huts aren't secure." Lance had stopped thinking like a policeman. He was now one hundred per cent father, and Jeff Thornthwaite represented a shining example of parental care.

"I know it's only a theory," said Gilda, "but should we get Veronica to a doctor?"

"The poor kid's been through enough," decreed Lance. "If the quacks got hold of her, she'd never recover. Just knowing that Leyton's dead will be the best thing for her. Jeffrey's saved

Australia a lot of bother and expense, and he had the right to shoot the pervert, in my opinion. It's what any father would do."

"It's certainly what my Dad might have done, whether he had the right or not," said Gilda, imagining the relish her trigger-happy father would have felt as he disposed of a child-molester. "But how do we prove any of it without getting a doctor involved? Jeffrey Thornthwaite's not going to confess."

"It's nothing more than a theory that he might have killed Clive Leyton, and I'm not about to persecute a father who was put in that situation by a pervert. Leyton's the one who's guilty, and he deserved what he got, so justice has been done. As far as I'm concerned, the official line can be that Leyton was insane, committed suicide, and his wife removed the gun because of an insurance policy clause, just as Wilbur Fairfax said."

"There's a slight snag with that story. According to Dulcie, Clive Leyton didn't have any life insurance. It went against his newfound beliefs."

"Typical of the man!" sneered Lance. "Couldn't give a damn if his kids survived or not. Who cares how a brute like that dies? Sooner or later, a crazed politician's going to give an order, and half the world will be vaporized while everybody else faces an agonizingly slow death, yet no police will be sent in to arrest the mad politician for murder. I sometimes wonder why we pretend a single life matters so much."

"I'll resign when I start to believe that," said Gilda.

"You could be right, but I didn't think any of us had a future last October, and all we've gained is borrowed time."

"Then I reckon we'd better make the most of it." Australia had once seemed very far away from bombs and blitzes, but no country would be distant enough to escape the aftermath of nuclear detonation. Anzac volunteers had travelled to the other side of the world to fight, but the next war zone was going to invade both Australia and New Zealand, and threaten every man, woman and child in the South Pacific region. "I'm glad I don't have kids," said Gilda.

"I used to think that the atom bomb kept us safe, as nobody would be fool enough to start a nuclear war, but I underestimated human stupidity." Lance sighed, angry at the fate that he had no power to avert. It made effort and ambition futile, and his decision to stay in a bleak marriage until his daughters left home had become a life sentence, because his kids would never be given a chance to grow up. They were among the last children on earth, and if Jeffrey Thornthwaite's swift justice meant that Clive Leyton's daughters had a happier time of whatever days remained, then Jeffrey Thornthwaite deserved a medal.

****

"Oh, Dulcie, I'm so sorry," cried Elaine, as she glanced around to see who was climbing up the steps of Hut 34. "I'm so very sorry. It's awful, the worst thing —"

"I've just dropped in to say goodbye," Dulcie said, to avoid the emotion of condolences. "Mr Webb's arranged for us to go to another hostel. He did tell me the name, but I've completely forgotten it. I wanted to apologize for not remembering about Veronica this morning. Is she any better?"

"Don't worry. Vron's fine. Dulcie, I can't believe any of this."

"I know, and what's dreadful, what makes me feel so much worse, is that Clive and I had a big quarrel this morning," confessed Dulcie. "I expect Veronica mentioned that he said the girls couldn't go to school today because of the film show?"

"No, Vron didn't say a word to me," replied Elaine, unsurprised. She found it difficult to take an interest in a child's limited world, an indifference that Veronica had sensed and therefore rarely bothered her mother with details. "Vron lives in a dream half the time, and she never notices what happens around her. I blame books, but Jeff's always encouraging her to read."

"But she must have heard the entire quarrel. Clive said that the girls weren't to leave the hut, but after he went out to the toilet block, I told them to go to school, and they were off like greased lightning before I changed my mind. I must have the only children in the world who want to run away to school." Dulcie tried to smile, abandoned the attempt and continued, "Anyhow, when Clive came back, we had a horrible row and he threatened to charge up to the school, and I said that if he did, I'd leave him, get a job, save up and take the girls back to England. There's no harm in a film, and Clive used to go to the cinema most weekends before God spoke to him, but when I pointed that out, I'm afraid we yelled a bit. Poor Veronica will have heard it all. She must have."

"No need to worry. Vron was asleep the whole time. She couldn't tell the police a thing."

"She couldn't? Oh, I'm so glad that the police don't know about the argument," said Dulcie, sinking down onto the sofa as she sighed with relief. "I should have told them myself; I know I should have told them every single word we spoke this morning, but it would have made Clive sound like an awful father, and he couldn't help God picking on him. Besides, none of this has got anything to do with — with what happened."

"Of course not, and I wouldn't talk about family business either. It's private." Elaine did not add that she might be willing to tell the dark-haired and handsome Detective Sergeant Palmer whatever he wanted to hear. She was an adult, married, a mother, and yet Elaine had never progressed beyond the adolescent phase of plunging headlong into an immediate crush on every good-looking man she encountered. Her upbringing insisted that acquiring a husband should mean she stopped noticing other men, but Jeff's mockery alienated his wife, and Elaine suspected that her lack of education had attracted him as much as her appearance. With a wife both ill-informed and ill-read, Jeff would always feel superior, knowing that she could never challenge any of his opinions, and Jeff had an opinion about everything. When they first met, his wide-ranging interests had made him stand out from the other men Elaine dated, who droned on incessantly about football or work, and she had failed to spot how pedantic Jeff could be, because in those early days he laughed with her, not at her, and the change hurt. Jeff had a chip the size of a log on his shoulder for not living up to his potential, and Elaine was the person he tried to dump that weight of bitterness on. She had married expecting the Hollywood happy ending that would grant her every wish, but Jeff let Elaine down by not realizing that he was supposed to stay attentive and flattering.

"Of course, I talked a load of rubbish," Dulcie was saying. "I'd never have left Clive."

"No, of course not," agreed Elaine, perhaps a little too hastily.

"But I had to take a stand this morning."

"Of course you did."

"I can't believe that God would want the girls to miss out on a bit of fun now and then, but Clive said I didn't know what I was talking about."

"Jeff's always saying that to me as well: not about God particularly, but more or less everything else." Elaine tried to appear sympathetic, but she was thinking of herself rather than Dulcie. No matter what circumstances had created the situation, Dulcie was now free of criticism and could do anything she liked, anything at all. "I know it's much too early to make plans for the future —"

"But I have: lots of plans. I'm going back to England." Dulcie knew that the Leytons must stay in Australia for two years or pay the full fare of the Ten-Pound voyage that had brought them to the hostel, but she hoped that Clive's bank account would reveal unexpected riches. Until God intervened, Clive had been a cautious man, and that caution might mean Dulcie could liberate herself from Nissen huts, even if Clive had practically given away their Wolverhampton home. "Yes, I'm definitely going back to England as soon as possible. What if something happened to me, and the girls were left on the other side of the world all by themselves?"

Dulcie looked frantic with worry at the thought, and Elaine was conscious of being such an inadequate mother that she had never once considered Veronica's fate should both parents die.

"When the nuclear war starts, England's going to be annihilated, stuck right in the firing line between Moscow and Washington: at least, that's what Jeff says will happen," ventured Elaine, hoping to imply that the decision to emigrate had been taken with Veronica's best chance of survival in mind.

"I'd prefer us all to be wiped out by the very first bomb, rather than face a lingering death out here. If we stay in Australia, I might die of radiation sickness before the girls, and leave them ill. No, much better if we die together, then I don't have to think about it." Dismissing World War Three, Dulcie turned to more immediate matters. "I feel exactly like a refugee. I can only pack the clothes on the washing-line. The police won't let me take anything out of the hut because they want to search it or whatever they do, and I've got hardly any money right now. The bank account's in Clive's name, he cancelled all the insurance policies after God spoke to him, and I haven't had a job since I was married. I've heard it's easy to get work in Australia though. Is that right?"

"Yes, it's the easiest thing in the world out here. I haven't got any qualifications at all, and only worked in a shop for a year or so after I left school, but now I could get a job in any factory I chose, and the wages are good." Elaine reached for her purse, and tipped its entire contents into the empty pocket of the apron that Dulcie was still wearing. "It's not much, but I can write a cheque if you need a loan until things are sorted out, and I don't even have to ask Jeff for a penny. I've got my own bank account now."

"You'll never know how you've helped me today." Dulcie suddenly started to cry, and Elaine promptly joined in as the most tactful response, but Dulcie's remark about a police search of the hut sounded an alarm in Elaine's mind as loud as the wartime air raid sirens that she had heard so often as a child.

****

"The Luger's not in its box," Elaine whispered, the moment Jeff appeared in the hut's doorway.

"Yes, I know. I checked earlier, and I've been waiting for you to say something."

"Keep your voice down. The police are next door. Where have you hidden it? I think you should get rid of that gun altogether. You could be arrested if the police search the hut and find a pistol."

"They'd be luckier than me," said Jeff. "I can't find it anywhere. Tell the truth for once, Elaine. You've thrown the gun away, haven't you?"

"I've never even touched it. You know I won't have anything to do with that Luger. I've told you for years that I don't like having it around. Stop fooling, Jeff; this isn't a joke. If the police catch you with a gun, they might make us go back to England, and I couldn't bear that. In fact, I wouldn't bear it. I'd sooner die than live in Acton again."

"Don't be absurd," scoffed Jeff, amused by the histrionics.

"Oh, all right, I'd rather be in Acton than dead, but I don't want that as my only choice. I love living in Australia, and I can have a much better time out here."

"Residing in a Nissen hut and working in an ice-cream factory." Jeff smiled at such low expectation from life, but he had no idea of the hopes and dreams that constantly flitted through Elaine's mind.

"This is just temporary, and I'm not afraid of working to get what I want."

"We'll all be radio-active and glowing in the dark long before then," decreed Jeff. "If we get another couple of years, we'll be lucky. The world's not going to see 1970, Elaine. Don't you realize there's no future for any of us? Are you that stupid?"

"I suppose so, because nothing you say will stop me trying to live the way Australians do. I want a house, and a car as well, and a television: everything Australians have got." Being told she was stupid had once convinced Elaine that she must be stupid, but now she felt secure enough not to care about Jeff's opinion. They were both factory workers doing the same job on the same conveyor belt, and Jeff's scorn of her intelligence seemed hollow when Elaine knew that she was considered the more efficient employee, and at times she almost pitied Jeff for his limited outlook. He was stick-in-the-mud while she planned to soar to heights that her parents would have deemed unreachable. Elaine had left a lot more behind in Acton than a domineering mother and a drab daily routine. "I won't risk being sent back to England, not for anything, not for anyone."

"And that's why you threw the Luger away, isn't it?"

"I didn't even touch it, but I wish I'd got rid of that gun months ago, years ago," said Elaine. "I wish I'd thrown it away before we left London. If the customs men had found a pistol when we arrived at Port Melbourne, they might have sent us straight back to England on the very next boat."

"They weren't going to disembowel a child's tattered and cherished teddy bear," laughed Jeff, proud of his resourcefulness. "Anyway, I got the idea of hiding the gun inside a toy from that film you insisted we went to see, so you ought to approve."

"This isn't a joke," protested Elaine. "Jeff, this is serious."

"Especially if you were seen throwing the Luger away. What a stupid thing to do, today of all days."

"But I didn't, Jeff. Perhaps Vron took it."

"Don't try and put the blame on her. Vron doesn't know a thing about the Luger. I've made sure of that. In fact, nobody but us knows of its existence, unless you lent the gun to Dulcie Leyton this morning. And stop trying to look so innocent. You're no actress."

Elaine was a far better actress than Jeff had ever realized, but she capitulated. "Well, as long as the gun isn't in here, that's all I care about. It just wasn't safe, having a loaded pistol around."

"It isn't safe sleeping in a Nissen hut that anybody can break into."

"Nothing ever happens on the hostel," retorted Elaine, and Jeff laughed again.

"I don't think Clive Leyton would agree with you, and his death proves how right I am."

"Oh, you're always right," snapped Elaine.

Back in England, the Luger had been a mere curiosity, the war souvenir taken from a German who had been overpowered by Jeff at the very moment that the pistol went off, leaving a Colonel dead and giving Jeff the double satisfaction of having shot an officer and acquiring a Luger, along with the bullets that might have had his name on them. At any rate, that was Jeff's account of the gun's dramatic history, but he also happened to be the ex-RAF man who assured his daughter that he had stood in the back of a Lancaster, tennis racquet at the ready, to lob out any bouncing bombs that bounced so high, they came back inside the plane that had just dropped them. When Elaine cowered in air raid shelters, Jeff had been a fearless warrior who cared nothing for authority, and he still thought of himself as a dashing rebel, but six weeks in Australia had altered Elaine. She was no longer a housewife reliant on a man to bring home his wages. She earned her own money, and the lifestyle that Australians took for granted was beyond anything she could have achieved in England. Hostel rents were high, but Elaine still managed to save, and planned to have a large detached house with a garden one day, perhaps on the coast, and so the slightest threat of deportation terrified her.

"We need that Luger for protection," argued Jeff. "Where is it, Elaine? I don't feel safe in this hut without a gun. How long are you going to go on pretending that you didn't get rid of it?"

"And how long are you going to go on introducing me to people as the old ball and chain?"

"What's that got to do with it?"

"Nothing. Everything. I don't know."

"That's the trouble with you, Elaine. You never think."

Jeff was wrong. Jeff was very wrong. In Acton, Elaine had drifted through whole years in a hopeless Hollywood fantasy of a better life that she could never have. In Australia, all she wanted seemed within her grasp, and Elaine had decisions to make that required a great deal of thought indeed.

5

"I checked with Hardy Spicer's," said Gilda.

"And Jeffrey Thornthwaite's alibi doesn't stand up to scrutiny of course," declared Lance. "I'd be willing to bet a month's pay that he arrived late for his job interview."

"You'd lose your money. He didn't turn up at all."

"I should have guessed. He wouldn't leave his daughter alone after the ordeal that she'd been through," said Lance, the warmth of approval in every syllable. "Jeffrey stayed with Veronica all morning, and heard everything that happened in the other side of the hut. When we went back to the manager's office, he sneaked out, got rid of the gun, and then made a big show of returning to the hostel as though he'd just stepped out of a train at the station."

"I looked through my notes, and Jeffrey didn't claim to have attended the interview. He merely said that he left the hut shortly after his wife went to work, because he had to get the eight-ten to be at Hardy Spicer's on time. Jeffrey also didn't say that he actually caught the train."

"Clever," Lance commented, admiring the way that Jeff Thornthwaite had left himself room for manoeuvre.

"There's a chance that Constable Dexter might have seen him when Jeffrey finally did leave the hut."

"No, that'd be far too basic a mistake for a man as clever as Jeffrey Thornthwaite. He'll have made a point of not going anywhere near a policeman." Lance smiled, appreciating the intelligence behind Jeff's hypothetical actions. Criminals were normally stupid, mere parasites governed by greed, and it was a novelty for Lance to have the felon dead and a wronged party the suspect. Jeffrey Thornthwaite had apparently cleansed the world of vermin, and Lance was forced to applaud, whatever the law's opinion.

"There's no proof that Jeffrey ever had a gun. It could have been Clive Leyton's," said Gilda, "We've only got Dulcie's word that he was a pacifist."

"But Dulcie Leyton didn't miss a job interview. No, I reckon that when Jeffrey went out to the toilet block, Clive Leyton heard him leave and thought he'd gone to the station. Leyton knew that Veronica was on her own in the hut, because he'll have heard what Elaine told his wife about the kid not going to school, and so he decided to pay Veronica a visit."

"But Dulcie would still have been around."

"She'd assume that he'd gone out to the toilet. Dulcie was occupied with the kids and then the laundry, so Leyton grabbed his opportunity."

"But Jeffrey must have been back in the hut by five past at the very latest, if he planned to catch the eight-ten train, and Elaine went to the factory about ten to. That only leaves fifteen minutes unaccounted for, at most."

"Enough time for a pervert," growled Lance.

"Why didn't Jeffrey confront Clive Leyton straightaway?" asked Gilda. "He wouldn't know that Dulcie was going to be conveniently absent in the laundry-room if he waited."

"It took him some time to get the whole story out of Veronica. As soon as Jeffrey heard Leyton's name, he snatched up his gun, and the rest we know."

The rest they were guessing, thought Gilda. "I still reckon that the child ought to be seen by a doctor. Jeffrey's lawyers will want physical evidence of an attack if he's charged."

"Jeffrey wouldn't give permission for Veronica to be examined, and I can't insist. We've nothing solid against him."

"There's the missed Hardy Spicer's interview."

"He'll find a way to explain that," predicted Lance. "Jeffrey's determined to protect his daughter, no matter what, and he should be left alone to do it."

"But if he killed a man?"

"It's only a theory," said Lance, pretending to back down from certainty. He believed that Jeffrey Thornthwaite had shot Clive Leyton, but plainly would prefer not to act on his belief.

Was Lance prepared to suppress evidence, knowing that prosecution would do added harm to Veronica Thornthwaite? Gilda's father would have bludgeoned his way to the truth, whatever the consequences, and she could hardly doubt his method and Lance's at the same time. The only hope was another suspect, even though that possibility could ruin the lives of three young girls. "I think Dulcie Leyton's too good to be true. No woman could be that obsessed with housework."

"You haven't met my wife," Lance muttered.

****

They heard Jeffrey Thornthwaite stop and chat to Mavis Webb outside the manager's office.

"Overconfident," said Lance. "It might be his downfall."

"Unless he's innocent," suggested Gilda.

"He is. Leyton's the guilty one."

106

An unproven hypothesis, made yet more doubtful by a smiling and relaxed Jeff who stood in the doorway, a convincing picture of a man with nothing on his conscience. "Mr Webb says that you want to see me."

"Yes, sit down for a minute," said Gilda. "We need to check something."

"OK." Jeff strolled into the store-room, apparently without the slightest concern at being summoned for police questioning.

"You didn't go to your job interview." Gilda knew that she ought to feel rather like a gambler who had just produced a possible winning card, but Veronica Thornthwaite got in the way. "According to Hardy Spicer's, you didn't show up."

"That's right," agreed Jeff, untroubled.

"But you told us that you left the hostel to catch the eight-ten train," said Gilda.

"And I did."

"How come, if you had no intention of doing the job interview?"

"I had every intention when I got the train," replied Jeff, "and every intention right up to the very moment I stood at the factory gate. Then I changed my mind, turned around and walked away."

"Did you speak to anyone while you were outside the factory?" asked Lance.

"Not a single solitary person," Jeff said cheerfully. "I can't provide a shred of proof, but that's what happened."

"How come you changed your mind about the interview?"

"Because the factory looked exactly like the one I'd worked in back home, and that was enough to put me right off the idea. I left England to start a new life, not continue the old one."

"You work in a factory now," Gilda pointed out.

"Yes, but it's small, and I don't have to waste hours every week travelling to get there and then get back. I made a snap decision that the extra money wouldn't be worth the loss of time. But why did you bother checking to see whether or not I showed up at a job interview?" Jeff enquired, amused. "Are you under the impression that I shot Clive Leyton?"

"It's routine to check what we're told," said Gilda. "I'll even check that your wife arrived at the ice-cream factory in time for the eight o'clock shift."

"In case Elaine was passionately in love with Clive, and shot him when he refused to elope with her?" mocked Jeff. "I think you're greatly overestimating Clive's power of attraction."

"Did you speak to anybody on the train?" asked Lance.

"Not that I remember."

"Did anyone else from the hostel travel on the eight-ten, or the train that brought you back?"

"I didn't notice," said Jeff. "There were some people waiting for the eight-ten, but I didn't recognize any of them, and the train I caught to get back was almost empty."

"Were you the only person who got out at Watson Valley Station?"

"No, there were a few other people. One of them was a blonde in a purple dress, whose heel got stuck down the side of a grid on the platform, and she toppled off her stilettos, then dropped a bag that fell under the train. I got out of that station fast, in case anybody expected me to be the gallant rescuer and crawl beneath an engine to retrieve lipstick and powder puff for the damsel in distress."

Jeff smiled at the memory, but both Gilda and Lance knew that he might have witnessed the platform scene from the steps going up to the station without leaving Watson Valley at all that day. And he could have seen a crowd waiting for the eight-ten any morning of the week as he walked to the ice-cream factory for an early shift.

"That's it," said Jeff. "The Invisible Man's testimony."

"Were you in the Army during the war?" asked Gilda.

"Don't insult me. I was in the RAF and, yes, I know about guns, but I haven't fired one since the war and don't have access to any now. Feel free to search the hut if you don't believe me." In Jeff's opinion, the questioning was over and he stood up. "My wife's in the canteen, and I must get back to Vron. After what happened this morning, I don't like leaving her alone in that hut."

"No, I'm sure you don't," said Lance.

Jeff sauntered out of the room as nonchalantly as he had strolled in, a man with self-assurance enough not to care if he had been believed. Jeffrey Thornthwaite was a factory worker with the arrogance of an emperor.

"He doesn't sound like he's lying," commented Gilda.

"He's lying," declared Lance. "It's quite clear to me that Jeffrey never left the hostel this morning until he sneaked out later on. I reckon he hung around that bit of road by the manager's office, waiting for one of the Webbs to spot him apparently returning from the station."

"Or perhaps he's got a girlfriend," suggested Gilda, "and spent a few hours with her instead of bothering with the job interview. After all, he won't get many opportunities to escape when he works in the same factory as his wife."

"He killed Clive Leyton. Every instinct I've got tells me that Jeffrey Thornthwaite killed Clive Leyton."

"And every instinct Inspector Fairfax has tells him that Clive Leyton committed suicide and Dulcie got rid of the gun."

"Leyton would have put the bullet in his head, not his chest, if he wanted to die," Lance decreed. "The man was ex-Army."

"Ex-Army Pay Corps."

"It'll be the same basic training. He'd know about guns."

"I wonder what Dulcie Leyton did in the war," said Gilda.

"Probably sat at a school desk until the duration. Jeffrey Thornthwaite fired that shot."

"How come an ex-RAF man didn't aim at Leyton's head?"

"Jeffrey was in a rage," decided Lance. "He just saw Clive Leyton and fired the gun, too angry to aim properly."

"Then why only one shot?" asked Gilda.

"Presumably because the gun only had one bullet in it."

"Jeffrey learnt about guns during wartime, and so he'd be trained to kill, not wound. Even in a fury, I reckon Jeffrey would automatically aim for the head at close quarters, especially when he knew that he could only have one shot."

"If you had kids, you'd understand."

Lance was annoyed by the supposed lack of sensitivity, but Gilda felt that she could easily understand Jeff Thornthwaite's instinctive reaction, assuming the reaction had happened in the first place. "If Jeffrey killed Clive, then the gun must still be on the hostel or somewhere around the station. It's a small search area."

"And when it turns up, we won't be able to connect it to Jeffrey Thornthwaite. He'll have made sure of that," said Lance, unable to keep approval out of his voice.

****

The Kendricks claimed to have seen nothing and heard nothing, and made it plain that neither of them ever intended to see or hear anything. They occupied the four remaining rooms in Hut 33, with the Yoxalls on the other side of partition walls, and had had the Leyton family next door as well as the Thornthwaites, but still the Kendricks claimed to know nothing about the events of that morning. Two parents and six children from Northumberland, their accent sounding more like a foreign language than English to Gilda, the Kendricks were short, solid, dark-haired, blank-faced and determined to offer no help at all.

"We keep ourselves to ourselves," declared Sidney, convinced that he was bragging about a virtue. "It's none of my business what those Leytons get up to."

"What did they get up to?" asked Gilda.

"I told you; it's none of my business." Sidney shifted his weight on a canvas chair that looked too rickety to support his bulk, and he added, "I've never been one to pry into other people's concerns."

"And nor have I." Sidney's wife Rose also sat on a canvas chair outside Hut 33, attempting to relax in shade that was very little cooler than sunlight, and she pressed her lips together firmly, disapproving of whatever scandal they were expected to make public.

"So none of you were here at eight o'clock this morning," Gilda concluded.

"Did we say that? There's no call for you to put words in our mouths," objected Sidney. "We might have been here, or we

111

might not have been here, but either way, we don't know anything."

"Nothing," agreed Rose.

"What time did your kids leave for school?"

Rose and Sidney glanced at each other, calculating the extent of their involvement with the police if they revealed even the most minor of facts. "Ten minutes or so before eight o'clock," Rose said at last. "They've got a fair distance to walk."

"Were you both in the hut then?"

Rose and Sidney exchanged another glance, and Gilda felt thankful that Lance was not there. The stubborn Kendricks would have already destroyed his limited supply of patience. "I didn't hear anything," Rose declared eventually.

"So you were here in the hut at eight o'clock," decided Gilda.

"I go to work then." Rose spoke defiantly, seeming to anticipate a challenge from Gilda.

"You've got a job in the ice-cream factory?"

"No." Rose sat bolt upright, affronted at the assumption. "I work in the hostel canteen."

"Then you know Mrs Yoxall."

"No, she doesn't," snapped Sidney, apparently defending his wife's reputation from slander. "We had nothing to do with the Yoxalls even before our rent money got stolen out of the manager's office. You ask Mr Webb what happened, if you want to know about those Yoxalls."

"I work the canteen lunch shift; she does breakfast and dinner." And the lunch shift was a cut above the other two, Rose's tone implied. "She's always eating a second breakfast when I get there. One breakfast isn't enough for Irma Yoxall."

112

"Did you see her in the canteen when you arrived this morning?" asked Gilda.

"She was stuffing her face as usual. Those Yoxalls should be made to pay extra rent to cover the amount she eats, even though they'd only steal the money."

"Where do you work, Mr Kendrick?"

Gilda turned to Sidney, who pondered the repercussions of a possibly damaging revelation before he answered, "I've got a job in the ice-cream factory."

"Did you work the eight o'clock shift this morning?"

"Yes," Sidney acknowledged, slowly and warily.

"So you left the hut about ten to eight."

"A quarter to," declared Sidney, delivering a reproof. "I like to be there early."

"What time does the canteen shift begin?"

"I work all the hours I'm paid to work," announced Rose, glaring haughtily at Gilda. "If I'm a few minutes late, I stay a few extra minutes at the end."

"So you were late for your shift this morning?"

"Only a couple of minutes," Rose protested. "Our Rita couldn't find a hat, and she had to run to catch up with the others, but I wouldn't let her go to school on such a hot day without a hat. The teachers always kick up a fuss. But I didn't hear anything."

Gilda felt tempted to ask what exactly Rose had failed to hear, but reckoned that such a question from a policewoman would make Rose clam up entirely, and Gilda tried an indirect approach. "Did you see Jeffrey Thornthwaite at any time this morning?"

"No," conceded Rose.

"Did you see Clive Leyton?"

"No, I didn't see him." Rose shook her head, and for the first time there was no hesitation, strengthening Gilda's suspicion that Rose had heard, rather than seen, something.

"Are the Thornthwaites noisy neighbours?" asked Gilda.

"We've no complaints," said Rose.

"Unlike some," muttered Sidney.

"Who do you mean?"

"I mean what I mean," Sidney replied austerely.

"Children have to play," declared Rose, suddenly coming to life. "And the Leyton girls are no angels. None of our daughters are pregnant, and none of our daughters get shouted at either."

"Did you hear Clive Leyton shout at a child this morning?" Gilda would have preferred Rose to volunteer the information, but Rose Kendrick was never going to volunteer anything.

"He was always shouting. Supposed to be so religious, but it's his daughter that's pregnant."

"What time did you hear him shout this morning?"

"A bit after eight. I was glad that my kids had gone to school. We never raise our voices in this family, no matter what," Rose declared primly, and Gilda believed her. The Kendricks were far too stolid to go in for extravagant displays of emotionalism.

"Which child was Clive Leyton shouting at?"

"I didn't look around to find out which of the girls was screaming. I had to get to work."

"Where did the screams come from?"

"I don't know. Behind me somewhere. Hut 34. I told you; I didn't look to see what was going on," said Rose, proud of her self-restraint. "I don't nose into other people's business."

"But it was definitely after the school kids had left?"

"Oh yes. They were all gone, long gone."

"And you're sure that it was Clive Leyton you heard?"

"I don't tell lies," stated Rose, insulted by the question.

Gilda had thought that she wanted to know the truth, but the truth she wanted was confirmation that there had been no attack on Veronica Thornthwaite, and Rose Kendrick's account of Clive Leyton and a screaming girl came as a blow with a force that was almost physical.

****

Gilda was writing a summary of her notes for the benefit of Detective Sergeant Palmer, when a shadow darkened the storeroom, and she glanced up to see Hubert Webb in the doorway.

"What's the story behind missing rent money, the Kendricks and David Yoxall?"

"Nothing that could ever be proved," replied Hubert, loath to reveal any discord on his happy hostel. "It seems that Mr Kendrick put his rent money on the counter in my office, turned for a moment to take the letter my wife handed him, and the money vanished. He suspects Mr Yoxall, who'd just left the office but was nowhere in sight."

"Just like the rent money."

"Yes, just like the rent money. But never mind all that. Look!" Hubert held up a shoebox in both hands as a votive offering, and it was easy to guess that whatever the box's contents, he considered them to be of the utmost importance. "Young Eric Fenton gave me this a few minutes ago. He found it under some bushes at the back of the ice-cream factory. The

115

children know that they shouldn't play there, but boys will be boys."

Gilda took the box, lifted its lid and saw a handgun inside: a handgun without a silencer. "Where's the boy now?"

"Outside. The pistol's a Luger," added Hubert, unable to resist airing his knowledge. "I last saw one of them in Germany, right after VE Day, and the sight of it immediately whizzed me straight back in time."

"Yes, I can imagine." But Gilda found it harder to imagine Hubert Webb as part of a cold-blooded military machine, routinely handling firearms and just as routinely dealing with death. After the drama of war, life in a hostel office must have seemed a mundane fate, but perhaps Hubert had chosen the job for that very reason. "Were you in the Army?"

"Yes, the complete Tommy Atkins in another life, another world, and more like half-remembering an old film than it once being real. I didn't touch the gun, of course, but young Eric's fingerprints are sure to be all over it, and probably those of his friends as well."

"That was my first thought, but it mightn't be the gun used this morning."

"Nobody's ever found a gun around here before, and the fact that it's a German pistol doesn't mean much." The investigation had moved into an area where Hubert could display some expertise, and he now regarded himself as practically one of the investigating team. "Any serviceman stationed in Germany could easily get hold of a Luger, so perhaps I should tell you now that Mavis is my only alibi for early this morning, although I did go into the canteen to pick up the weekly order at about half-past eight."

"Duly noted. I'd better see where the Luger was found before Eric takes all his mates on a guided tour of the spot," said Gilda, pushing the paperwork to one side.

"The factory security guard's going to be furious that the children have got under the fence again, but everything you tell them at that age just goes in one ear and out the other. You won't scold Eric, will you?"

"How can I? He's apparently succeeded where we've failed."

"Yes, indeed." Hubert decided that his hostel residents had been praised, and he went out of the store-room smiling proudly as he beckoned to a fair-haired six-year-old boy, who reluctantly moved to the forefront of a group of children. Gilda left the shoebox on the table, closed and locked the door, and then smiled at Eric in the hope of reassuring him, but he seemed overwhelmed by the prominence of his rôle.

"Would you show me where you found the gun, Eric?" asked Gilda.

The boy nodded, turned around and ran towards the canteen, pursued by the other children, all eager to see the Luger's former hiding-place and share the importance of Eric's moment in the limelight.

"They think it's a game," said Hubert, in case Gilda should conclude that the hostel's younger generation were insensitive. "It's like a cowboy film to them."

"Yes, it must be." Gilda followed Hubert to the back of the canteen, and climbed onto a grass verge that hosted swings and a slide, metal dazzling in the sunlight. A bunch of small girls, playing with a skipping-rope in the shade, glanced up and then hurried to tag-along when the sight of Eric rushing past with his entourage offered greater entertainment. The crowd came to an abrupt halt in front of a wire fence that separated hostel land from the stony clay behind the factory building, and Eric looked at Gilda as he pointed to a cluster of scrawny bushes growing on the barrier's other side.

"Stand back," Hubert called, as the children surged forward to get a closer view. "You might destroy vital clues."

The gun had probably been tossed into the undergrowth, rather than carefully placed there, and Eric was likely to have trampled over any clues, vital or otherwise, but Gilda smiled at the kids standing in a fascinated semi-circle by the fence and then smiled at Eric until her facial muscles began to ache. "Did you find the gun on top of the ground, Eric, or buried in the earth?"

Eric whispered something that Hubert bent down to hear. "It was lying on the ground," he reported. "Children, go and find Detective Sergeant Palmer. Tell him that a gun's been found, and he's to come here at once."

Amused at the idea of Lance being accosted and then given orders by a pack of excited kids, Gilda surveyed the narrow tunnel the boys had made under the fence into the bushes, and she knew that Lance's dignity would never permit him to squirm through the gap. A walk along the full length of the boundary to the road and then onto factory land would be the next event of the day.

"When the burglar made his escape, he must have thrown the Luger away in a panic," decided Hubert, glad of any opportunity to exonerate his hostel. "He fled across the road to hide behind the Rec, got rid of the gun, sprinted to the railway crossing and then vanished over the paddocks. Much less chance of being spotted if he took that direction than if he ran up the hill."

"It's a possibility," said Gilda, but it was also a possibility that either Jeffrey Thornthwaite or Dulcie Leyton had done the throwing away, whether or not in panic. The culprit might have a closer connection to Watson Valley Migrant Hostel than its manager was prepared to admit.

"I'm glad that the case is nearly solved," said Hubert.

****

"Jeffrey Thornthwaite's even cleverer than I thought," Lance remarked with grudging admiration as, accompanied by an acrid smell of ammonia, they skirted the ice-cream factory's square mass of concrete. Gilda and Lance had walked across the forecourt, and then veered to the left-hand side of the building without anyone stopping them to ask what they were doing, and as there was no window at the back of the factory, whoever had deposited the Luger could easily have avoided being seen. "When Jeffrey found out that Dulcie Leyton had insisted on waiting for her kids by the Recreation Hut, he decided to cloud the evidence. Jeffrey knew that if the gun was found nearby, she could have been the person who took it there, and he's hoping we'll think that she had the Luger on her all morning until she felt it was safe to ditch the gun at last."

"Perhaps that's exactly what happened," said Gilda, recalling the bulging pocket in Dulcie's apron. "She made a fuss about waiting for her kids hours before they actually appeared."

"Jeffrey Thornthwaite's behind all this; I know it. And I bet there never was a silencer on the gun. We only assumed that, because Veronica supposedly managed to sleep throughout the whole morning."

119

Hubert Webb stood on guard by the hostel side of the wire fence, and he waved a hand, but it was to waft away flies rather than an endeavour to attract Lance's attention. However, Hubert need not have volunteered for sentry duty because there was nothing for him to protect: no silencer, no footprints in a clay as hard as cement, no cigarette ends, no litter, no strand of clothing caught on bushes, no traces even of Eric Fenton or any other trespassing hostel child.

"I felt sure that there'd be one clue at least," Hubert said in disappointment.

"The gun will be sent to Melbourne for examination, and it could be very useful evidence," Gilda offered Hubert as consolation, but she had little hope of the Luger revealing any fingerprints except Eric's, unless whoever had abandoned it was extraordinarily careless or stupid.

Lance stood by the fence and looked around. They were directly opposite the Recreation Hut, but it only had one door, and that was in its wooden side and faced the canteen. There was no opening in the waves of corrugated iron in front of them, and although the canteen had windows, the view from them was obstructed by the slide and swings of the children's play area. Whoever dumped the Luger had presumably known the locale, because the railway tracks as well as the first house on the hill slope were hidden by gum trees.

"At least you've got the Luger to show Inspector Fairfax," remarked Hubert, searching for comfort.

"Thanks to Eric," said Gilda.

"Yes, and despite the risk of being told off for trespassing on factory land, Eric knew how important it was to hand the gun

120

over to me," declared Hubert, and he could not have sounded more proud had Eric been his son. "That's a very responsible action for a child his age."

Gilda nodded, hoping to seem appreciative of Eric's maturity, and then she hurried to follow Lance who had started to walk back towards the factory. A bitter smell of ammonia again filled the air, and Lance sighed, apparently suspecting that it had been released with the sole purpose of annoying him. "The Luger's going to be useless as evidence against Jeffrey Thornthwaite," he said. "A waste of time sending it to Melbourne. That gun will have been wiped clean of prints, and I bet Jeffrey's never shown the Luger to anybody. He knows he's safe."

"Perhaps if I talked to Veronica —?" suggested Gilda.

"Jeffrey will have told her to keep quiet, and that's exactly what the poor kid wants to do. She'd just clam up, and I reckon Jeffrey won't even tell his wife what happened."

"If it did happen. David Yoxall had a grudge against Clive Leyton, and seems the type who could easily turn violent." They had reached the side of the factory building, and Gilda decided to save herself a second journey. "I'll go and check that Yoxall was here at eight o'clock, as he claimed. I wouldn't trust that man's word about anything."

"I don't trust any of them," said Lance.

****

The factory manager was the owner's son, a son in his mid-forties who considered himself a debonairly handsome playboy, in spite of the weight that was steadily adding to a stomach already bulging over trouser belts. Neville Arlen had the money and the car that, in his opinion, made a plain-faced middle-aged man irresistible in the eyes of every young female lucky enough to behold him, and the fact that so many succeeded in resisting his fascination, Neville was easily able to attribute to shyness brought on by awe at being in such exalted company.

However, Detective Senior Constable Gilda Garfield turned out to be disappointingly unattractive, and so there was no need for Neville to exhibit the full splendour of his personality. "How come you're asking me about guns and trespassers?" he snapped. "Talk to the security guard."

"OK. And I need to check who worked the eight o'clock shift here this morning."

"Then ask one of the foremen," said Neville, dismissing Gilda with a wave of a hand. "I'm the factory manager."

A manager with a singularly empty desk, Gilda noted. "Did Clive Leyton get on with his fellow workers?"

"Ask them. How should I know?"

"Were you happy with his work?"

"I wouldn't have recognized the man if I saw him," declared Neville, who was soon bored with any conversation not centred on himself. "I've got an entire factory to run. I don't have time to fiddle about with minor details of shifts and workers."

"Then who does?"

"Whichever foreman's around," replied Neville, sighing at the dreary woman's persistence.

"Would that foreman be in charge of the wage office too?"

"Of course not. That's Mrs Quentin's job. She's further along the passageway, if you must bother her. The door's got a notice on it that says *Wage Office*."

"That should save a thief valuable time. He won't have to blunder around the place looking for cash," commented Gilda, and Neville glanced suspiciously at her. Nobody made fun of the magnificent Neville Arlen, but Gilda Garfield seemed unaware of the rules.

"My Dad's got friends who are in politics, high up in politics, so if you tell the newspapers anything about our factory, the Chief Commissioner's going to hear."

"I'll consider myself cautioned," said Gilda. "Do you know a David Yoxall?"

"Never heard of him. Go and see Mrs Quentin or a foreman or whoever you like. I've got work to do," announced Neville, picking up a glossy magazine that he flicked through to gaze at even glossier cars.

Leaving the boss's son to his labours, Gilda went out into the passageway. The wage office door was wide open, a sign of the distance that separated workers from the cash in their next pay packet, and Gilda saw an empty desk that had presumably been Clive Leyton's. The second desk in the room was almost hidden under a clutter of paperwork, but the woman behind it looked up with a relaxed smile.

Gilda had expected the female who outranked Clive Leyton to dress as severely as Mavis Webb, but Nanette Quentin wore a beribboned pink frock that would not have been out of place at a barn dance, and the yellow curls hanging down her back made her look much younger than forty. "I couldn't believe it when I heard the news: not Clive Leyton," said Nanette, hurriedly replacing the inappropriate smile. "But I knew something must be wrong the moment I arrived here this morning. He was always at his desk when I opened the door, even though we don't officially start work until nine."

"Had Clive Leyton appeared worried lately, or somehow different perhaps?" asked Gilda. "Did he have any problems at work?"

"I don't think so." Nanette hesitated, and then grimaced. "We're not supposed to speak ill of the dead, I know, but he was the problem around here: in my opinion anyway."

"Clive didn't like a woman running the office?"

"No, of course he didn't." Nanette was surprised that the question needed to be asked, and Gilda knew exactly what she meant. "He made a point of informing me quite a few times that his wife hadn't gone out to work since their first daughter's birth, and he never actually said that I was a lousy mother, but he certainly thought it."

"So you wouldn't describe Clive Leyton as the most easy-going and broad-minded of men."

Nanette struggled to keep her sombre expression from crumpling into a smile, and failed. "I couldn't bear the man. He used to tidy up after me. All right, that doesn't sound much, but he'd have a superior look on his face, and it drove me wild."

"Did you ever meet his wife?"

"He wouldn't have allowed that to happen," replied Nanette. "I'm divorced. It might have given her ideas."

"Did he ever mention God to you?"

"Mention! He more than mentioned. Clive Leyton had a direct line to the Almighty, or so he claimed, and I got into the habit of leaving the office door open as often as possible. Those puritanical religious types are usually the worst."

"Did he seem a danger to women, to girls?" asked Gilda, doing her best to make the question sound casual.

"I didn't like being alone with him; that's all I can say."

"Did he ever try anything?"

"I made sure that he didn't get an opportunity," declared Nanette. "It was probably my imagination, but better safe than sorry."

"What made you distrust him?"

"I don't know for certain. Instinct, I reckon, but the man's dead, and it doesn't matter now."

It might actually matter a great deal, and Gilda persevered. "Was it the way that he looked at you?"

Nanette paused before replying, and then shook her head. "I don't know what it was. Just a feeling I had, but the phoney religious hooey put me off him from the start."

"Did he talk to any of the other women who work here?"

"I doubt it. He never left the office during his breaks. He'd just sit there, reading a Bible like he was cramming for a written exam." There was a silence as Gilda scribbled in her notebook, and then Nanette was unable to resist asking, "Who shot him? His wife?"

"We don't know yet who fired the gun. What makes you think it might have been Mrs Leyton?"

"Because I'd end up killing a husband like that. Good on her, if she did. I hope she gets away with it."

"Perhaps I should now enquire what you were doing between eight and nine this morning," said Gilda, amused.

"Getting the kids off to school, and walking to work. And yes, before you ask, I do go past the hostel on my way here. I live up at the top of Bethanyville Avenue, and I suppose I could easily have made a detour to the Leyton hut. I don't know which one it is, but I might have got the number from the factory records." Nanette looked intrigued at the idea of herself as murder suspect, and added with a laugh, "Should I be sending for a lawyer?"

"You went past the hostel this morning? Did you see anyone or — or anything?"

Nanette frowned in thought, and then shook her head again. "I don't remember seeing anybody at all, but it probably means that I didn't notice. I was thinking about my kids and the school holidays, and hoping that the bank would deliver the cash early this week, because it's such a rush to make up the wage packets when the money's late. You know the usual jumble that wanders through your mind."

"But you'd notice if something appeared odd as you went by the hostel?"

"I reckon so." Nanette sounded doubtful, however, frowning again as she attempted to recall a journey that would soon have escaped her memory but for Gilda's interest in it.

"You didn't hear anything?"

"Like gunshot? Now that I'd remember. No, it was just another morning for me."

But not for Clive Leyton who, if he always arrived at the office before Nanette Quentin, had presumably been dead by the time she walked past Hut 34. "When did you get here this morning?"

"About five to nine, but if you need the exact minute and second, you can check when I clocked-in."

"Does everyone clock-in when they get here?"

126

"Everybody. Except Neville Arlen, and that's just as well. After all, his father might check the record. But by an odd coincidence, the less we see of Mr Arlen junior, the more smoothly things run in the factory."

"Can I have a look at this morning's shift rota?"

"I don't have it yet. We're paid a week in arrears, but there'll be a copy on the factory notice-board, and a foreman will probably be able to tell you who was late or who didn't turn up for work this morning, without him even needing to take a glance at the clocking-in record. Do you think somebody working here killed Clive Leyton?"

"I don't think," replied Gilda. "I wander around collecting details that other people assess. Quite a dull job, really."

"Dull! You're talking to somebody who works in a wage office."

Nanette stood up and led Gilda along the passageway, then down a second corridor, the thudding reverberation of machinery louder with each step. They turned a corner, and were suddenly on the factory floor, and it seemed impossible that a product as bland as ice-cream could originate in such a complexity of engineering, all of which looked as though it ought to manufacture aeroplanes or ocean liners to live up to its full potential and justify so many white-coated and white-hatted workers. Nanette unpinned a sheet of paper from the notice-board by the door, beckoned a tall man to follow her, and then she retreated down the passageway.

"I can't hear myself think in that din, but nobody working in there seems conscious of the racket and they talk to each other quite happily without even having to shout," said Nanette, handing Gilda that day's shift rota. "Rod, did everyone turn up at eight o'clock?"

"I don't know." Rodney Fryer took off the peaked cap covering his dark hair and shrugged. He was a handsome man in his early thirties, and appeared relaxed despite working in the midst of continual noise. "I had the morning off, and I've only just arrived. You'll have to check who clocked-in and when."

"Could somebody get a mate to clock-in for them?" asked Gilda, and both Nanette and Rodney smiled.

"It's been known," conceded Rodney, "but instant dismissal if you're caught."

"We've got a good mob here," declared Nanette, "apart from a few exceptions."

"David Yoxall's down for the eight o'clock shift," Gilda remarked, glancing at the rota.

"You've just hit the bull's eye when it comes to exceptions," said Rodney.

"Is that repulsive Dave Yoxall a suspect?" demanded Nanette, and then she added regretfully, "But you won't tell us, of course. Rod, if you think a woman in charge of a wage office is unusual, here's a female detective. This is all about Clive Leyton. Have you heard what happened to him?"

"Everybody in the post office was talking about it, but I never thought of Dave Yoxall," said Rodney. "I assumed the meek and mild wife had finally flipped."

"Did you know Clive Leyton well?" asked Gilda.

"I'd seen him around the factory, but I don't think I ever spoke to him," Rodney replied.

"Then how do you know what his wife's like?"

"Just about everybody I work with here comes from the hostel, and I hear them talk. There are three Leyton daughters and a downtrodden wife who cleans a hut all day every day. You'd be surprised at the amount of hostel gossip I could tell you." Rodney treated Gilda to the film star smile of a man confidently attractive: a man who felt that he could rely on his looks to get him whatever he wanted.

"David Yoxall," said Gilda. "Any gossip on that particular individual?"

"Lazy, stupid, bad-tempered, belts his wife and kid, drinks, gambles away any money he gets hold of, relies on his wife to pay the bills. How much more do you want?"

"I've never heard anything good about him either," said Nanette. "England must have forgotten that criminals aren't transported to Australia any more."

"Look no further if you want the most violent man on that hostel," added Rodney.

"What about Jeffrey Thornthwaite?" asked Gilda.

"Him!" Rodney looked astonished, and demanded, "Is he on the list of suspects?"

"I'm interested in all the hostel people," Gilda replied. "What's the gossip about Jeffrey Thornthwaite?"

"He's a good worker, although not as clever as he thinks Jeff Thornthwaite is." Rodney's tone was stilted, but his dislike of the man could not be disguised "I haven't heard that he was violent. Is he?"

"Not as far as I know."

"Then how come you're asking about him?"

"Because he works here. Any more gossip about Jeffrey?"

"Conceited. Laughs at people and tries to make them feel stupid." To judge by the expression on Rodney's face, he was speaking from personal knowledge rather than merely repeating gossip, and whatever the memory, it made him angry.

"What about Sidney Kendrick?"

"Reliable. Always clocks-in before anybody else on his shift. Hates David Yoxall. Something about stolen rent money. Well, if no more gossip's required, I've got to get back to work or Australia will be crying out in vain for ice-cream."

"Thanks, Rod," Nanette called, as he hurried down the corridor, and then she turned to Gilda. "I'll show you where we clock-in, and print out a copy of this morning's record."

"That'll be a great help." Gilda followed Nanette, and looked down at the shift rota again, suddenly realizing that one name she had expected to see was missing.

6

Lance was drinking fruit juice and eating a slice of madeira cake, courtesy of Mavis, when Gilda returned to Hubert's storeroom. The electric fan continued to whirr, but Mavis had been right when she told Gilda that borrowing it would make very little difference to the stifling air indoors.

"One and a half discrepancies," reported Gilda.

"David Yoxall wasn't at the factory this morning," said Lance. "I knew that man had something to hide."

"No, he was there, but clocked-in forty-three minutes late. Elaine Thornthwaite's the main discrepancy. It was her day off, and yet Jeffrey made a big thing of how his wife wouldn't have gone to work and left Veronica if Dulcie Leyton hadn't promised to keep an eye on the kid."

Lance looked intrigued as he contemplated such a major flaw in Jeff's account of the morning's events. "Why should he go out of his way to emphasize the point? How come he wants to place his wife firmly off the hostel at the time when Clive Leyton was killed?"

"You're going to answer yourself by saying that Elaine shot Clive Leyton, and Jeffrey's trying to cover for her."

"They were in it together," decided Lance. "She was the one who snatched up the gun, when they finally got the story out of Veronica."

"I think Jeffrey's too intelligent to claim that his wife went to work when he knew she didn't. It's too easy an alibi for us to check," Gilda pointed out. "His tale of going to the job interview and changing his mind could be true, and we'll have difficulty proving that it isn't. If he's lying, it was a clever story invented by a clever man."

"I suppose," conceded Lance, regretfully abandoning his picture of an incensed Elaine emptying the contents of a gun into the pervert. "So, wherever she was, Jeffrey presumably thought that she'd gone to work."

"It must have been something important for her to leave a sick child alone in a Nissen hut."

"Not all mothers are that devoted."

"I know, but mine died when I was a kid, so I cherish illusions about how perfect my childhood would have been if Mum had lived." Gilda laughed, attempting to make her words sound flippant, but she was telling Lance the exact truth. A very young girl once blamed her mother for dying, and had felt ashamed ever since. Gilda wanted Elaine to have a noble and watertight reason for deserting her daughter, because anything else was too much a reminder of a seven-year-old child's anger. "I expect considerably higher standards of behaviour from mothers than from fathers."

"There's probably a boyfriend," said Lance. "What else could it be?"

"Let me consult my idealistic imagination. What about Elaine suffering from a serious illness, refusing to burden her family with the worry, and so she's secretly going for medical treatment?"

"Elaine Thornthwaite's the healthiest invalid that I've ever seen, and if she's visiting a doctor, he's the boyfriend," declared Lance. "Besides, Elaine's the type."

"What type?"

"The type of wife who gets bored and wanders off."

"How could you possibly know that?"

"Instinct," said Lance, and then added as Gilda looked unconvinced, "Elaine didn't stay with her sick kid this morning, and yet she had a day off work. Family can't mean much to her, so she's the sort who'd cheat on a husband."

"You're as unrealistic as me about the maternal instinct. After all, according to Jeffrey Thornthwaite, he didn't stay with Veronica either."

"Yes, he did," insisted Lance. "Whatever Jeffrey says, I'm certain he didn't leave his daughter alone this morning, except for the few minutes he needed to pretend that he was returning from the station. Go and confront Elaine. She'll talk more freely to another woman."

"Not when that woman's in the police force," said Gilda.

****

Jeffrey was in the hut, and Gilda could hear him speaking to Veronica, but Elaine sat outside on a canvas chair in the shade, her dark curls tied back in a pony tail, and she looked up cagily as Gilda approached.

"We know that you weren't at the factory when Clive Leyton died," said Gilda, to stop Elaine having time to think. "We know that this is your day off."

It was a moment that Elaine had been expecting, and she nodded slowly, almost glad to face the consequences and get them over with. Yet still she was reluctant to let Jeff hear what she would say, and so Elaine stood up and walked across the road to put some distance between herself and her family before replying to Gilda. "I didn't tell you any lies. I told them all to Jeff."

133

"That's none of my business. I just need to know where you were this morning between eight and nine o'clock."

The Recreation Hut loomed in front of them, forcing Elaine to turn and walk up the hill to get even further away from the hostel. "I was with a friend of mine."

"And will this friend back up what you say?"

"Yes, he'll back me up. Rod's not married. I suppose you think that I'm a terrible mother, but Veronica only had a stomach upset, nothing serious, and she's OK now." Elaine looked like a schoolgirl about to be scolded, although ready to acknowledge what she considered to be the main betrayal in the whole mess. Jeff had had years to win a wife's loyalty, in Elaine's opinion, and the failure was his.

"I need the name and address of your friend."

"Rodney Fryer."

"The Rodney Fryer at the factory? The foreman?"

"Yes, him. He lives in a flat at the side of the greengrocer's by the station. Are you going to tell Jeff?"

"I've got no reason to," said Gilda, and she was surprised to see a look of disappointment cross Elaine's face. "If Rodney Fryer confirms you were with him, that's the end of the matter as far as we're concerned."

"He'll confirm it. Rod's asked me to leave Jeff, to get a divorce."

And you want me to break the news to Jeff, thought Gilda. "Thanks for answering my questions. I'll have a quiet word with Rodney."

"It just happened," said Elaine, almost pleading for Gilda's sympathy. "I'd never done anything like this before in all the time

134

that I've been married, and I married very young. I was only seventeen."

"You don't have to explain to me."

"I know, but it's different in Australia. Nobody gets divorced in England, yet it seems quite common over here." Elaine apparently imagined she was offering a reason that would make Gilda understand, but Elaine herself was the person who needed to believe that what she had done was justifiable. "Rodney and I belong together. We recognized it the instant we met, like we'd known each other for years. Rod says that he never got married because he was waiting for me to show up."

"It's better not to talk about private things," advised Gilda. "Whenever I've done any confiding, I always end up sorry that I didn't keep my mouth shut."

"I suppose so," said Elaine, and she sighed.

"I won't have to bother you any more. Thanks for your help."

Gilda walked back down the road towards the hostel, but Elaine stayed where she was, wishing that she need never return to Hut 34. The white-painted houses on the hillside looked cool and fresh, despite their heat-withered gardens, and the sight represented freedom to Elaine, who tried to picture herself living in one as Mrs Fryer with husband Rodney, an almost forgotten Jeff Thornthwaite very far away in the past. Then Elaine sighed again, and reluctantly began to make her way back to the Nissen huts.

In ten married years, not once had Elaine suspected Jeff of even glancing at another woman, but now she hoped that the story of the missed job interview at Hardy Spicer's had been invented to give him a morning of illicit sex. Elaine knew how easy

135

it was to ignore marital vows, and everything would be effortlessly simplified if he left her for somebody else.

Jeff never praised Elaine's appearance, but Rod swore that she was better-looking than Sophia Loren and Ava Gardner put together, and although Elaine knew that his words were as insubstantial as moonbeams, it felt wonderful to be flattered after so many years of the ridicule that made Jeff think himself witty. If he had found another woman, the entire situation would be neatly solved, and Elaine could then be free with no blame attached to her, free to live with somebody who thought that she was special and said so.

The voyage to Australia had been an exciting novelty, and Elaine yearned to keep the feeling that adventures could happen and that life would smile on her. With Jeff, there seemed to be nothing ahead but growing old and eventually watching Veronica rush off to parties with boyfriends, assuming that Jeff's daughter ever lifted her nose out of a book, and Veronica was Jeff's daughter with Jeff's interests, inheriting nothing from her mother in that studiously dull nature. Elaine had thrown away so much life by marrying young, and she wanted those wasted years back. She wanted a second chance to live.

****

Lance smiled, confident of the answer that he would get. "Well, is Elaine the type or isn't she?"

"Lucky for me that we didn't have a bet," said Gilda. "At eight this morning Elaine Thornthwaite was with factory foreman Rodney Fryer, who lives in a flat at the side of the greengrocer's by the station. Not exactly the most romantic of addresses for an assignation, but I guess it signifies luxury when your home's a Nissen hut."

"He doesn't live on the hostel? That's interesting."

"It might be part of his attraction. Anyway, Rodney's asked Elaine to leave Jeffrey, and I got the impression that she probably will, if she gets up enough courage."

"Does Rodney Fryer realize that, I wonder?" Lance was rapidly forming another theory, and Gilda smiled.

"I thought you'd decided on vengeful father Jeffrey Thornthwaite as killer."

"That doesn't mean the case has been closed," Lance pointed out, adding pensively, "I assumed that it was one family to each hut when we first arrived here."

"So did I, but Rodney will know better."

"He and Elaine won't be discussing neighbours when they're together. If Rodney imagined that only the Thornthwaites lived in Hut 34, he might have jumped to the conclusion that any man he saw inside had to be Elaine's husband."

"He works with Jeffrey Thornthwaite and knew Clive Leyton by sight, so Rodney wouldn't mistake one for the other."

"He'd be standing in sunlight looking into a dark hut, and just see the outline of a man."

"Yes, but at the time Clive Leyton was killed, Elaine says that she and Rodney Fryer were together, so they'd have to be co-conspirators, and surely Elaine would describe in detail the way the hut's divided up, before sending Rodney to gun down her husband," said Gilda, regretting the loss of that particular scenario because it would have meant there had been no assault on Veronica Thornthwaite.

"Perhaps Rodney Fryer's the Watson Valley Don Juan, Dulcie Leyton's another of his conquests, and Rodney obliged her by removing an unwanted husband."

"A true Don Juan wouldn't care whether a woman had a husband or not. In fact, he might prefer married women to stop the chance of long-term entanglement. If Dulcie's acquired a lover, he doesn't have to be Rodney Fryer," said Gilda, and she shook her head in bemusement, trying to picture the life that Dulcie claimed to lead. "There has to be something more going on. She doesn't have a job. A canteen provides all the family meals so no cooking or shopping for her to do, and she's only got three small rooms to clean. There isn't even a wireless in the Leyton side of the hut. How did she pass her time when the husband was in the wage office and the kids at school?"

"Believe me, Dulcie could find plenty of housework to do if she set her mind on the task, and then she'd be able to whine about how hard she had to slave and how nobody appreciated her efforts," snarled Lance, glaring at the face he saw in his mind. "I'm beginning to think that there could be something in Wilbur Fairfax's suicide theory. Clive Leyton might just have had enough of it all."

"He could simply have walked away."

"With three kids dependent on him?"

"You think that their father's suicide would be less traumatic for them? More likely it was Dulcie who'd had enough."

"You've never been married, have you?" said Lance, making his words sound more like an accusation than a query.

"The longer I do police work dealing with families, the less likely I'll ever be to marry." Gilda was supposed to go out for a meal with Jerome Henderson that evening, and she usually had a good time with him. He was generous as well as a glib talker, but only when the topic of conversation centred on Jerome Henderson, and thirty or forty years of togetherness sounded more dull than idyllic.

"Marriage is so easy to get into, and so hard to get out of," complained Lance.

"I think that's exactly what puts me off," admitted Gilda, "and I can't imagine wanting to be with the same person every day for years and years."

"A prison sentence," said Lance.

A week earlier, Jerome had asked Gilda to marry him. She laughed and said no, but he suggested that perhaps the matter ought to have a little more thought than half a second. Jerome was a businessman with a successful construction company, and he aimed at even greater success. An inch or so taller than Gilda, Jerome had blond hair and a lined face that made him look older than thirty-eight, but his outlook could sometimes be juvenile. He seemed to imply that it was Gilda's last opportunity to acquire a husband, and he might have been correct, but with misery and betrayal apparently the marital norm, it appeared that Gilda had made a sensible choice when she instinctively turned Jerome down flat. Marriage could so easily become her personal prison sentence, the way it presumably had for the wandering Elaine and possibly for housework-obsessed Dulcie as well, and Gilda wanted more from life than dreary domesticity, continual lies and a bored husband who complained to colleagues about her shortcomings. Lance was speaking of his own situation, but he had just helped Gilda free herself from the fear that she might be making a mistake if she rejected the chance of a conventional happy ending.

****

"I reckoned you'd be returning here soon," said Rodney Fryer, sounding amused.

Machinery roared in the background, and Gilda wondered how anyone could bear to work in a factory day after day. She walked down the corridor to escape the worst of the noise, and asked, "Is there some place we could talk for a few minutes?"

"What's wrong with here and now? I can't leave the floor for too long."

"OK. You were off work this morning."

"That's right." Rodney leaned against the wall, untroubled by police questions. If anything, he gave the impression of enjoying himself: a man who believed things were going his way. "You want me to tell you where I was this morning and who was with me, but you already know or you wouldn't be here now."

"I still need confirmation," said Gilda.

"And you shall have it. I was in my flat all morning, and so was Elaine." Rodney smiled complacently, proud to be the factory Lothario.

"What time did Mrs Thornthwaite arrive and leave?"

Rodney frowned, his smile abruptly gone. He had not liked to hear Elaine called Mrs Thornthwaite. "She was with me from five minutes to eight, and stayed until one o'clock."

"You're sure it was five to eight?"

"Yes. We joked that she was a few minutes early for her shift. That's one of the oldest cover stories: an extra shift at the factory." Rodney tried to laugh and present himself once more as a carefree womanizer, embarrassed at having even momentarily revealed the depth of his feelings for Elaine.

"Did anybody see you together?"

"Only if they peered through the window. No, that wouldn't have done them any good because I didn't open the shades until this afternoon." Rodney was smirking again, but his reaction to Elaine's married name had made matters clear. It was no casual affair for him.

"Do you know which hut Mrs Thornthwaite lives in?" asked Gilda, to try and knock Rodney's confidence with another reminder of Elaine's life with a husband.

"It's the hut at the far end of the first row." Rodney did not like the question any better than Gilda had thought he would, and she imagined him standing opposite Hut 34 in midnight darkness, brooding over lurid mental pictures of Elaine and Jeffrey in bed together.

"Have you ever been inside the hut?"

"No." A snapped-out answer, but more resentful than defensive. The Nissen hut was where Elaine lived with her family, and the separation of the two lives was yet another reminder of Elaine's reluctance to free herself from what Rodney doubtless regarded as the past. "Does Jeff Thornthwaite know that Elaine was with me this morning?"

"Only if she's told him."

"Oh." A faint hope had flickered and then vanished. Rodney might be sure of Elaine when she was with him, but the rest of her life remained off-limits to Rodney Fryer.

"Do you have a gun?" asked Gilda.

"Which part of a foreman's job in an ice-cream factory do you think requires him to be armed with a gun?" said Rodney, grinning. "No, I don't have a gun. And no, I didn't mistake Clive Leyton for Jeffrey Thornthwaite this morning. I wouldn't risk the death penalty when Elaine's going to get a divorce. She's just waiting for the right moment to leave Jeff."

There could never be a right moment to tell an unsuspecting husband that the marriage was over, but it seemed to have nothing to do with Clive Leyton's fate, whoever Elaine eventually decided to live with. Gilda closed her notebook, wondering if she would have been less inclined to laugh at the idea of becoming Mrs Henderson had she sensed even an iota of Rodney's infatuation accompanying Jerome's proposal.

"Elaine and I are getting married," Rodney announced, as though Gilda had argued the point. "She's not the sort of woman who roams from bed to bed."

That appeared to be precisely what Elaine Thornthwaite was doing, but Gilda nodded. "I've got to check the whereabouts of hostel residents this morning; that's all. I don't need to know anything more."

"What will you tell Jeff Thornthwaite?"

"Nothing. You've confirmed Mrs Thornthwaite's account and, as I said, that's all I need to know. Clive Leyton's death is the only police matter. Thanks for answering my questions."

"No problem." The foreman's problem was Elaine's indecision about taking the final step and leaving her husband, and Rodney looked let down to realize that the police investigation would apparently not act as a catalyst.

"Oh, one more question. Do you know Clive Leyton's wife?"

"You mean Clive Leyton's widow." Rodney shook his head, but Elaine was still preoccupying his thoughts and he spoke absently. "Mrs Leyton's never had a job here, so I haven't even met her. Why do you want to know?"

"Just routine."

"Elaine and I are definitely getting married," declared Rodney, and he folded his arms, prepared to defy the world.

****

"Well? Do I arrest Elaine Thornthwaite for murder?" asked Lance.

"Not at the moment. Rodney Fryer agrees that she was with him from eight this morning," Gilda reported. "So unless we can get evidence of a vast conspiracy, Elaine's in the clear."

"Not in her husband's eyes, if he ever finds out what she's doing. Of course, Jeffrey might be glad to get rid of Elaine. She wouldn't be much of a loss, despite her looks."

Lance grunted contemptuously, and the disdain in his voice would have helped Gilda to make a decision, had she not already suspected that marriage to Jerome Henderson might easily end up as one of the stupider mistakes of her life. "Well, unless Elaine dispatched Rod to kill Jeff, and somehow the wrong husband was shot, I reckon the passionate foreman and the accommodating wife can be put to one side."

"But Jeffrey Thornthwaite can't be."

"Or Dulcie Leyton. And David Yoxall still has to explain why he was forty-three minutes late for work, something that he neglected to tell us. There's also the fact that most of the men living on the hostel will be ex-military, so the Luger could have

143

been anybody's. And what about Oskar Hauser? He was around at the time of Clive Leyton's death."

"A musical murderer, you reckon?" Lance looked amused, and then added, stubbornly loyal to his instinct, "The Thornthwaites are the ones with secrets."

"Everybody's got secrets."

"Perhaps, but they don't usually have as many as the Thornthwaites."

Only one family secret was established, and that belonged solely to Elaine, who apparently had a watertight alibi for the time when Clive Leyton died. The rest was merely guesswork, and there seemed to be no reason why Gilda should not contribute to it. "What if Clive had an affair, and Dulcie found out?"

"An affair with a three-year-old," muttered Lance.

"An affair with anyone at all." And yet, Gilda sounded unconvinced. In spite of there being no irrefutable proof, she was unable to free her mind from Lance's belief that Clive Leyton had been a child-molester who deserved to die.

"Why would Dulcie bother to kill her husband when she could walk out with the kids, leech off Clive for the rest of his life and get away from a talkative God at the same time?" To Lance it was a simple solution, but Gilda could imagine any woman in Dulcie's circumstances being daunted by the prospect of such drastic action.

"She's in a strange country with no money of her own, no family support and no job."

"Then there must be an insurance policy, whatever she claims," said Lance. "But Dulcie didn't need to do a thing because Jeffrey Thornthwaite obliged."

"I'll go to Watson Valley Station tomorrow morning, and ask the people waiting for the eight-ten if any of them caught that train today," decided Gilda, "One of them might recall seeing Jeffrey Thornthwaite."

Lance shook his head. "Nobody will have seen him. The Invisible Man; that's what Jeffrey called himself, the Invisible Man."

7

Despite the sweltering heat of the store-room, Detective Inspector Wilbur Fairfax had managed to fit another hostel visit into his busy schedule, and looked as though he expected to be thanked for his consideration by both Lance and Gilda. "Have you got enough on Leyton's wife to make an arrest yet?"

"Not yet," replied Lance. "And there are other possibilities."

"Every migrant living in Watson Valley's a possible suspect. I'm more interested in probabilities."

"Then Dulcie Leyton probably removed the gun because her husband killed himself, but there's a man in the next hut who had a grudge against Clive Leyton. David Yoxall seems the violent type, and it wouldn't surprise me if he had a record."

Wilbur shook his head. "He couldn't get past the emigration process with a criminal record. What century do you think it is?"

"He might have used a dead brother or cousin's birth certificate to grab himself a whole new identity," suggested Lance. "It could be worth checking on the family with the English police."

"I'll contact them," said Wilbur, who liked telephones and telegrams better than the tedious slog of going through statement details. "But it's Leyton's wife who'll end up arrested."

"The likeliest possibility," conceded Lance.

Gilda waited for a mention of an additional possibility, but apparently Wilbur was not to be informed of Lance's theory about Jeffrey Thornthwaite, or even of Veronica's presence in the next room at the time of the shooting. Wilbur might not have listened to any further speculation when Dulcie Leyton was convicted in his mind of trying to cover up her husband's suicide, and Lance could offer no proof of Jeffrey's supposed actions, but the omission still surprised Gilda because Lance usually liked to broadcast his opinions.

"Well, I have to disappear now and play Melbourne politics." Wilbur stood up and he sighed in a show of reluctance to leave. "It's Ed Bixby's retirement swill, and I'm making a speech. Get hold of that life insurance policy, and you've got Dulcie Leyton's motive in your hands."

"There isn't a policy," said Gilda. "After the voice ordered him to emigrate, Clive cancelled all their policies because taking out insurance implied a lack of trust in God."

"Is that what Dulcie told you?" Wilbur laughed as he went out of the store-room. "There's a life insurance policy for Clive Leyton somewhere, and with a suicide clause. Find it."

"Wilbur scents promotion in the air; that's why he's determined to hang around Melbourne," said Lance, slumping back in his chair. "It's not worth the bother of checking, when Fairfax the clairvoyant knows all the circumstances surrounding Clive Leyton's death, but perhaps we should give the tax-payers value for money, and ask David Yoxall what he was doing prior to his arrival at the factory forty-three minutes late for a shift. And there's lover-boy Alan as well. He had plenty of time to shoot Leyton and get to school afterwards if he ran. Even the puniest kid can be a thug with a gun in his hand."

"Oskar Hauser was in the same hut as Clive Leyton until going out to work, and Oskar admits that it was close to nine o'clock when he left," Gilda reminded Lance, "although a few complaints about Beethoven aren't much of a motive for murder."

147

"They've been committed for even less reason." Lance heaved himself to his feet unenthusiastically, pushed back a chair, and headed towards the door. "Yoxall first. Beethoven can wait."

"Perhaps it's as straightforward as the Inspector thinks." Gilda followed Lance out into what felt like a solid wall of heat, and she paused to lock the store-room door. "Perhaps Clive Leyton did kill himself, and everything else is a sidetrack."

"Perhaps, but there was no point in telling Wilbur about Jeffrey Thornthwaite," Lance said, answering the question that Gilda would not have asked. "There's nothing to link Jeffrey to the death. No proof at all."

"None," agreed Gilda. A child's scream, a shouting man: evidence of nothing, and yet the entire basis of Lance's theory. "Is it likely that Veronica would have slept right through a shooting in a room the other side of a thin partition?"

"Nobody's found a silencer, but that doesn't mean there wasn't one on the gun."

Dazzled by sunlight reflected off silver roofs, they crossed the road and began to walk along the front row of huts. Families were sitting on chairs near to their blue-painted doors, and radio music mingled with snatches of *Hancock's Half-Hour*, but as Gilda and Lance went by, the wirelesses might as well have been silent because the two outsiders were scrutinized intently by every group that they passed.

"This must be how film stars feel," said Gilda, nodding at Sidney and Rose Kendrick who pretended not to notice.

"Film stars?" repeated Lance, but he spoke absent-mindedly, gazing at the end of the row. The Thornthwaites were sitting in front of Hut 34, a family façade with Veronica on the steps, her parents either side of her on chairs. Elaine looked up, possibly hoping that the moment of decision had been made for her, and Veronica looked down, perhaps fearing more questions, but Jeff smiled confidently, challengingly, as Lance and Gilda turned onto the path that led between Huts 32 and 33, leaving the Thornthwaites to another night of pretence.

Constable Dexter was no longer guarding the ex-Leyton section of the Nissen hut, rooms with closed doors and closed windows, a temporary memorial of the day's drama that left David Yoxall totally indifferent. He sat on the steps of 33 smoking a cigarette, two empty beer bottles beside him, and he lurched to his feet when he saw the visitors. "What's this country? A police state? I've got rights."

"So have we," retorted Lance, "and one of them is to ask questions during an investigation. You didn't clock-in at the factory this morning until forty-three minutes after the eight o'clock shift began."

"What's that got to do with you?" demanded Dave. "I don't have to say a word. Do you think I'm stupid?"

Lance ignored temptation by asking a question of his own. "How come you were late for work this morning?"

"None of your business," Dave roared. "This is persecution, and you're not going to treat me like dirt. I'm no thick-headed factory labourer that you can push around. I could have been a singer, if that doctor hadn't mucked up my tonsils."

"Then sing out what you were doing between ten minutes to eight and seventeen minutes to nine this morning," said Lance.

"I'm not paying a penny for any brat, and the law can't make me," announced Dave.

Wirelesses were being switched off, allowing the cicadas to take over from Tony Hancock as listeners along the row of huts tuned in to a more interesting conversation, but the smaller kids took a few steps back when Dave turned to his audience and started bellowing. "Mind your own business, you —"

"Be careful of your language in front of children, Mr Yoxall," snapped Lance, as a reminder of the authority that he could wield.

"They're all jealous of me," Dave shouted, waving a fist at the onlookers. "Sinatra himself said to me, 'Dave, he said, 'Dave, I wish I had a quarter of your talent.' Those were his very words. 'Dave,' he said —"

"Where were you at ten to eight this morning? Answer the question."

Lance was coming close to arresting Dave, and removing such belligerent stupidity from the midst of a hostel teeming with children seemed a good idea, whatever the reason. David Yoxall clearly had a problem controlling himself, and was probably a drunk: one that Gilda could easily imagine turning aggressive over the most trivial of matters, and gossip, usually a wild distortion of fact, appeared to be accurate when it maintained that Yoxall was violent toward his wife and son.

"I don't have to say anything," declared Dave, imbecility personified.

"Oh, just tell them." A woman stood in the doorway behind Dave, her voice shrill and harsh. Gilda had been picturing an intimidated wife, listless after years of beatings, but Irma Yoxall looked prepared to do her share in any boxing match. A stout woman, with large arms and legs that looked almost stick-like in comparison to her bloated body in its tight dress, Irma had short straight gingery hair pushed back behind her ears, and it accentuated the wizened face of someone who failed to realize the shrivelling effects of strong sunlight. "Just tell them that you were late for work because you're a bone-idle drunk who can't wake up in the mornings."

"You shut your gob," retorted Dave. "I haven't got a cushy number in a canteen, swigging tea all day and stuffing cake down my throat. No, I'm slaving in that factory hour after hour: all the hours God sends. You ask anyone, and they'll tell you that I'm the best worker they've got over there. Neville Arlen himself said to me, 'Dave,' he said, 'Dave, I only wish I had your management skills.' Those were Nev's very words. 'Dave,' he said –"

"More likely he told you to take a running jump," scoffed Irma.

"Shove it where the sun don't shine."

There had never been much chance of Jerome persuading Gilda to become Mrs Henderson but, after that example of domesticity, there was no chance at all. Lance stood back, allowing the Yoxalls to screech at each other, as he waited to see exactly how antagonistic they would get. Dave was a fool, but possibly a dangerous one, although the watching families seemed to regard the scene as nothing out of the ordinary, indicating that the couple routinely traded loud insults.

"Were you here with your husband at eight o'clock this morning, Mrs Yoxall?" asked Gilda, unable to bear the row any longer.

"No, I was still at work. I start my first shift in the canteen at five," replied Irma, self-righteously smug. "And that means I can't stay up half the night drinking."

"I've got insomnia," yelled Dave. "My brain's too active for me to sleep, and it's nothing less than a miracle that I go on: a miracle. Those were the doctor's very words. 'Dave,' he said to me, 'Dave, it's a miracle, nothing less than a miracle, that you survive with all your problems.' His very words —"

"Oh, shut it," said Irma. "Alan was in the canteen having breakfast around half-past seven, and then he went straight to school, so this layabout was on his own in the hut at eight o'clock. And if you lock him up, it'll be the best thing that's happened to me in years."

Once upon a time, Dave had presumably proposed marriage and Irma accepted, or even vice versa, but the result showed how easy it was to waste life shackled to the wrong person. "Mr Yoxall, were you alone from half-past seven?" Gilda asked.

"Mind your own business. I don't have to tell you a thing. I'm not stupid," snarled Dave. "And those Leytons aren't getting a penny out of me."

"They'd have a job, when he drinks and gambles the lot away," said Irma. "Do us all a favour, arrest the old git, bung him in prison, and then lose the key."

"It's no crime to be alone in a hut," shrieked Dave, "and that's where I was until I went to work. If I'm arrested, I'll make sure the Prime Minister hears about it."

"Then spare Bob Menzies the deep anguish that he'll feel at the news, and answer a few questions," said Lance. "Did you hear any sounds coming from Hut 34?"

"Him! Hear anything!" jeered Irma. "An atom bomb could blitz the entire hostel, and he wouldn't hear a thing after he's had a skinful the night before."

152

"That's not true," protested Dave. "I heard a kid scream. It woke me up."

"What time was this?" Lance demanded.

"I don't know. Around eight o'clock. Does it matter?"

"What did you do?"

"What was there to do? Kids are always screaming their heads off. I've got my own problems."

"Was it a young child's scream?"

"I don't know."

"Boy or girl?" asked Lance.

"A kid," replied Dave, irritated by what he perceived as nagging. "Just a kid. The hostel's full of them."

"Was it a scream of terror, of laughter —?"

"A scream, that's all."

"Could you say where the scream came from?"

"How should I know?" Dave retorted in exasperation. "A kid screamed. I woke up. That's it."

"Was the sound from indoors? Outdoors?"

"One or the other. Look, I've got things on my mind —"

"Like where I hide my purse now," said Irma.

"I told you, I never touched your purse," shouted Dave.

"No, course not," said Irma. "Those pound notes unfolded themselves and walked away of their own accord."

"Mr Yoxall, did you see anyone when you went out?" asked Lance.

"I might have. I don't remember."

"No, he wouldn't," agreed Irma. "No chance of that. He can barely focus on the ground beneath his feet after he's been drinking most of the night."

"It's a medical condition," growled Dave. "I've got vertigo, just like James Stewart in that film."

"More like a drunk in any film," remarked Irma.

"Shut up!"

"Shut up yourself!"

"What did you hear after the child screamed, Mr Yoxall?" Lance demanded, struggling to retain some patience.

"Nothing. A car. Some man."

"What man?"

"How should I know? Just a man."

"Was he talking, singing, laughing, shouting —?"

"I didn't listen. I told you, I've got things to think about."

"A hangover to think about," said Irma.

"So you heard a child scream and then a man's voice," Lance reminded Dave. "What happened next?"

"I went to the toilet."

"Did you hear gunfire at any time?"

"No, I didn't. I'm not taking the rap for shooting that Leyton nutter, and don't you forget it."

Assuming that truculent Dave was telling the truth, someone else had been frustratingly near events surrounding the death of Clive Leyton and, like Oskar Hauser and Rose Kendrick, chose not to listen. Perhaps it was an inevitable result of so many lives crammed in a small area, forcing people to ignore their neighbours as much as possible, but David Yoxall kept glancing up to assess how his testimony was received. It could have been the reflex action of a habitual liar, but Gilda felt fairly sure that Dave wanted to hide something. "What time did you come back to the hut from the toilets?" she asked.

"I didn't. I went straight to work."

"So you spent three-quarters of an hour in the toilet block?"

"I met one of my mates and talked to him for a bit."

"Even though you were late for work?" Lance looked sceptical, and Irma laughed stridently.

"He thinks being late for work's normal. That's why he's always getting the sack. And the mate he ran into would either be collecting bets or wanting a loan repaid."

"Are you talking about unlicensed gambling?" Lance sounded more resigned than shocked, but Dave reacted as if a bolt of lightning had hit him.

"She's a liar," he shrieked. "And she can't prove a thing. And neither can you."

"What's the name of your mate?" asked Lance.

"I don't rat on mates," shouted Dave. "And I'm not saying another word that'll get twisted around against me. I wouldn't do anything illegal. I'm not stupid."

"Huh!" commented Irma.

****

"Did you believe a single word of what David Yoxall just said?" Gilda asked Lance, as they walked away from the huts and crossed the road. "I know that another account of the child's scream backs up what Oskar Hauser and Rose Kendrick told us, but I'm beginning to doubt the whole thing now that David Yoxall says it happened."

"If that man informed me I was an Australian, I'd check my birth certificate to make sure," replied Lance. "Oh, no! Look who's hot on the trail."

"This is a very happy hostel." Hubert Webb stood outside his office addressing a tall, thin, brown-haired man in his mid-thirties, and Lance muttered irritably at the mere sight.

"The vultures are starting to circle."

Bryce Chesney was too untidy to be likened to any bird, and he often gave the impression of being absent-minded, but he had still managed to be first reporter on the scene that day.

"Could be worse," said Gilda. "It might have been his wife."

"Don't even mention that woman," groaned Lance.

"The younger children are in the Recreation Hut," Hubert was saying. "There'll be organized games for them every day during the summer, and the teenagers have dances."

Bryce was actually writing down the details in a notebook, because he knew better than to alienate anyone who might later become a useful source, and he merely nodded at Lance and Gilda as they walked past.

"He won't be quite so relaxed when a few other reporters show up here," Lance remarked, torn between indignation at being practically ignored and the wish not to be bothered by a rabble of journalists.

"Bryce will get more copy out of a hostel manager than you, and he knows it," said Gilda. The air inside the store-room was suffocatingly hot, and she switched on the electric fan but with very little hope of lowering the temperature. "I wonder what Bryce is going to make of David Yoxall?"

"That's obvious. Yoxall's a liar as well as a half-wit."

"What about his tale of being woken by a child's scream? If the other kids had left for school or were in the kindergarten, it must have been Veronica he heard."

"Yes, but Yoxall's an unreliable witness," declared Lance. "Imagine him giving testimony in a courtroom."

"He'd certainly liven up the proceedings."

"What court and what proceedings?" Bryce Chesney stood in the open doorway, fanning himself with the notebook he held. "It's like a furnace-room in here. How do you stand the heat?"

"Wait until you go inside one of the Nissen huts," replied Gilda. "I don't know how the migrants can bear living in them."

"But they're all happy, and such nice people," said Bryce, consulting his notebook. "How come nice and happy people are going around shooting each other?"

"No comment," said Lance. "Get out. We've got work to do."

"So have I. Hubert Webb doesn't believe that any of his nice families could possibly be involved, but someone shot Clive Leyton. So why did it happen? Robbery? A merciless gang targeting Nissen huts?"

"The police continue their inquiries," said Gilda.

"Did the wife have a hand in it? Oh, by the way, talking of wives, congratulations, Gilda."

"Thanks. What for?"

"Your engagement."

"What engagement?"

"But you must be engaged to Jerome Henderson," protested Bryce. "My informant's known the man for years, and she's a most reliable source."

"Not this time."

"You're mistaken, Gilda, very mistaken," Bryce said firmly. "My wife's never wrong and never will be wrong. Even if Millicent has to march you and Jerome into the nearest jeweller's at

157

gunpoint, you'll find yourself wearing an engagement ring before the week's over."

"Not while I've got any say in the matter."

"You haven't," declared Bryce. "Millicent has spoken. Now, if I'm ever found shot, she'll undoubtedly have aimed the gun at me. What about Clive Leyton's wife? Is she equally decisive?"

"There'll be a press statement in due course," said Lance. "Get out."

"Try David Yoxall, Bryce, Hut 33," suggested Gilda. "He's not stupid, as he'll tell you himself."

"I'll trade information," offered Bryce.

"You haven't got any, or you wouldn't be in here on a fishing expedition," retorted Lance.

"People won't talk freely to the police, but they like newspapers. I'll pick up things that you won't even get near."

"Then go pick them up. Nobody's stopping you." Lance despised Bryce Chesney who, as well as being a reporter, was the reporter who had married his editor's daughter, a move that Lance regarded as cynical opportunism. To others, it seemed more likely that the determined and forthright Millicent Hatton had married the hapless Bryce Chesney, but Lance rarely found a reason to change his mind.

"At least give me the facts," Bryce pleaded, turning to Gilda.

"And get myself demoted? Not a chance! You're on your own, Bryce."

"The story of my life."

"Not when the newspaper's editor happens to be your father-in-law," Lance said, unable to resist so satisfyingly barbed a comment.

"You've no idea how isolated a situation it is," lamented Bryce. "The whole office assumes that I'll go running to him with the slightest piece of gossip, and so I'm the permanent outsider."

"Nice play for sympathy, but it won't work," said Gilda. "Why not visit the happy hostel residents? You'll find practically everyone at home now."

"Wait until my spellbinding personality charms the sensational truth out of the migrants. You'll be sorry then."

"Not as sorry as you'll be if you go on obstructing police work any longer," said Lance.

"Attempt to stifle press freedom. I can see the headline now." Bryce sauntered out of the store-room, and Gilda wished that Lance had been less hostile. A little collaboration with a journalist could sometimes produce helpful information, but Lance's scorn of Bryce Chesney would ensure that there was no exchange.

"Conceited fool. He always uses other people to get him where he wants to go," Lance declared.

"He's right about the migrants not talking freely to us though," said Gilda. "They're in a new country, and won't want to get themselves mixed up in a police inquiry, but a reporter asking them about hostel life might be different, and any difference in David Yoxall would be an improvement."

"David Yoxall, Oskar Hauser, Dulcie Leyton, Jeffrey Thornthwaite." Lance said the names aloud as if he hoped that the sound would offer enlightenment, but he was just repeating syllables. "Rose Kendrick too, and the Webbs as well, for that matter. Every one of them had an opportunity to kill Clive Leyton, and none of them liked him."

159

"We don't know that about Dulcie," objected Gilda.

"After so many years of marriage, and then God interfering? I'd say that she was a very likely suspect. David Yoxall's the most violent, and stupid with it, but Jeffrey Thornthwaite's motive is the strongest."

"Assuming that his daughter was assaulted."

"Yes, of course," said Lance, waving away the detail. "Then there's Oskar Hauser. Not much of a motive, unless he was having an affair with Dulcie."

"The affair was supposed to be with Rodney Fryer a couple of hours ago," commented Gilda. "Dulcie's certainly got a more active social life than mine."

"Are you really going to marry Jerome Henderson?" asked Lance. "Do you know that his company was investigated for fraud a few years back?"

"Yes, I know, and that he was cleared of all allegations."

"No smoke without fire. Has he ever tried to get information out of you?"

Jerome Henderson's main topic of conversation was Jerome Henderson, and Gilda replied quite truthfully, "He never shows any interest in my work."

"Well, be careful all the same. Mud sticks."

"And mud could also put out a fire, as well as its smoke."

"And put out your career at the same time. Ask yourself why Henderson's so eager to be seen around Melbourne with you."

The implication was that no man would consort with a woman as plain as Gilda Garfield unless he had a nefarious hidden agenda, and she smiled at Lance's low opinion of her allure. "Perhaps Jerome's desperate. After all, isn't the statistic

160

something like ten men to every one woman in Australia? I might be poor Jerome's last chance."

"Or his last chance to pretend that he's got nothing to hide." Once a suspect, always a suspect, according to Lance, no matter how little evidence he had to support his belief. Jerome Henderson was one step ahead of the law, and Clive Leyton had been a child-molester whoever shot him because, despite the flimsiest of foundations, possibilities became probabilities and then certainties the more Lance mulled things over. Instinct occasionally worked for him, but he relied too much on it, and Gilda was beginning to think that Clive Leyton's killer might never be charged if Lance refused to take notice of testimony that failed to support a theory rooted primarily in imagination. Any contradictions in a statement were going to be dismissed as irrelevant, and perhaps Lance's experience in the job meant that his was the right approach, but doubts were starting to nag at Gilda's mind about Lance's inflexible conclusions.

"If Jerome had something to hide, Millicent would have found out ages ago, and then got all the gory details printed in her father's newspaper," said Gilda. "I was surprised when she married Bryce, because Millicent and Jerome were an item for quite some time."

"Keeping company with Desmond Hatton's daughter doesn't add anything to Jerome Henderson's reputation," declared Lance.

"Perhaps Jerome likes to live dangerously."

"Make sure that you don't, if you want to keep your job."

Lance saw no reason why a policeman should be denied his own life off-duty, but he regarded women as too gullible to make level-headed judgments, yet commonsense told Gilda that Jerome had asked her out because he needed to be seen with another woman, any woman, after Millicent Hatton had departed to marry a man who should have gone unnoticed when the successful Jerome Henderson was around. He hoped to prove something to Millicent, rather than gain access to the limited police knowledge available to a low-ranking insider like Gilda, and it was an adolescent reaction to unaccustomed failure, therefore typical of Jerome.

"If I get thrown out of the force, it'll be my own fault, not Jerome's," said Gilda, "and probably something to do with me making snap decisions that are way off target. I don't think David Yoxall can really be as dim-witted as he pretends, but he's not intelligent and yet thinks he's clever. That can be a dangerous combination."

"His account of the screaming child backs up Oskar Hauser and Rose Kendrick," Lance pointed out.

"Yes," Gilda conceded.

"If anything, despite the obvious lies, Yoxall's version of events puts Jeffrey Thornthwaite at the top of my list."

"It might not have been Veronica who was heard screaming. The sound could have come from a nearby wireless: a very loud wireless."

Such dubious speculation had Lance raising his eyebrows and shaking his head, and Gilda knew that he was right. One of radio's tinny voices would never be mistaken for a nearby child.

"It could have been any kid screaming," argued Gilda, but she knew that Veronica Thornthwaite seemed to be the only child not on her way to school or safely in kindergarten at the time of Clive Leyton's death, and the thought made Gilda frown.

****

Bryce Chesney crossed the road, aware that he was being watched by many eyes: an unusual occurrence for a journalist expecting to be the observer, not the observed. Children, who had been running around, paused to stare at the interloper, and adults sitting in the shade of their huts stopped talking as the stranger approached, making Bryce feel like a gatecrasher at a family gathering.

Hubert Webb had pointed out Hut 34, and as Bryce drew nearer, he was surprised to see a man, woman and child sitting in front of its open door. The final bars of Beethoven's Seventh Symphony swirled away, but the family looked as though they were waiting for something to happen and suspected that Bryce might be the herald of whatever was coming next.

"This *is* Hut 34?" he asked.

"According to the number on the door." Jeff Thornthwaite was not hostile, merely superior, and prepared to give no more information than the exact amount requested.

"I've got the wrong hut then," said Bryce. "Do you know where the Leyton family lived?"

"Yes."

"Which hut was it?"

"34."

"Go around to the back," said Elaine, impatient with Jeff's condescension.

"Families don't get a hut to themselves?" queried Bryce.

"Only if they've been foresighted enough to have a dozen kids," said Jeff.

163

"Did you know the Leytons?"

"Yes."

"Are you from England, like them?"

"That's right."

"My parents were English," remarked Bryce, making an over-friendly attempt to chat. "They came from a place called Acton. That's in London. Do you know it?"

"I've heard the name Acton before," replied Jeff.

Bryce needed a link, a bond that made him an ally, but Jeff was clearly unmoved by family origins, and Bryce tried again after spotting the metal badge pinned to Veronica's dress. "Good rowing, Argonaut."

"Not another one," sighed Jeff. "What's she joined? The Australian equivalent of the mafia?"

Once, in years long-gone never to return, Elaine had thought Jeff amusing. That day, he was simply irritating, and she had to fight back the sudden urge to start an argument: a private spat that would have become a public one within seconds as gossip sped throughout the hostel. Jeff had to be silenced instead, and the stranger sent on his way. "It's a waste of time looking for Dulcie Leyton and her daughters around here. They left the hostel this afternoon."

"Yes, I know," said Bryce. "Mr Webb told me."

"Then why were you pretending to look for them?" asked Jeff, smugly proud of revealing a flaw in the outsider's story.

"I'm not looking for the Leytons. I want to see their hut, get some idea of hostel life, talk to people who know them, and —"

"You're a reporter," declared Jeff, his tone implying that he had wide experience of journalists and their devious ploys.

Veronica was awed by her first sight of a newspaperman, but she lived in a world where publicity played no part, and Jeff looked scornful, Elaine indifferent. Bryce was accustomed to Melbourne politicians and businessmen eager to get their version of events into print, but migrants without a place in a new society disconcerted him, and he was left with triteness. "It must have been a great shock when you heard what happened to Mr Leyton."

"No, it's an everyday occurrence on this hostel," said Jeff. "Life's one drama after the next here."

"Did you know the Leytons well?"

"Not at all, it seems."

****

"Why were you so unpleasant to him?" asked Elaine. "He's just trying to do a job."

"I wasn't in the least unpleasant," protested Jeff. "I merely chose not to do his job for him."

"He only wanted a bit of information about the Leytons. How's he going to get it without talking to the people who knew them?"

"His problem, not mine."

There was no reason why Jeff should have discussed Clive Leyton with a reporter, and it had probably been kinder not to gossip about Dulcie and the children, but Elaine was annoyed by whatever Jeff did. "It's nearly time for your shift," she said, attempting to hide her exasperation.

"I don't think that I'll go in tonight."

"Why not?" demanded Elaine. As soon as Jeff had gone, she would send Veronica to bed, and then hurry out to Rodney. Elaine

165

had been clock-watching for hours, longing for the night's arrival, and the thought of being trapped inside an airless hut with Jeff appalled her. "You've got to go to work; you've got to."

"It isn't safe, you and Vron alone in this hut tonight."

"Why not? Dulcie won't be coming back to shoot us, as well as Clive."

"Did Mrs Leyton kill Mr Leyton?" asked Veronica in surprise.

"Don't tell the police. It's a secret," said Jeff. "But Mum's right. There's nothing for you to worry about, Vron, nothing at all."

"So there's no reason for Dad not to go to work tonight, is there, Vron?" urged Elaine.

"It's still been an upsetting day, and I don't think that Vron's fully recovered from whatever made her ill this morning," argued Jeff, signalling to Elaine that he meant more than he said. "She isn't her usual self."

"She's just missing Audrey. Jeff, if you want to get Vron off this hostel, money's the only thing that'll do it."

Jeff knew that Elaine was right, but she had not lived through his day. "I still think it'd be better if I stay here."

"There'll be policemen hanging around all night. No cause for you to hang around as well, when you could be earning money."

"I suppose not." Jeff gave way reluctantly, and Elaine felt that prison gates had been opened especially for her.

****

The door and the window beside it were closed at the back of Hut 34. Not realizing that he could break into any hostel hut he chose, Bryce merely pressed his face against the panes of glass,

166

vainly attempting to peer inside, although conscious that there was an onlooker.

"Oy! What are you doing?"

A thickset man heaved himself to his feet, red face glistening with the effort. He had been sitting on the steps outside Hut 33, and Bryce remembered Gilda's mention of a possible source. "Mr Yoxall?"

"Who wants to know?" demanded Dave. "Are you with the police?"

"Nothing so exalted. I'm a journalist."

"I could have been a journalist," Dave retorted, apparently under the impression that Bryce had just denied so obvious a fact. "The editor of the *Sheffield Telegraph* told me that if I'd work for him, his paper would be as famous as the *Manchester Guardian*. 'Dave,' he said —"

"Then you'll understand all about deadlines. Did you know the Leyton family well?"

"Thieves and liars, the lot of them, trying to con money out of honest men. I'm not stupid. I recognize extortion when it jumps up and slugs me in the face, and extortion's the only word for it. Yes, out-and-out extortion, when my boy wouldn't even go near that girl, let alone knock her up. 'I'll see you in hell before I part with a farthing for any brat,' I told Leyton."

"He accused your son of getting his daughter pregnant?" Bryce felt let down. He had hoped for a more sensational story behind the death of a migrant, but humanity would insist on petty motives and pettier squabbles. However, Detective Senior Constable Gilda Garfield had been unexpectedly kind when she directed Bryce straight to the killer.

"Leyton put the story all around the hostel," fumed Dave. "He was bent on getting some mug to pay for the brat. I knew what his game was. I'm not stupid. He just didn't want to admit that his daughter had gone with a German."

"What German?"

"The one in the room right next door to the little tart. Easy enough for her to slip out at night and pay him a visit. The war's over, as far as I'm concerned, but Leyton was determined to hide the truth and put the blame on Alan. I'm not the one who's going to pay, I told Leyton; you are. That's exactly what I said to him: my very words."

"How did Leyton react?"

"I didn't waste my time hanging around to find out. Nobody gets away with trying to con me, and you can print it in your newspaper that Dave Yoxall's no fool."

A swaggering half-drunk bully, perhaps made more of a bully by wartime access to guns, was likely to regard killing as a routine way of dealing with enemies, and Bryce asked, "Were you in the Army?"

"I'm no shirker. They wanted me to be an officer, and Montgomery himself said, 'Dave, if I had you on my staff, the war would have been won years ago.' Those were Monty's very words."

Hubert Webb had told Bryce all about the finding of a Luger and his belief that it was probably a war souvenir used to kill Clive Leyton. Ex-soldier David Yoxall seemed to have little grasp on reality, and would certainly think himself clever enough to get away with murder. A few more drinks inside Yoxall, and he might start to brag about the ease with which he hoodwinked the police.

What had at first appeared to be a predictable case, a wife freeing herself without the formality of divorce, had twisted in the direction of a blustering fool's resentment, and Bryce wondered, if he returned with some whisky, how much of Yoxall's rant he would be able to get past the newspaper's lawyer and into print by the next morning.

Dave had turned to the couple sitting further along the row outside Hut 31 and, even though the audience members looked more resigned to their fate than enthralled, he was launched on a tale of Field-Marshal Montgomery seeking Dave Yoxall's advice about war strategy, and Bryce backed away to examine the far side of Hut 34. Two doors were side-by-side, and it would certainly have been easy for a girl to leave one room and join her German lover in the next, but the young man, listening to Beethoven's *Kreutzer Sonata* as he sat on the wooden steps in front of his open door, smiled when he saw Bryce.

"Firstly, I come from Vienna, and am therefore not German but Austrian despite the *Anschluss*. Secondly, no baby, whether half-German, half-Austrian or wholly English in origin. Thelma Leyton is thirteen, and to her I am a decrepit old man, not a boyfriend. Mr Yoxall is a buffoon, but a dangerous one."

"Why do you say that?" It was a question Bryce hardly needed to ask, and Oskar smiled again.

"What conclusion have you reached after listening to the man?"

"Pretty much the same," admitted Bryce. "Are you sure that there's no baby?"

"Quite sure. You hear a great deal through the thin walls of these huts."

"Yoxall believes in the pregnancy."

"He believes many things, most of them with no basis in actuality."

"Did he threaten Clive Leyton?"

"Mr Yoxall has threatened everybody on the hostel at one time or another," replied Oskar. "Why should Mr Leyton be an exception? It appears that Mr Yoxall enjoys great influence in political circles because the Governor-General of Australia is a close personal friend, happy to oblige Mr Yoxall by using wide-ranging powers to imprison the Leyton family and then return them to England."

"How did Clive Leyton react?"

"By speaking on behalf of God, and informing Mr Yoxall that liars burn in hell for eternity, but Mr Yoxall seemed untroubled by the prospect."

"Clive Leyton was religious?"

"In his opinion."

"But not in yours."

Oskar shrugged. "My opinions are of no importance, and I consider myself ill-equipped to speak for God."

Bryce felt uncomfortable with the Almighty butting into everyday life. Reporting a ceremony in the cathedral was a different matter; people expected mention of God at such occasions, but a migrant hostel on a weekday meant that a Supreme Being was definitely out of place, and Bryce recoiled from the topic. "What's Mrs Leyton like?"

"Happier than during past years, I imagine." The music stopped, and cicada song filled the hot evening air, but Oskar was unable to appreciate the sound of an alien continent. He stood up, went into his room and turned the record over to vanquish the native insects with European magnificence.

"Why did you emigrate?" asked Bryce.

"My old life had come to an end, and I hoped for another. It would be a similar answer from anybody on the hostel, apart from Mr Yoxall who doubtless emigrated to Australia at the request of the Governor-General and possibly Prime Minister Menzies too. Mr Leyton was another exception, because God ordered him to come here."

The young man from Vienna appeared to be a religious fanatic, determined to get God a mention in Bryce's copy, but a swift detour would nip that ambition in the bud. "Were you here in this hut when Clive Leyton was killed?"

"What time was he killed?"

"I don't know for sure."

"Then how can I be sure if I were here or not?"

"You'd have heard a shot," Bryce pointed out.

"Not necessarily when I play music, but Mr Leyton would have had a glorious death if it happened before I went to work, a death without fear, because it was accompanied by the Ninth Symphony no less."

"Whose ninth symphony?"

Oskar shook his head sadly at Bryce's ignorance. "There is only one Ninth Symphony in my opinion, the Ninth Symphony of Beethoven, and it always succeeds in making me feel brave enough to tackle anything a day might bring, even death."

"Well, it's better than taking to drink," said Bryce. "Does David Yoxall think that he's considered to be the supposed baby's supposed father?"

"No, that honour has been awarded to his fourteen-year-old son Alan."

"What's he like?"

"He plays football," replied Oskar, as though the one fact said everything required about Alan Yoxall.

"He's the hostel Romeo?"

"No, the hostel team reserve goalkeeper."

Clearly the God devotee knew nothing useful, and there was no point in wasting time with further questions, so Bryce nodded and strolled away. Dave Yoxall could wait until some whisky was acquired, and exploring the hostel took priority. It felt like visiting a new world, as foreign to Bryce as Australia must have seemed to a newly-arrived migrant, and he wandered through the rows of Nissen huts, wireless music following him, along with an increasing group of children. He tried to talk to a few adults, but word had already spread that he was a Melbourne reporter, and the migrants were wary of saying the wrong thing. Then, in a chance moment of good luck, he spotted Gilda Garfield by herself outside the manager's office, leaning against the wall in a patch of shade. Bryce dodged behind a hut to shake off the kids, and hurried across the road before Lance Palmer put in an appearance.

"Thanks for the tip, Gilda."

"What tip?"

"David Yoxall, of course."

"Yoxall?" Gilda smiled, and added in disbelief, "You're thanking me after the experience of meeting him?"

"It was an experience all right. He's chief suspect; that goes without saying."

"You know I can't possibly comment, Bryce."

"Was that Luger the gun used to kill Clive Leyton?"

"The results aren't back yet, and I shouldn't even tell you that much." Gilda could see Veronica Thornthwaite sitting on the steps of Hut 34, and was glad that Bryce had been sidetracked away from the child. David Yoxall could look after himself. "You'd better make the most of your exclusive. The rest of the journalist pack will arrive here before long."

"You're right. I haven't a minute to spare." Getting his hands on a bottle of whisky would have to be the next item on Bryce's busy agenda, but still he remembered to do a little buttering up. "You're a sport, Gilda, a real sport. Thanks again for the tip."

"No comment," said Gilda.

****

Alan was in his bedroom listening to the wireless, Irma at the canteen working the second half of her split-shift, and a drunken Dave talked as freely as Bryce had guessed that he would, but unfortunately all information centred entirely on the astounding life and amazing times of the multi-talented David Yoxall, dearest friend and confidant of the famous.

Nightfall had made little difference to the temperature inside the Nissen hut and, uncomfortable in the heavy heat, Bryce mentioned Clive Leyton's name again and again, but the only result each time was a short rant about Dave Yoxall not being fool enough to part with a farthing for any half-German Leyton brat; then, after another swig of whisky, Dave would return to the fascinating topic of his genius, and the many overwhelming tributes paid to it by the world's movers and shakers. Cruel circumstance had forced David Yoxall into anonymity, but that was no reason to deny all-comers a judiciously edited version of his memoirs.

"And after I led that bayonet charge up the beach, General Eisenhower himself told me I deserved nothing less than a medal. "Dave,' he said —"

"How much money did Clive Leyton actually demand?"

"He wasn't going to get a penny, whatever the thief demanded. Do you think I'm stupid?" snarled Dave. "Anyway, I'd just captured the machine-gun when Eisenhower came over to congratulate me in person. He'd seen the whole thing, and Ike himself said to me —"

"Where did you get that whisky?" shrieked Irma, clomping up the hut steps. "I knew it was you stole that money out of my purse."

"I never touched your purse," shouted Dave. "Are you calling me a liar?"

"Yes!" retorted Irma, snatching the whisky bottle. "And as I've paid for this, I'm finishing it off."

Dave howled in anguish as the treasure was wrenched from his grasp, and Bryce prudently decided on retreat. He was ready and willing to be an investigative journalist up to a point, and that point had definitely been reached when a drunken killer was about to go berserk. The swearing and screaming followed Bryce as he walked away from the hut, and he could easily picture David Yoxall killing Clive Leyton or anyone else Dave had a grudge against, which reduced police work to collecting a few facts prior to the inevitable arrest. Bryce Chesney's copy would probably make the next morning's front page with a byline, assuming that no Melbourne hullabaloo pushed him to the paper's interior, and one day he would be able to write an eye-witness account of Yoxall domestic life, although the full story might have to remain off the record until after Dave had been charged with murder. It was not a tale destined to shake Melbourne to the core, but Bryce would be glad to produce copy almost worthy of the Hatton family. He was very aware of being a disappointment to his father-in-law, a man who seemed able to scent a story even before it happened, and Bryce's wife Millicent was bounding ahead in radio news, but Bryce himself had always been more at home in the back blocks of journalism. He liked to talk to centenarians about their memories of colonial life or to interview the young and ambitious, rather than ply worthless no-hopers with drink, but the Hatton family were all high achievers, and Bryce felt obliged to succeed in their world using their methods. Any débris left behind was for someone else to clear up.

8

Pale-blue sky, birdsong and all the bright freshness of early morning went unnoticed by a dazed Hubert Webb, who was saying over and over, "I can't believe it. I just can't believe it. No, I simply can't believe it."

Proud of his front-page byline, and even prouder of having beaten his colleagues to the story, Bryce joined a group of journalists gathered around Hubert outside the Watson Valley manager's office. "Believe what?"

"Another death," wailed Hubert. "We'd already had three on the hostel this year, three of them, and things are only supposed to happen in threes and then stop. There shouldn't be a fourth. I just can't believe it. Not another death."

Irma Yoxall! Beaten to a pulp! Slain by her drunken husband!

The morning sun was warm on his face, but Bryce felt cold. He had supplied the whisky and then walked away when David Yoxall turned violent. Yet, instead of remorse, Bryce was ashamed to find himself wondering if he had been spotted leaving the Yoxalls' hut. To report crime was one thing, but to be involved in it? Unthinkable for a Hatton son-in-law. Rival newspaper editors would relish the opportunity to slam into Desmond, and Millicent was going to be even more exasperated by her husband's fecklessness should she ever hear about the whisky, but as Irma Yoxall had passed beyond help, there seemed no point in allowing a boozed-up thug to destroy Bryce Chesney's prospects. Stout denial was the coward's solution, the hypocrite's solution, but also a comfortingly possible escape route.

"There's never been anything like this at Watson Valley Hostel before, never," protested Hubert, as though refuting an accusation of poor management from one of the reporters. "It's coincidence: nothing more than coincidence. Yes, that's all it is, coincidence."

"When was the body discovered?" asked Bryce, trying to seem casual but uncertain what his normal voice sounded like.

"Inspector Fairfax told me not to say anything because he'll be giving a press conference in a few minutes, and you'll get the facts then. I don't know them all myself." However, that was no reason for reporters to stop demanding answers to questions, and Hubert had started to look persecuted by the time Detective Inspector Fairfax strode out of the store-room, flanked by Lance Palmer and Gilda Garfield.

Wilbur Fairfax enjoyed talking to the press because he thought of himself as the friendly face of Victoria's police force, and considered that a good relationship with journalists was an essential part of his job, especially when speaking about a case that had already reached the headlines. Eager reporters were lined up, notebooks open at the ready, and behind them stood clusters of migrants who had paused on their way to the canteen for breakfast. Wilbur approached his audience, and despite it being too sombre an occasion for a smile, he basked in the attention.

"I've got a short statement to make," Wilbur announced, "and then perhaps I'll answer a question or two, but I haven't much time to spare as I'm sure you realize. Now, to begin at the beginning, just before six o'clock this morning, the body of a man was found on the path outside the —"

"A man!" gasped Bryce, before he could stop himself, and journalists looked up from notebooks, pausing in mid-scribble to glance at him.

Wilbur gazed reprovingly at the reporter attempting to muscle his way into the Fairfax limelight, and then continued, "He's not yet formally identified, but the man is believed to have been a resident of Watson Valley Migrant Hostel."

Both Gilda and Lance noted the deliberate build-up of suspense by Wilbur, who knew the identity of the hostel's ex-resident as well as they did. It was the sole aspect of the death that had no question whatsoever surrounding it.

"Is it connected to the Leyton killing?"

"Was he shot?"

"Is it another murder?"

Wilbur, that master of press briefings, waited until the journalistic uproar had faded away before he spoke again. "It's far too early to say exactly how the second death occurred or the reason why it happened. My officers and I continue our investigation. That's all for now."

Bryce had never thought that he would feel so happy to learn of an unidentified man's death, but life was completely altered by the news that the body had not formerly belonged to Irma Yoxall, and Bryce Chesney, reporter, was freed to join in the clamour around Inspector Fairfax. "Who found the man?"

"One of the migrants: a migrant whose name is not being given out at the moment. Now, if there are no more questions —" Of course there were, and Wilbur fielded them with good-natured grace. He was unable to share any further information, simply because he knew little more than had already been revealed, but luckily Wilbur never minded repeating himself when journalists were listening.

"Why the big mystery?" wondered Gilda. "The migrants all know who's dead. A reporter could ask any one of them and find out who it is."

"Wilbur likes to think that he's the puppet-master," said Lance. "He'll summon the press again to announce the name officially after it's already been printed in every Melbourne newspaper."

Lance was right. Public statements and press conferences were Wilbur's favourite part of the job, and he was visibly congratulating himself when he finally turned back toward the store-room. "That went smoothly. The wireless people should be here soon, and probably television as well. Let me know the minute they arrive."

Gilda started to follow Lance and Wilbur into the store-room, but a frantic Bryce Chesney clutched her arm. "The migrants are saying it's David Yoxall's body. Is that right, Gilda? Is Yoxall dead? How did it happen? Was he murdered?"

"Inspector Fairfax would get me kicked out of my job if I confirmed or denied anything before he did," Gilda replied. "You'll have to wait for the official word."

"But the migrants seem positive that it's David Yoxall. What time did he die?"

"Why not ask one of the migrants?" Gilda shook off Bryce's grasp and escaped, leaving him to wonder if she had just dropped a hint that the hostel dwellers knew all the answers. Other reporters appeared to think so, and were pursuing migrants into the canteen, but Bryce recalled Hubert Webb. The press statement had been delivered, presumably freeing the manager from his vow of silence, and Bryce hurried into Hubert's office.

"When did David Yoxall die? Was he shot? Is it another murder?"

"I don't think anyone knows yet, although I'm sure it was an accident or else a heart attack." But Hubert looked more worried than certain of anything, and he moved restlessly around his office, unable to settle. "It would all happen just before Christmas. Not that death's easier for families to cope with at any other time of year, but you know what I mean."

"Did he die inside the hut?" demanded Bryce, replaying his mental film of a drunken Yoxall brawl, but with Irma's fist aiming the fatal punch in the revised screenplay, and a mortally-wounded Dave tumbling backwards down the steps.

"As Mr Yoxall was found outside the toilet block, he must have tripped, hit his head on the path and died there. It's the likeliest thing to have happened, don't you think?"

"Yes. Yes, of course." Whether likely or not, the idea came as a relief, and with a bit of luck, Irma might have got herself too drunk to remember Bryce Chesney's part in the previous night's proceedings. "Was there a head injury?"

"It looked like it to me. I asked Mrs Yoxall if she and Alan wanted to move somewhere else, but she said that she'd prefer to stay right here in Watson Valley with all her friends." Hubert was gratified at the compliment to his hostel, despite having been surprised to learn that Irma had any friends. She was a foul-mouthed woman, stridently bad-mannered as well as unpopular with her fellow workers, and Hubert had hoped to solve the problem of Irma's confrontational nature by seizing the chance to

180

purge his canteen and offload the maverick onto another hostel, but it was typical of life that the nice Mrs Leyton had chosen to leave while the unpleasant Mrs Yoxall refused to be dislodged.

"Who found the body?"

"A young Viennese. A horrible discovery to make, even though he seemed calm enough when I saw him, but I suppose the shock still hadn't sunk in."

A calm young Viennese? It seemed too much of a coincidence, but Bryce recalled the non-German accused by Dave of fathering the avaricious baby so eager to grab at Yoxall money with single-minded resolve. "You mean the Austrian in Hut 34?"

"Yes, that's him. Of course, he wasn't close to the Yoxall family but, all the same, you'd expect more of a reaction, yet you never can tell which people are able to cope. It was often the swaggering brutes who went to pieces during the war, when the quiet ones just got on with the job."

"What's his name and where does he work?" A hostel feud turned violent would free Bryce of any responsibility for the death, and he took out his notebook, remembering that he was a journalist dedicated to uncovering the truth, even if it would be convenient for him should certain parts of the previous night's truth remain a little hazy.

"I doubt that Oskar will be able to tell you anything more than you already know," said Hubert.

"I just need the facts of the accident confirmed," Bryce explained, but the confirmation he wanted was of a second murder: a murder that had no connection with the amount of whisky inside David Yoxall at the time he died. The Hatton family would not approve of being linked even in the slightest way to a drunken Pom, and if Irma identified her husband's booze supplier, Bryce foresaw numerous complications destined to end his career abruptly, as father-in-law Desmond Hatton would certainly not hesitate before distancing himself from son-in-law stupidity. Should it turn out that David Yoxall had been deliberately targeted and killed, it was going to be the best news that Bryce Chesney might hear all summer.

****

The day was one of the most enjoyable that Irma Yoxall had ever known. Her work colleagues brought cups of tea and snacks over from the canteen, Mavis Webb asked if Irma needed any help, her neighbours offered to run errands, and most wonderful of all, she would never again have to see her boozing, gambling, swearing, shouting husband.

Sixteen years earlier, Dave Yoxall had seduced a young and gullible Irma Hobson by telling her that he was a war hero whose story had been bought by a Hollywood producer now urging Dave to immortalize his exploits by starring as himself in the forthcoming epic. However, Alan became a more imminent production, and Irma's level-headed parents kept the would-be film idol supplied with booze until he was safely married to their daughter and the Hobson family's respectable reputation secured.

But at last the day of freedom had arrived, and although Irma started the morning with a hangover, it miraculously cured itself the moment she had official confirmation that she was a widow. By ceasing to breathe, David Yoxall gave both Irma and Alan the happiness that his continued existence would certainly have denied them, and it was the first time in years that Irma had been the centre of attention. She savoured every glorious minute, and even police questioning added zest to the day.

"I know it'll be very difficult, so take as much time as you like," said Gilda. "Some of the things that I ask are going to seem intrusive, and I'm sorry, but I have to —"

"Oh, that's all right," declared Irma, as gratified as she was surprised to find herself considered a delicate flower.

"Did your husband have anything to drink last night?"

"He was sozzled out of his mind as usual."

"He drank a lot?"

"A lot! He was a drunk. His six o'clock swill went on twenty-four hours a day."

"He was always falling down," added Alan. He stood supportively beside Irma, but his slight figure made him look more in need of protection than she ever would.

"When I got in from work last night, there he was, finishing off a bottle of whisky with one of his layabout mates," Irma reported.

"Do you know the name of this mate?" asked Gilda.

"No idea. I never saw him before. Tall, thin, brown hair, probably in his thirties, nothing special."

"I think I heard him say his name was Bruce," offered Alan, frowning in an attempt to remember. "But I was listening to the wireless in my room."

"Anyway, whatever his name, he slunk off when *I* came in." Irma folded her arms and looked scornful at the memory of a weak-kneed coward, and Gilda had no problem imagining Bruce fleeing into the night.

"Did you have a quarrel with your husband?"

"Yes, of course I did. If you'd been working a four-hour shift in a steamy kitchen on a scorching summer night, and then came back to find your bone-idle husband boozing away the money, wouldn't you have a fight with him?"

"What happened next?"

"He went out and I went to bed. I do split-shifts in the canteen, and the first one starts at five every morning."

"Where did your husband go?"

"I haven't a clue. He went out every night, gambling or drinking, probably both." Irma shrugged, resigned to what she apparently regarded as normal married life, and Gilda determined to reject Jerome Henderson's second proposal as emphatically as she had his first.

"What time did your husband return?"

"I don't know." Irma gave a contemptuous snort, and added, "He wouldn't come back while I was still around."

"When did you get up?"

"Half-past four, but that sounds worse than it is because you get used to waking early."

"After you got up, I suppose you went down to the toilet block?"

"Where else would I go?"

"And you didn't see —?"

"He wasn't on the path then. Or if he was, I didn't notice," replied Irma, as indifferent as to a piece of litter. There was no hypocrisy in either her or Alan. David Yoxall had blighted their lives, and they were now rid of him: a straightforward honesty that said more about Dave than the family left behind.

"Your husband had a history of falls?"

"Whenever he got drunk, and that was every day he had money," said Irma. "My money, if he could get his hands on it, because he'd gamble his own away minutes after being paid."

"Do you know where he gambled?"

"I just know he did."

The question that Gilda really wanted to ask was why the hard-working Mrs Yoxall had not deserted the no-hoper husband years before. Irma would be better off in every way without a thieving drunk making life miserable and, for once, a death seemed to have no sorrow whatsoever surrounding it. "Alan, did your father come back to the hut after your Mum went out to work?"

"I didn't hear him," replied Alan. "And I usually did."

"The whole hostel usually heard Dave," Irma commented.

"I only woke up when Mr Webb knocked on the door to check that I was all right," said Alan.

"The Webbs have been ever so nice," remarked Irma. "I can't think why I didn't like them much before."

"So your husband almost certainly didn't come back to the hut this morning," Gilda concluded.

"That's probably what he was trying to do when he fell down the path," replied Irma. "Dave would watch until he saw me go over the road to the canteen and then he'd sneak in, hoping that I might have started hiding money inside the hut again, but even locking my purse up in a suitcase overnight wasn't enough to keep it safe from him."

"He smashed the piggy-bank my Gran gave me when I was a kid," added Alan. "There were only a couple of pennies inside it, but he didn't know that."

"Mrs Webb asked me if I needed any money," said Irma. "It was before Dave died that I had no money. I think he could smell it like a bloodhound."

"When he left the hut last night, did your husband follow the mate he'd been drinking with?" Gilda had given up all pretence of commiseration, as neither Irma nor Alan needed or wanted sympathy. It was their day of liberation, not mourning.

"I don't know where he went or anything about his latest mate. Dave never managed to keep one for long because he'd always wind up stealing from them, and then they'd arrive on the doorstep expecting me to pay up," said Irma, relating facts rather than complaining. "You're police so you can ask around for this Bruce, but there's no need to bother me with the details. He'll be a gambling drunk and Dave owed him money, but I'm not forking anything out and you can tell that to Bruce. I heard the same story over and over again for years."

Jerome Henderson would get a phone call cancelling their dinner date, Gilda decided. He seemed unlikely to turn into a David Yoxall, but she was not fond enough of Jerome to take the risk of possibly ending up as a second Irma. Lance had been right when he described marriage as a prison sentence, but it was an avoidable fate, and Gilda had already started running in the opposite direction.

****

Quietly confident and in complete control of himself, Oskar Hauser sat in the store-room. He had found a body only a couple of hours earlier, yet appeared as unmoved by the event as a hospital worker, and Gilda wondered about his background.

186

Oskar was too young to have many memories of the Second World War, but perhaps his family's experience of the German occupation had made him resilient or simply taught Oskar to hide emotion. Whatever the reason, he certainly gave the impression of being more concerned about his job than David Yoxall's fate.

"At the most, I can only stay for twelve minutes. I must reach the delicatessen by nine o'clock."

"Then tell us in twelve minutes or less what happened this morning," ordered Lance.

"You already know what happened. I found Mr Yoxall on the path outside the toilet block."

"Go back a little," said Gilda. "What time did you get up?"

"A few minutes before six o'clock."

"How come you were around so early when you don't start work until nine?" asked Lance, prepared to be sceptical of any answer from someone so self-assured.

"I was hot and uncomfortable," replied Oskar. "I decided not to stay in bed any longer, but to go and take a shower."

"What made you wake up?"

"No shout or cry disturbed me. I merely woke up."

"And?"

"And I left the hut. I saw a bundle of clothes outside the toilet block, and as I walked down the path, that bundle became Mr Yoxall." Oskar sat back as though his testimony had now been completed.

"Did you see anyone else about?"

"No. I went to Mr Webb's office, but of course it was too early for him to be at work, so I knocked on the door of his house instead."

"Where does he live?" Gilda had not given the matter any thought, but realized that she automatically assumed the Webbs would inhabit a Nissen hut.

"Mr and Mrs Webb live beyond the office in the house at the corner of the road: the house with a willow tree in its garden. Mrs Webb telephoned for a doctor, and Mr Webb came with me to see if he could do anything for Mr Yoxall, but too late."

"Did you know that David Yoxall was dead when you found him?"

Oskar paused to consider Lance's question, and then said, "Mr Yoxall no longer looked alive, but I knew that he drank a great deal of alcohol and you use the term dead-drunk in this country. I was undecided."

A dead drunk. David Yoxall's epitaph. A pointless end to a futile life. There seemed nothing further to say, and Gilda stopped writing in her notebook.

"You're quite sure that no one else was around?" persisted Lance.

"Early morning is the only silent time on the hostel, and the footsteps I heard were my own."

"Did you move Yoxall at all?"

"No, and nor did Mr Webb. He merely checked for a pulse, and then we waited until the doctor was there. Mrs Webb brought him to us, and Mr Webb went to make sure that Alan Yoxall was safe."

"Safe?" queried Lance.

"Safe," repeated Oskar.

It was the correct word to use when two deaths had occurred so close together, and one of them almost certainly murder. Hubert Webb would have been worried by the thought of Alan alone in a hut that anyone could enter, and Gilda was able to imagine Hubert's trepidation as he approached the door. She and Lance had known before their arrival in Watson Valley that the doctor said a fall was the likely explanation of Yoxall's head injury and death, but as Hubert Webb went to find Alan, he only knew that a migrant had been shot less than twenty-four hours previously and civilization seemed to have abandoned his hostel.

"What did you do next?" asked Lance.

"After I heard that Alan was safe, I finally took the shower," replied Oskar. "But I had to go to the other toilet block because Mr Webb locked the nearer one in case clues were inside that ought to be preserved."

"Had you ever seen a dead body before?" Lance hated dealing with emotional witnesses, but Oskar's serenity made him suspicious, although Lance was uncertain precisely what he suspected Oskar of. Shock sometimes took hours to manifest itself, but usually gave some sign of its presence, and Oskar appeared entirely placid.

"Yes, I have seen death before, many years ago: so long ago that perhaps I imagine remembering scenes that I only heard about. No, I might not have seen death before." Oskar looked unsure of himself for the first time, shook his head, and then stood up, adding, "Perhaps any other questions could wait? I must go to my job now."

Oskar hurried out of the store-room, and Lance turned to Gilda. "What do you make of that bit of nonsense? Doesn't know whether or not he's seen a dead body before today. That's one thing you don't forget, can't forget."

"He'd have been very young even at the end of the war," said Gilda, but Lance was unimpressed.

"You remember things that happened in your childhood more clearly than later events. What's he playing at?"

Probably nothing, thought Gilda. Oskar Hauser had discovered a body, gone for help, and now wanted to get on with his life. It was the air of superiority that Lance objected to, rather than any discrepancy in Oskar's version of the morning's drama, because Lance expected a shop assistant to be in awe of his authority, but that particular shop assistant had the air of a Governor-General. The police were servants in Oskar's mind, and Lance resented it.

"These migrants are a weird mob," he declared, "but it seems a very strange coincidence that people Oskar Hauser dislikes end up dead."

"If Hubert had ever organized a hostel popularity contest, neither David Yoxall nor Clive Leyton would have been among the prize-winners," Gilda pointed out. "And would Oskar put himself forward as finder of the body if he gave it a shove down the path? At least there's no reason to connect Jeffrey Thornthwaite with this death, even though, as you predicted, I couldn't find anyone at the station who recalled seeing Jeffrey catch the eight-ten yesterday or return later on. The ticket-collector remembers the stiletto-heeled blonde prostrate on the platform, and remembers her in impressive detail, but no sighting of Jeffrey at all."

"Of course not. The Invisible Man saw the blonde from the steps going up to the station or possibly from the road. He wanted to be able to describe, as a minimum, one of the passengers who got on or off that train." Lance grudgingly prepared to acquit

Oskar for the time being, but suspicion remained. "There's something about that Hauser. He doesn't ring true."

"He doesn't have to, especially as David Yoxall was a drunk who probably tripped over his own feet. If this is another murder, it's a clever one." Gilda regretted her words as soon as she had said them. To Lance, clever meant one person, and that person was Jeffrey Thornthwaite.

"Yoxall saw him go into the Leyton hut yesterday morning, heard gunfire and then tried a spot of blackmail," Lance decided. "Yes, typical of Yoxall. Australia's much better off without his sort."

Jeffrey Thornthwaite: public philanthropist? "If Clive Leyton was shot because of Veronica, it could have been done in a rage, but rigging an accident shows premeditation."

"It might not have been rigged," argued Lance. "When David Yoxall demanded money, threatening to tell us what he'd seen, Jeffrey punched him and sent the stupid drunk sprawling down the path. If everything came out, Veronica would be in a courtroom, forced to relive Leyton's attack, perhaps even help send her own father to prison, and Jeffrey wouldn't be able to protect her from any of it. No, when he hit Yoxall, it was in a split-second of fury."

"Jeffrey does seem fairly prone to these split-seconds of fury," commented Gilda.

Lance frowned, but the criticism he sensed was of Jeffrey the devoted father, rather than doubt of a scenario that cast Jeff in the rôle of avenging angel. "His actions are completely understandable," Lance declared. "The instinct to protect your child is probably the strongest of all."

191

"No doubt, but why did the two men meet at five in the morning? It must have been around then, if David Yoxall did encounter Jeffrey of the lethal punch, because Oskar discovered the body at six, and yet there was no sign of it when Irma went back and forth at half-past four."

"A chance meeting," said Lance, not to be daunted. "Jeffrey woke early, and he went out to the toilet block, just as Oskar claims to have done. David was on his way back to the hut, knowing that Irma would have gone to work, and he decided it was the perfect opportunity to make some easy money when he saw Jeffrey."

"If that's what happened, then there isn't any reason not to believe what Oskar says," Gilda pointed out.

"No," Lance conceded, but he was reluctant to distrust his instinct, and that instinct continued to suspect Oskar Hauser, even when he was apparently blameless.

"It's possible that Irma could be lying, and she did see her drunk of a husband flat out on the path and left him there," suggested Gilda, easily able to imagine an exasperated Irma storming past the horizontal Dave as she hurried to get ready for work.

"We've got no evidence of it," Lance stated, ignoring the fact that he had no solid evidence of his Thornthwaite theory or of Oskar's deviousness. "You might as well say that Irma killed her husband."

"OK, I'll say it. Jeffrey's lethal punch actually belongs to Irma, or she could have tripped up the drunk or pushed him down the hut steps." Gossip maintained that David Yoxall had been violent, but Irma was no terrified wife, beaten into submission.

She had coped for years with a blustering fool, and done her fair share of screeching abuse, and that situation was not going to alter drastically in one night. "I think Irma's shown amazing restraint. If David Yoxall had been my husband, I'd have killed him before the first wedding anniversary."

"While we're suspecting the wife, why not the son?"

"Alan seemed too calm to have anything on his mind. In fact, they were both completely relaxed." Gilda tried to recall the slightest tension in either Irma or Alan, but Dave's death was more an unexpected holiday for them than a grief. There had been no hesitation before replying to each question, yet the answers appeared unrehearsed. Straightforward, thought Gilda: that was how she would describe Irma and Alan. "I'm fairly certain they've got nothing to hide."

"You can never tell for sure," objected Lance.

"No, but they didn't even try to pretend that they were upset, and I reckon most people would, if only for the sake of appearance."

"Most people don't have a David Yoxall in the family, or a Clive Leyton either."

"Dulcie was upset," remarked Gilda.

"Dulcie was agitated," said Lance. "That's not quite the same thing."

Clive Leyton had either been murdered or committed suicide; David Yoxall, in all likelihood, fell while drunk. Irma's husband had died as abruptly as Dulcie's, but the two deaths were not really comparable, although Gilda suspected that Irma would have been unfazed no matter what removed Dave from her life, and it probably never occurred to Irma that anyone might be studying her reaction or questioning what she said. Irma was freed and she could only rejoice.

****

Yet again the Kendricks claimed to have seen nothing and heard nothing, and claimed it with steadfast resolve.

"We keep ourselves to ourselves, as I told you before," declared Sidney. "Live and let live. Well, perhaps they're not the right words to use at the moment, but you know what I mean."

It was still early in the morning, but the Nissen hut had already absorbed enough of the day's heat to make the interior stifling, and Gilda found herself continually glancing at the door to check that it really was open. Rose and Sidney both had a day off work and were impatient to take their children on a family excursion to Melbourne, but David Yoxall retained the power to aggravate people even after his death.

"Did you hear Irma Yoxall come back to the hut last night when she finished work?" Gilda asked.

"We had the wireless on all evening," said Rose. "It's the sole way to get some privacy in these huts."

"I've heard that your family had trouble with David Yoxall." Lance was trying to hurry through the questions, having no real interest in the Kendricks because they did not feature in the story he had built up around Jeffrey Thornthwaite, unless as witnesses, and that possibility both Rose and Sidney were determined to shun.

"Just about everybody on this hostel had trouble with David Yoxall," said Rose.

"Everybody," echoed Sidney.

194

"You told me about him stealing your rent money," Gilda prompted.

"Yes," growled Sidney, unable to remain aloof at the bitter memory of that vanished money. "We still owed the rent and had to pay it again, even though Yoxall stole the cash right off the counter in the manager's office. I know that I can't prove a thing, but David Yoxall nabbed our money."

"He won't be nicking money where he's gone," predicted Rose, grimly satisfied with the retribution meted out by fate.

"So you didn't hear any sounds at all from the Yoxalls last night," Lance informed the Kendricks as he stood up, eager to get out and breathe fresh air again.

"No," said Rose. "Nothing worth mentioning."

"What isn't worth mentioning?" asked Gilda, re-opening her notebook.

"Oh, nothing much."

"Nothing much about what?" Gilda persisted.

"We don't know why they were yelling," replied Sidney.

"That's when I turned up the wireless," added Rose. "We don't want the children repeating the sort of language that those Yoxalls use. The kids would get into trouble at school with their teachers."

"So you heard the Yoxalls arguing last night." Lance sat down again, regretting any testimony that condemned him to further time inside the clammy hut.

"We were planning to catch the very next train," Rose protested, realizing that she had said too much. "I promised the kids that we'd take them out today, and you're making us lose time."

"Then save time by telling me quickly what you heard," said Lance.

"Nothing. Just shouting."

"There isn't anything to tell," declared Sidney. "They shouted every day. We didn't listen."

"What time was this?" asked Gilda.

"Nine? Ten? Somewhere around then." Sidney looked annoyed at being considered a gossiper, but he was more than ready to speak ill of the dead. "Yoxall sounded drunk, like on every night of his life, but we never listened to whatever they screamed at each other."

"How long did the shouting go on for?" Lance knew that he had to ask the question, but as Irma freely acknowledged fighting with Dave, back-up from the Kendricks was unimportant.

"Five minutes? Ten minutes?" Rose shrugged helplessly because the evening had been one of many, a part of hostel routine. With the wireless volume as high as it could go, Yoxall family matters were muted to mere background noise that hardly registered.

"It'd stop whenever *he* went out," Sidney muttered.

"Did you hear any more shouting later on?" asked Gilda, and both Kendricks shook their heads.

"It was quiet for the rest of the night, so *he* must have stayed out the whole time, drinking and gambling," reported Sidney. "At least, that's what I've heard he did, and on our rent money too."

"Did either of you leave the hut before six this morning, or at any time during the night?"

The query was a waste of breath because neither Rose nor Sidney would be likely to admit to wandering around the hostel on

196

the night that a rent money thief died close to their hut, and the Kendricks reacted as though they had been directly accused of slaying the drunk. "Nobody left this hut until long after Yoxall was found, and you police were already here by then," Sidney declared, rigid with indignation.

"That's right," snapped Rose.

Lance opened his mouth to snap back, but Gilda stood up, pocketing her notebook. "Thanks for your time. You've been a great help," she said, turning towards the door and hoping that Lance would follow. Wilbur Fairfax had warned Lance about abruptness, and added that the State of Victoria now expected its police to be courteous as well as firm because gone were the days of shooting first and asking questions later. It was a wild exaggeration of Lance's usual method of working, but Wilbur regarded all those who failed to kowtow before him as out-of-control mavericks endangering his chance of higher and higher promotion. Lance was at the top of the hit-list should there be any more complaints about police ruthlessness, and he already had enough problems to deal with at home.

After a moment of hesitation, Lance stalked out in Gilda's wake. The sunlight was hot, but felt almost cool after the heat inside the Nissen hut, and Gilda was about to comment on the welcome freshness, when all thought of empty chat vanished at the sight of Veronica Thornthwaite sitting by herself on the steps of Hut 34, eyes fixed on a book. Correct procedure could go walkabout. It was too good an opportunity to miss, simply because of the lack of a parent.

"Good rowing, Argonaut," called Gilda, startling Veronica out of the story that she had been reading, and for a split-second the child looked frightened, as well as wary. "Have you heard about David Yoxall?"

Veronica nodded her head, glancing back into the hut as if she wanted to retreat.

"But it's not always sad when someone dies, is it?" added Gilda, noting that Veronica immediately adopted her blank expression before twisting around to look inside the hut again. "What time did your Mum and Dad get up this morning?"

"Her Mum probably got up at approximately half-past six so that she could be at the factory by eight o'clock. Her Dad didn't have to get up at all this morning because he was on night-shift, and it's far too hot in the hut to start sleeping now." Jeff appeared at the door, looking amused to have thwarted the attempt to interrogate Veronica behind his back.

"You were at the ice-cream factory all night?" Lance made no effort to keep scepticism out of his voice, unable to accept any statement that contradicted the theory he now regarded as established.

"This time the Invisible Man's got more alibis than you could shake a stick at," Jeff said, cheerfully relaxed. "Why are you asking about us? Do you think that we helped Dave Yoxall shuffle off to Buffalo? Of course, I can't speak for Elaine as I wasn't here, but I don't picture her roaming the hostel with malice aforethought last night. And there's no point asking Vron, because she wouldn't hear her Mum either leave the hut or return. I think Vron could sleep through an earthquake."

"That's more or less what you said yesterday," commented Lance.

"It just goes to show how consistent my testimony is."

198

"How well did you know David Yoxall?" asked Gilda.

"Hardly at all," replied Jeff. "I was inclined to avoid the man."

"When was the last time you saw him?"

"That's difficult to say for sure." Jeff thought, furrowed brow, absent stare: the very picture of a man thinking. "Monday's usually the same as Tuesday on the hostel, and Tuesday's the same as Wednesday, which is the same as Thursday etc. It's only lately that we've gone in for sensationalism. I saw David Yoxall in the canteen a few days ago: saw and heard. He was complaining rather loudly because there were no chips on the menu."

"When was the last time that you spoke to him?" enquired Lance, with no expectation of being told the truth.

"A month or so back, when we first arrived here. One conversation with David Yoxall was more than enough. I steered well clear of him after that." Jeff was speaking with absolute self-assurance, making Gilda wonder if he might be daring them to prove that his words were a lie. Perhaps Lance had been right to think that overconfidence would be Jeffrey Thornthwaite's downfall.

"David Yoxall lived in the very next hut to you," Lance pointed out. "Are you saying that you never even said good day to him?"

"I'm saying exactly that," agreed Jeff. "Anyone can be the Invisible Man in a crowd. There's always a horde of people around wherever you go on the hostel, so it's easier to shun somebody than you'd imagine."

"You worked with David Yoxall as well. Did you never talk to him in the factory?"

199

"You're not allowing for the distances created by rank. I'm a highly-skilled technician who stencils addresses onto boxes, while Dave Yoxall merely stood looking clueless at a conveyor belt." Jeff studied his listeners, possibly checking to see how credible he had been, and it seemed odd to Gilda that such a glibly-resourceful man should apparently be content to spend his working-life as a factory hand.

"Do you have to stay inside throughout a shift, or can you go out during breaks?" asked Gilda.

"Did I leave the factory with the sole purpose of shoving a drunk down a path?" Jeff smiled at the absurdity of the idea, and Gilda admired the calmly convincing way he spoke, before she recalled that Jeffrey Thornthwaite might actually have played no part in Yoxall's death. "Why would I deliberately go AWOL from work in order to trip up someone who fell over on a daily basis?"

"You tell me," said Lance. "You didn't like the man."

"There are lots of men I don't like, but they don't all wind up dead at the end of a path outside a toilet block."

Jeff was quite right because one of the men he disliked had been shot, and Lance continued, "What singled David Yoxall out? What made him different?"

"He was the stupidest man I ever encountered," replied Jeff, complacently certain that nobody could criticize his own intelligence.

"Was David Yoxall stupid enough to be a blackmailer?" asked Lance, attempting to use his favourite shock tactics.

"Definitely," said Jeff, without the slightest hesitation. "Why? Was Yoxall blackmailing someone? Well, he certainly got his comeuppance in that case."

Nothing was going to shake Jeffrey Thornthwaite, especially with Veronica as audience at his feet. He stood on the top of the hut steps, looking down at Lance and Gilda, and an outright accusation of having killed two men would make Jeff laugh, because he knew that the police had no evidence against him. Veronica was the only potential weak link, assuming Lance's theory had any validity, and Jeff seemed determined that his daughter would never be alone.

"He isn't even going to sleep after a night-shift," Lance remarked, as he and Gilda crossed the road on their way back to the store-room.

"Perhaps he's an insomniac," said Gilda. "But he's right about it being far too hot inside a Nissen hut today for anyone to be able to sleep."

"He left the factory during one of his breaks, and met David Yoxall at a pre-arranged time under the pretence of handing over some money. Yoxall was too stupid to recognize what a mistake he'd made in taking on a clever man like Jeffrey Thornthwaite."

"I still don't have complete faith in your theory," confessed Gilda. "David Yoxall could easily have survived a fall. It seems more like chance that killed him, rather than a deliberate attempt to silence him."

"It wasn't deliberate. Jeffrey knew that Yoxall would never talk to us, and even if he did, we'd want to know why he hadn't said anything the first time we spoke to him. Jeffrey told Yoxall to go to hell, and punched him to make the message even clearer." Lance nodded approval of his revised scenario. Jeffrey Thornthwaite was restored as the passionate man of integrity, defending a daughter from further trauma.

"It could have happened that way," conceded Gilda. "But whatever's been going on around here, one thing's certain. Veronica looked frightened when she saw us."

"Of course, poor kid. After what she's been through, Veronica just wants to forget, and she'll probably realize the danger that Jeffrey's in. It'd be cruel to force any daughter to give evidence against her own father."

"Would a child think that far ahead? But something's frightened Veronica, and she's nervous that we'll find out. Have you noticed her sudden blank expression when we get a little too close to whatever it is?" Gilda felt uneasy at the idea of dragging any truth out of a young girl so desperate to pretend that nothing was wrong, and there should have been a gentler alternative because, according to Lance, two men had died who did not deserve to live, yet justice and kindness seemed incompatible in the case. "We'll have to question Veronica again sooner or later."

"Later," decreed Lance.

9

"Why didn't you tell me about this story?" demanded Millicent. "I could have had an exclusive."

"You don't let me know when you've got a lead," Bryce pointed out, but his wife was in no mood for reason.

"I could have had the story on air yesterday afternoon," lamented Millicent, distraught to think of the lost opportunity to broadcast her voice. "You should have told me, Bry. My job's the future. Newspapers will be extinct in a few years."

"Then I hope that you're preparing to keep an unemployed husband in idle luxury."

"Not while so many factories are short-handed," Millicent retorted.

They were standing outside Hubert Webb's office, and Bryce wondered what his wife would say if he told her the full story, including the bottle of whisky that might have contributed to a second death at Watson Valley Migrant Hostel. She forged ahead through life, never seeming to make mistakes or question herself, even though Millicent knew that she had only been given a job in radio because of the Hatton surname. Very aware that she was good-looking, slim and fair-haired, Millicent aimed at television as an eventual goal after she had become a name in radio news, and Bryce had no doubt that his wife would achieve everything she wanted.

"Just let me have a few details," pleaded Millicent.

"Not a chance," said Bryce, forcing a laugh. "You'd steal all my hard work."

"Mum warned me against marrying a newspaperman," sighed Millicent. "But I wouldn't listen."

"If you want full coverage of the story with every nuance explored, feel free to read my copy. You'll find it on today's front page under a byline."

"Divorce proceedings are started with less provocation," said Millicent. "At least give me a couple of hints, Bry. Are the deaths connected?"

"Ask the police."

"Lance Palmer? He wouldn't tell me what day of the week it was. He hates journalists, and so do more influential people it seems. Dad said that there's been pressure from on high not to give as much prominence to the Watson Valley story. Someone doesn't want the British papers to pick up on it. Not the most ideal of publicity for the Ten Pound Pom scheme: emigrate to sunny Australia and get shot."

"Is your father listening?" The story's demise could be Bryce's salvation, assuming that a certain bottle of whisky got buried along with it.

"You don't know Dad at all if you think some jumped-up bureaucrat can dictate what he puts in the paper. The interference is more likely to make Dad front-page the story for a week."

"Then I'll go and chase up my sources on his behalf," said Bryce, barely able to hide his disappointment. "I do hope that you're not going to follow me."

"Of course not," scoffed Millicent. "You'd deliberately take me on a wild goose chase. Anyhow, you might be tracking a false lead, and I've got to get my copy written by lunchtime, so I can't afford to amble about like you all morning."

"Then I'll amble away and leave the real work to others more dedicated than me," said Bryce. "You're late getting to the party though."

"Don't remind me," groaned Millicent. "How did you manage to be first reporter on the scene?"

"I never name my sources." Bryce walked off, heading in the direction of the railway station, and Millicent's competitive nature made her yearn to outdo him. Despite his years of journalistic experience, Bryce was usually no rival at all, but that time he had somehow stumbled on news almost certain to be reported internationally as well as across Australia, and Millicent wanted her name attached to it. When Gilda Garfield appeared in the doorway of the room next to the manager's office, Millicent rushed up to her.

"Don't even attempt your customary 'we're both women struggling in a man's world' approach," said Gilda. "I'm immune to it, and you know quite well that neither of us has had to do any struggling."

"I wasn't going to say something so clichéd," Millicent declared, abandoning the speech that she had been ready to launch into. "I missed the press briefing, and just need a few facts. Are the deaths connected?"

"No comment," replied Gilda. "And if Sergeant Palmer sees me talking to you, I might find myself a struggling woman after all: a struggling unemployed woman. Why don't you ask Bryce for the details? He was here most of yesterday."

"I can't get a word out of him. That front-page byline has gone to his head. Incidentally, while we're on the subject of husbands, congratulations."

"Thanks, but your source has got it all wrong. I'm not engaged to Jerome Henderson."

"Why not? He's rich. What more do you want? Grab him."

"You didn't follow your own advice and grab Jerome," remarked Gilda.

"No," conceded Millicent, "but I fully intended to, and then got sidetracked by a front-page story about wheat prices. There are times when I wonder why, but I thought that if a man could get that no-hoper copy into the headlines, he had to be worth marrying."

"The price of wheat isn't Jerome's strong point, so perhaps that's why there's no engagement story here."

"I'll settle for a few facts about the hostel one. Are you expecting to make an arrest soon?"

"No comment," said Gilda.

"Was the second victim shot as well?"

"No comment."

"I've got to have something by midday," said Millicent in frustration.

"And I've got to get back to work before Sergeant Palmer spots me wasting time."

"Tell him you turned the tables and pumped me for information, and I let slip that there's been an attempt to persuade my father to drop this particular story from the paper. Somebody high up doesn't want bad publicity for the Ten Pound Pom scheme."

"What somebody wants and what somebody gets are often two different things." It was not Gilda's problem, because any pressure descending from on high would land on the shoulders of

Inspector Fairfax, and Wilbur enjoyed dealing with people who were close to what he regarded as the centre of power.

"Well, don't say that you weren't warned." Millicent smiled, pleased to be more worldly-wise and better informed than Gilda. "They're not going to tolerate bad publicity for the Ten Pound Poms."

"Whoever *they* happen to be, their toleration will just have to put up with any inconvenient reason behind either of the deaths."

"I don't think that truth's a problem, as long as it can be kept quiet."

"This is Australia," declared Gilda. "We're not living in some Iron Curtain dictatorship."

"No, we're living in a country desperately short of workers, and relying on a steady stream of migrants to arrive over the next decade."

Millicent sounded as if she expected a Government-enforced conspiracy of silence to surround the hostel, and Gilda was amused at the wishful thinking of a journalist eager to uncover a political scandal. Whoever had killed Clive Leyton, the death was unlikely to end migration to Australia when murders were a daily feature in any European newspaper. Millicent was overreacting as usual, and Gilda had to get back to work.

****

Oskar recognized Bryce Chesney, but was too busy cutting slices of cheese for a customer to acknowledge anyone else when the shop door opened. Watson Valley's delicatessen was a bright and cheerful place to work in, and although the wages were not the highest that Oskar could have earned, he appreciated the quietness, and liked the opportunities of talking to people as it made time pass quickly. He also had the bonus of being valued by his employers because Helmut and Erika Schneider's limited grasp of English failed to include tax forms and any other officialdom, despite their twenty-four years in Australia. They spoke German to each other in a pretence of never having left Innsbruck, and as no children had been born to force them out into the new country, Victoria remained as foreign to them as on the morning they stepped off the boat in Port Melbourne. Driven out of their homeland by the *Anschluss*, the Schneiders must have realized that their Europe was long vanished, but still they talked about going back, while knowing that the journey would never happen. They were safe in Watson Valley, surrounded by people they trusted, and it was too late for the upheaval of yet another new life.

"Could I have a word?" asked Bryce. The shop door had closed behind the cheese-carrying customer, and there was no need for Bryce to make his sentence a question; the word would happen whatever Oskar Hauser answered.

"I have nothing to tell you. I found Mr Yoxall at the end of the path, went to the manager's house, and Mrs Webb phoned for a doctor. You will know more than I do by now."

"Did you realize that David Yoxall was dead when you found him?"

"It seemed likely, but I have no medical training." Oskar reached for a cloth, and began to polish an already pristine counter in a shop that was dazzlingly white, displays of food the only colour. A ceiling fan whirred monotonously but the cool air it distributed, whenever a refrigerated cabinet was opened, made what might otherwise have been an irritating noise into a reminder of luxury.

"Was David Yoxall shot?" asked Bryce. "Did you see a wound? Had he been bleeding?"

"I saw no blood." Oskar shook his head, as though trying to dislodge a picture in his mind, and he polished the counter more attentively.

"Were you bothered when Yoxall accused you of fathering the Leyton girl's baby?"

"As there was no baby, I gave the matter little thought, and certainly did not kill Mr Yoxall in revenge." Oskar looked amused, and Bryce had the uncomfortable feeling that he had made a fool of himself by asking a stupid question.

"Do you think it's odd that there should be a second death on the hostel the day after Clive Leyton was shot?"

"Most odd."

"What's your explanation?" enquired Bryce. "Coincidence?"

"Possibly, but I think — no, I speculate that Mr Leyton might have been killed in mistake for Mr Yoxall. Is that sensational enough for your newspaper?"

"Definitely, if it's what happened. But who'd want to kill David Yoxall?"

"Almost everybody who met him," replied Oskar. "However, to be more specific, perhaps the man who came to my room last week calling me David Yoxall and demanding the immediate repayment of a debt."

"Who was the man?"

"I would never ask such a person anything, merely tell him the correct hut number and hope that he goes away."

Oskar's wry smile made Bryce picture a gorilla-shaped gangster, and he demanded, "Do you know whether the man caught up with Yoxall?"

"I think not. A few moments later I heard Mrs Yoxall shouting, presumably at the man, and then all was quiet again. Had Mr Yoxall been inside the hut, she would have continued to shout."

"Did you tell all this to the police?"

"I remembered the incident only after I came to work. Then I thought that if one man had mistaken the huts, perhaps the same thing happened when Mr Leyton was killed."

Of course, Oskar might have invented the story of a thug's visit as cover for his own part in David Yoxall's death, but Irma was offered as corroborator, and Oskar did not know that Bryce would be very unwilling to go near the woman who might recognize him as her husband's whisky provider. A possibility existed that Oskar's theory about the Leyton killing could be right, and Bryce asked, "Is there a lot of gambling on the hostel?"

"Every migrant is a gambler, or we would still be in Europe," Oskar pointed out. "Gambling with the whole of life makes horses and cards dull, but Mr Yoxall would fail to comprehend that."

"This man looking for Yoxall, was he Australian?"

"I think so," said Oskar, but sounding far from certain. "There are so many English accents, and all are foreign to me. Mr Yoxall, I could barely understand."

"Oh, I don't reckon it matters who the visitor was or where he came from. There's no evidence that he had any connection with either of the deaths, and the police aren't interested in guesswork," said Bryce, hoping to keep the new information to himself for as long as he could. "Most probably Yoxall tripped over his own feet on a sloping path without any assistance from gamblers. This is Watson Valley, where nothing's happened since Watson named the place, whoever Watson might have been."

"I doubt that the police would listen to me telling them how they should do their job." Nevertheless, Oskar was pleased to be given permission to keep his idea to himself, because he disliked being centre stage and could imagine Sergeant Palmer's reaction to an amateur detective with a melodramatic scenario.

"Can you describe him: the man who called on you by mistake?" Bryce added casually, planning an article about evidence having emerged of a link between unlicensed gambling and both deaths, whether or not that link existed in reality, but with liberal use of *allegedly* and *possibly*, his copy might sneak past the newspaper's lawyer and onto another front page, whatever chanced to be the truth. It could also move the police investigation away from the reason for David Yoxall's drunkenness that night, with a bit of luck, and Bryce felt that he certainly needed that luck.

****

"Would you answer a few questions, Inspector?" asked Millicent, appearing in the store-room doorway. "The one o'clock news bulletin needs a few details clarified before we go on air."

"There isn't anything to add to my last press statement."

Taken aback, Millicent stared in bewilderment at Inspector Fairfax. Usually her problem was not getting Wilbur to speak, but trying to stop the rush of words that poured out of him at the mere sight of a microphone. "Then perhaps you could recap events for the radio audience, Inspector. After all, your expert opinion —"

211

"There's nothing for me to be expert about, and we should be finished here by the end of the day," said Wilbur, but Millicent noted the surprised expression on the faces of both Lance and Gilda. "The medical evidence clearly indicates that David Yoxall had a fall and hit his head: an accident that can happen anywhere at any time to anyone. And Clive Leyton's death was in all likelihood an accident as well."

"An accident?" queried Millicent. "The man was shot."

"He'd kept a Luger as a war souvenir, and must have been cleaning the pistol when it went off accidentally."

"If you say so, Inspector, but Leyton couldn't have thrown the gun away afterwards," Millicent pointed out.

"Strictly off the record, his wife got rid of it. She was worried about a suicide clause in her husband's life insurance policy, and feared that the company might attempt to use the gun as an excuse to avoid paying out," said Wilbur, sighing at the thought of Dulcie's plight. "An understandable reaction when the poor woman's left alone with three young daughters to support."

"But you can now confirm the Luger was the gun that killed Clive Leyton."

"Of course it's the same gun," declared Wilbur. "How many guns do you think would be hanging around here? This is a completely safe environment for families, not some Wild West shanty town. There are no murders or suicides on any Australian migrant hostel, and no connection between the two accidents either. Nothing more than coincidence is involved here: tragic, yes, but still mere coincidence."

"My father told me that pressure was being applied to try and make him drop the story," said Millicent.

"What on earth are you implying?" demanded Wilbur. "We live in a free country, not a corrupt totalitarian régime somewhere in Eastern Europe."

"So you'll be happy to go on air and squash all sensational reports about the violence of life on these migrant hostels." Millicent knew that Detective Inspector Fairfax was a man who could never be bribed with money, but ambition meant that his principles had a tendency to bend in the direction of a prevailing wind when he realized the full truth might be a little inconvenient, as well as stand between him and promotion. However, Wilbur also liked to think of himself as dashingly proactive. "You really ought to say something publicly, Inspector, and end the rumours. It's a situation crying out for the authoritative voice of reason."

"Yes, I reckon it might help damp things down more quickly if I did an interview," conceded Wilbur, giving way to temptation. Lance looked scornful and Gilda battled to hide her amusement at the rapid about-turn, but Wilbur was too preoccupied to notice them. "Yes, it's the right time for me to make the press understand that there's no lurid copy to be had here, and that the migrants must be left to enjoy their new lives in privacy and peace."

"That's exactly what you ought to say on air to stop any more guesswork," urged Millicent, wide-eyed and ingenuous as she gazed at her prey. "It's just what's needed to bring all the wild speculation to a halt."

"Yes, a few firm words should do it," agreed Wilbur, the seductive enticement of a microphone luring him from the store-room. "I'll state precisely what happened here in Watson Valley, and leave it at that."

Millicent smiled, confident of her ability to demolish Wilbur's rhetoric and leave him faltering among the ruins of his reputation, but as interviewer and interviewee went outside, Gilda was less certain who would be the victor and who the vanquished. "Surely he can't talk his way around this one, even with an amateur like Millicent asking the questions. Nobody's going to believe a word that he says."

"Wilbur Fairfax can slither like a snake," declared Lance, "and he'll creep out of this swamp."

"Millicent's got behind-the-scenes gossip from her father though. That's what she meant about pressure being applied to ditch the story."

"She was the one applying the pressure: the pressure to make you talk," said Lance, contemptuous of reporters and their deceitful methods. "Why would anybody care what goes in Desmond Hatton's scandal-sheet? The days of newsprint are numbered and, let's face it, neither Leyton nor Yoxall could be described as a loss to Australia. Even their families are glad to be rid of them."

"But, according to Millicent, somebody's worrying about bad publicity for the Ten Pound Pom scheme, especially if the British newspapers pick up the story."

"They've got enough murders of their own to occupy them," said Lance. "Anyhow, Wilbur's probably right about David Yoxall. A drunk had a fall. End of story."

"And Clive Leyton was cleaning his Luger while reading the Bible," said Gilda. "But of course, I'm forgetting that Dulcie must have deliberately planted the book when she spirited the gun away because of that non-existent insurance policy."

"We've only got Dulcie's word that there isn't one, but she didn't kill her husband whether a policy exists or not, and the Government will just have to put up with the reason why Leyton was shot."

Lance spoke as though Jeffrey Thornthwaite had already confessed, and Gilda shrugged. "Perhaps they only check that migrants are healthy whites, but if the immigration department's letting child-molesters and gambling drunkards into the country, then I reckon the Government deserves some bad publicity, whatever the politicians want."

"Politicians!" Lance muttered derisively.

****

"But, Inspector, is there any evidence that Clive Leyton actually owned the Luger?" asked Millicent.

"Our investigations continue," Wilbur said, irritatingly unruffled. "And it's now clear that Mr Yoxall's death was an accident too."

"Has that been established beyond doubt?"

"The facts speak for themselves," declared Wilbur, but quite willing to help them become even more vocal. "You can't quarrel with facts."

"The fact is that Clive Leyton was shot, and the gun removed from the hut."

"All the evidence indicates a tragic accident," maintained Wilbur, "and the Leyton family has been co-operating fully, despite so catastrophic a loss."

"And then there was a second tragic accident only hours later?" Millicent added a distinct touch of scepticism to her voice, hoping to disconcert Inspector Fairfax, unaware that she was dealing with an expert manipulator.

"Yes, too right, too right," sighed Wilbur. "A terrible coincidence, and my compassion goes out to the families of both men: two hard-working families, filled with hope, eager to seize the opportunities of a new life in a new homeland. Indeed, I'm sure I can speak for the whole country in offering condolences."

Wilbur Fairfax, spokesman for Australia, lowered his voice as a sign that the interview had come to an end, but Millicent disagreed. "What's the evidence that Clive Leyton owned the Luger or any other gun?"

"A full statement will be made shortly," said Wilbur. "Exaggerated reports help nobody, and add to the family's distress. Our migrants need encouragement and friendship in the early days of their new lives. They need the generosity that all Australians are famous for, because we invited them here and they deserve much better from us than intrusive and inaccurate press reporting."

Millicent had thought that it would be easy. She planned to disarm Wilbur with a couple of insipid queries, before annihilating his ridiculous claims with one barbed comment, but she had a tendency to underestimate people, and Wilbur Fairfax was the veteran of many interviews. He had developed a bland technique of referring to undisclosed evidence while ignoring any inconvenient questions that he had no intention of discussing, and Millicent knew that she would sound hectoringly shrill if she kept interrupting him to demand straight answers, making the listeners' sympathy instinctively centre on the bullied Wilbur, no matter how ludicrous his assertions. It was one of the rare occasions when Millicent had no idea how to get her own way. "Who got rid of the gun?" she asked, trying to regain lost ground.

"There'll be a statement soon about the final few details, and we expect to close the investigation today: tomorrow at the latest. No arrests or charges are anticipated, and the migrants will be able to get on with their new lives in this great country of ours: the country that welcomes migrants with true Australian open-hearted warmth."

"If you've got evidence that Clive Leyton owned a gun, how can you rule out the possibility of suicide?"

"He had everything to live for," replied Wilbur with another sigh. "Clive Leyton was a devoted father, a family man who had a good job and a wonderful new life in our wonderful country. It's a tragedy that he should meet with an accident. Yes, nothing less than a tragedy."

"But how can you be so sure that Clive Leyton's death was an accident? What's the evidence of it? Is there a witness who saw the shooting?"

"Full details of the police investigation are going to be available very soon, and they'll show the folly of listening to wild rumour," said Wilbur, confident that before too long another drama would distract journalists, and then the Leyton case could safely be put to one side without awkward questions. He relaxed, and smiled benevolently at the microphone, knowing that a good day's work had been done.

"But who removed the gun?" Millicent demanded in frustration. "It couldn't walk off by itself."

"No, of course not, and the full details will be in my next press statement. Excuse me, but duty calls."

Wilbur ended the interview by smiling again and walking away, leaving Millicent bewildered at the unaccustomed defeat and baffled by the ease with which things had gone so wrong for her. If Bryce managed to get another front-page byline, Millicent hoped that she would be able to resist the impulse to make him the third victim of tragic coincidence because, with a little shrewd editing and juxtaposition of police fudging and the facts, he could make Wilbur Fairfax look the charlatan he was, but Millicent had neither the skill nor the time available to compete with Bryce when the lunchtime news bulletin was fast approaching. She would do her best, but Millicent knew that she had failed, and the thought rankled.

Millicent Hatton liked the feeling of superiority, of having deigned to marry a man without influence or money, and she had assumed that Bryce would always be in her shadow, but he was the journalist rejoicing in a front-page byline and she had been trounced by smooth-talking drivel. Millicent would have laughed at Bryce's humiliation if their situations were reversed, and she found herself imagining him gloating in victory.

The honeymoon was over.

10

It was steamily hot inside the canteen, but migrants, each carrying a tin tray and cutlery, queued patiently while Irma ladled out pasta and cheese sauce from a giant-sized container onto plates. Everybody had admired her bravery when she insisted on returning to work, and Irma felt like a wounded war hero, although a Christmas turkey escaped from its cage would have been a more accurate description. Suddenly she was popular, sympathetic smiles were aimed in her direction with people acting as if Irma Yoxall had become a close friend.

The canteen was managed by Domenico and Quinta Pancaldi who had never liked Irma's piercing voice or abrupt manners, but even they now appeared to regard her as a delicate porcelain figure liable to shatter at a hasty word, and because the Pancaldi family held the record for the longest stay at Watson Valley Hostel, they set the tone for the other migrants. Seven of the ten Pancaldi children had ventured out into Melbourne, but three were still in school and until they had been established in secure jobs, Domenico and Quinta would not think about spending money on themselves and moving from a hut to a house.

The Pancaldi couple shared the cooking, and stolid British palates, reared on watery vegetables and soggy chips, were forced to adapt to Italian food that was as alien to new arrivals as the country they had just landed in, adding greatly to the sense of reckless adventure. But the migrants had coped during a month at sea and followed up that experience with life in a Nissen hut, and so they could certainly tackle pasta.

Despite all menial tasks being part of an underling's job, Domenico did the washing-up that day, while Quinta insisted on wiping down the canteen's many plastic-topped tables as they became vacant, making it the first time in decades that Irma had encountered kindness, and she revelled in the attention. There seemed to be collective amnesia about David Yoxall's aggressive nature, but his widow would never forget or sentimentalize the departed drunk, and marvelled that she had not rid her life of him years before. He was no loss in any way, especially not financially, and returning to a quiet hut would become one of the day's pleasures. Irma knew that she was now able to save enough money to keep Alan in education until he got a few qualifications, and then she might even have her own house one day without Dave dragging his family down. Irma had never been encouraged to develop ambition, parents and teachers writing her off as factory fodder who would marry young, but now she felt re-born as a new Irma, an independent Irma, a powerful Irma who could have friends visiting the hut without Dave's stupid behaviour driving them away.

"If there's anything I can do to help, just ask," said Elaine Thornthwaite.

"Tell me how to get slim and beautiful like you," laughed Irma. "Not that I want another man. I've learnt my lesson."

Elaine had disliked Irma, linking the loud-mouthed stridency to Dave's drunken insolence, but even she was forced to admire the straightforwardness. Thornthwaite life had no honesty about it at all, and Elaine felt ashamed of her pose as the contented wife and mother, but she was prepared to pay a fine for deceit. "Are you OK for money, Irma?"

"I'll be rolling in it now that Dave isn't here to leech off me. It's wonderful to be free of him, and I only wish I'd known enough never ever to get married."

"We all marry too young," said Elaine, a generalization safer than a specific opinion. "It was the way we were brought up. Grab the first man who proposes in case there isn't a second following on behind."

"I wouldn't be without Alan for anything though," declared Irma. "He's nothing like Dave, and nothing like me either. He's — well, he's just Alan."

"Vron takes after Jeff." Elaine could not bring herself to go into motherly raptures, and the thought of Veronica barging in on her romantic new life with Rodney Fryer spoilt the dream, but Elaine was miserable with guilt to have so little maternal instinct that she wanted to leave her daughter as well as her husband. Such callousness went against everything she had been taught, yet Rodney appeared to love the flawed woman she was, not the paragon that Elaine felt she ought to be, and if Veronica had ever shown any sign of admiring her mother, things might have been different. It did not occur to Elaine that Veronica was merely the product of an upbringing by parents who never praised their child or each other.

"Why didn't I walk out?" asked Irma, bewildered that she had allowed herself to get trapped for no better reason than habit. "I was the one who earned money and put food on the table. Why did I waste all that time, when I could have simply dumped him?"

"It'd be such a huge step," said Elaine.

"Not really: not when it's so wonderful to be rid of the old git. I ought to have realized how easy it was, realized years ago. I should have rented my own place and moved there with Alan. Why didn't I just walk out?"

Presumably because of the same hesitation that stopped Elaine packing her clothes, leaving a note and departing from Watson Valley with Rodney. She needed courage, not self-analysis, but said, "There are some men who make you feel stupid, and you lose your confidence until you haven't got the nerve to do anything at all. You start thinking that you're such a fool, you must be headed for disaster, no matter what you decide, so you daren't make the decision."

"I still should have done more because of Alan," declared Irma, but she was astonished at her lack of enterprise, rather than conscious of not protecting a child, and she smiled in satisfaction. "Oh well, it's over and done with now."

"What are you going to do?"

"What I'm already doing: work in the canteen. The difference is that I'll be happy." Irma laughed raucously, delighting in the newfound freedom, and Elaine did her best to look sympathetic, but she was envious of such self-assured independence.

"It's so different for Australian women."

"What is?" asked Irma.

"Everything," said Elaine. "In England you're supposed to accept second-best as normal and be grateful for it, but out here women get divorced if they're not happy. They won't allow themselves to be trapped."

"And that's exactly what will never happen to me again. It's going to be *my* life from now on."

Elaine had done what her mother ordered, what teachers and employers told her to do, and what Jeff wanted. Even in Acton, when visions of a glorious Australian future haunted her imagination, the final decision to emigrate had been Jeff's. She was an also-ran in her own life, apologizing for being alive. "Have you noticed the way Australians don't say 'sorry' all the time like us? When one of the machines broke down at work, I apologized to the supervisor for holding up production, even though it wasn't my fault. Rod — the foreman laughed, and asked me if I was apologizing for a spot of sabotage."

"I'm never going to say sorry to anyone again," announced Irma, who had no history whatsoever of having apologized for anything. "I'll do exactly what I want from now on."

"Good on you," said Elaine, mimicking an Australian accent, and they both smiled.

"Let's have a drink to celebrate. Domenico Pancaldi gave me a bottle of wine. He said there was courage in it."

"If that's true, then I definitely could do with a drink," Elaine declared.

****

Bryce Chesney stood in the shade of the canteen building and re-read his notes in the hope that something would leap off the page, forcing him to spot what had previously been overlooked. Oskar Hauser talked of a mysterious visitor and gambling, but perhaps Oskar Hauser himself was the link between the two deaths. He had been in his room when both Clive Leyton and David Yoxall died, or so Oskar claimed, but no proof was on offer. Hauser's motive? Leyton might have believed Yoxall's allegations and been infuriated at the seduction of his thirteen-year-old daughter. He confronted Hauser who retaliated by pursuing Leyton with a gun: a German pistol that had found its way to the Hauser family during the Second World War. David Yoxall might have seen or suspected something, perhaps he even attempted blackmail, and of course would then have to be silenced: an easy enough task with a drunk and a faked accident on a sloping path at night.

Oskar suddenly appeared too good to be true: a young man, evidently well-educated, yet working as a shop assistant and seemingly content to live alone in one room of a Nissen hut with nothing to do in his spare time but listen to music. Although Bryce could easily understand anyone deliberately choosing a quiet existence, he decided that Oskar must have a nefarious reason for trying to pose as an anonymous migrant in a hostel, and if any files existed locally containing details of Oskar Hauser's former life, they were likely to be stored in the manager's office. Bryce left the shade of the canteen, and crossed the red clay that stretched between him and the information he sought.

The office door was wide open but, unfortunately, Hubert Webb sat at his desk, and the filing cabinets were behind him. However, the manager would undoubtedly be called away sooner or later, and Bryce was prepared to wait. "Do you mind if I stay in here for a while to cool off a bit? It's so hot today."

The temperature inside the office was only marginally lower than outside, but Hubert never suspected devious intentions, and he smiled a welcome. "I've lived in Australia for more than a decade, but I don't think I'll ever get used to the heat."

"Even Australians can't take it on days like this, but it must be worse for newly-arrived Europeans, particularly those from places where it gets really cold like Germany and Austria. I said that to someone from Vienna, an Oskar Hauser, and he agreed with me. He seems an unusual young man."

"Oskar? Unusual?" queried Hubert, looking surprised. "Why unusual?"

"Well, travelling alone to the other side of the world at his age."

"Lots of young men do the same thing, especially Italians for some reason. Perhaps there isn't much work in Italy."

"Is that why Oskar Hauser left Vienna? Unemployment?"

"Possibly, or he might simply have wanted a new start. I had a job in England, but just couldn't settle after the war, and hated the feeling of being trapped in an office for the rest of my days." Then Hubert laughed as he glanced around the room. "Yes, I'm still in an office, but this is no nine-to-five lock-in. It's a different job every day, and I'm forever dashing around the hostel sorting things out."

"Sounds like my line of work," claimed Bryce, trusting that Hubert would soon recommence his dashing. "Each day I meet new people, learn about their problems, and then try to help."

"Yes, that's it exactly," said Hubert, struck by the coincidence.

"You must hear so many reasons why migrants come to Australia. My father's story was almost the same as yours," revealed Bryce, keen to secure some fellow-feeling. "He caught the end of the First World War, and then found that he couldn't cope with the pettiness of being a London clerk after the nightmare of life and death in the trenches, He tried, he tried for years, until eventually he and my mother decided to give Australia a go."

"I know precisely how your father felt," declared Hubert. "You can't go back to routine or a pettifogging supervisor after the experience of war."

"And Australia's far enough away to change everything, apart from the language. That's what surprises me about migrants like Oskar Hauser: not only coping with a completely new life, but a foreign language as well."

"It isn't all that foreign a language for Oskar. His English is excellent: much better than mine," said Hubert. "I feel quite reproved for my sloppy manner of speaking whenever I talk to him. He sounds like a schoolmaster."

"He must be highly educated," Bryce remarked. "How come he works as a shop assistant?"

"I imagine it's a temporary thing to get some money together while he applies for other jobs. Most of the migrants take any work they can get, just to give themselves time to find their feet in a country where they don't usually have any family connections to ease the way."

For a resentful second, Bryce assumed that he was being mocked because of his advantageous marriage into the Hatton family, but Hubert was thinking of his own arrival in Australia, and he sighed nostalgically.

"My first job over here was in Brockoff's factory. We were allowed to eat as many biscuits as we liked off the conveyor belts, so I sampled the lot on a daily basis, and now I can't bear even the thought of any biscuit."

"If Oskar Hauser needs money, I'm surprised that he didn't go and work in the ice-cream factory. The wages must be better there than in a shop."

"I can't somehow picture Oskar inside a factory," said Hubert. "I think the noise would get to him, and he's not a mixer. He never goes to any of the dances in the Rec, but that might be because rock 'n' roll isn't his sort of music."

"Yes, I noticed the classical concert he was giving the area."

"A treat to hear, although Mr Leyton used to complain about it. I did suggest to Oskar that perhaps he might consider turning down the volume a little now and then, but he just smiled and said that he would when Mr Leyton turned his own volume down."

"Did Clive Leyton play loud music as well?"

"Oh no, Mr Leyton would never have done that," said Hubert, emphatically shaking his head. "I think Oskar simply meant that the family could get a bit noisy at times with three children."

"But Oskar got on OK with the Leyton daughters, didn't he?" Bryce remarked, rather overdoing the casualness. "I've heard that he was very friendly with the eldest girl."

"Oskar's friendly with everybody, and the Thornthwaites have certainly never objected to the music."

"But Clive Leyton did."

"He even asked me to move Oskar to another hut," Hubert recalled, and the memory of Clive Leyton made his tone automatically sombre, despite Hubert's regained freedom from a plethora of niggling complaints. "I don't think that Oskar would have minded, but there wasn't a free room available at the time, and I wouldn't permit a direct swap with another singleton because I like to get any place thoroughly cleaned, and repainted if necessary, before someone moves into it. This hostel might only have Nissen huts, but I'm determined that they'll be huts of the highest standard."

When he agitated to get Oskar Hauser moved, had Clive Leyton been trying to silence Beethoven or shift a young man away from the vicinity of a daughter? The latter reason offered Bryce a chance of better copy, and he asked hopefully, "When was all this trouble?"

"Oh, it wasn't trouble," declared Hubert, surprised at such a dramatic interpretation of his words. "We never have trouble here. It was merely that Mr Leyton preferred silence to music. Not that there's ever silence on the hostel. Nearly everybody's got a wireless, and a couple of the families even have a television. You can tell which ones they are by the crowd of children gathered in a semi-circle around the door as they stare inside the hut."

"Oskar Hauser seems to be quite a loner," said Bryce, ignoring the digression. "Doesn't he even have a girlfriend?"

"I've no idea, but he appears happy enough with his own company. It's good to be like that, especially when your homeland's in another hemisphere, and Oskar will make a success of his new life."

"How do you know?"

"I can always spot the people who won't be able to settle out here, always, every single time," said Hubert, proud of his mystical insight. "Some migrants begin saving for the fare back home the minute they see the hostel, but the majority have more determination, and Oskar strikes me as the type who'll put up with a lot before he admits defeat. Of course, there's a possibility that he might not have anything to go back to. Oskar never gets letters from Europe, and so perhaps he hasn't any family members left. That could be the reason why he decided to make a completely new start in life."

"Yes, perhaps." Or perhaps Oskar Hauser had departed from Vienna without leaving a forwarding address. The more Bryce heard, the more instinct told him that there was copy heading in his direction. "You'd think Oskar would cling to his own country in the absence of family."

"It probably hits each person in a different way," said Hubert. "Some cling, I imagine, but others can't bear to be reminded of their past. A few migrants even invent a story, so that they don't have to talk about what really happened to them."

"How can you tell?"

"One might say that he's a Londoner, a Londoner with a distinct Liverpool accent, or someone mentions eating lunchtime sandwiches by the sea when supposedly working in the Midlands: little discrepancies like that. It's usually because the person doesn't want to talk about something unpleasant, rather than a deliberate attempt at fraud, but most people have bits of the past that they'd like to ignore. I expect it applies to you as well."

"No, there's nothing hidden in my life. I'm far too boring to be a man of mystery." Bryce gave a resigned shrug of his shoulders, but there was one fact about him that he preferred not to reveal. Bryce had gone to school in Australia, knew the country's history and geography, planned his whole future in Melbourne and yet loved the solitude of the outback along with its Dreamtime stories, although Bryce had never actually seen an Aborigine in real life. His thinking was Australian, his hopes were Australian, everything about him said white Australia, but Bryce Chesney had been born an Englishman, not leaving his native land until the age of five. It was a mere fact, nothing to be ashamed of, and he readily acknowledged English parents, but still he never corrected the assumption that he was Australian-born. "What discrepancies have you noticed about Oskar Hauser?"

"I was never in Vienna so I wouldn't spot anything." Hubert shuffled some forms to make a tidier pile, put the paperwork into a desk drawer and then stood up. "I'm sorry, but I've got to ask you to leave now. The office has to be locked whenever I go out. I'm sure that you'll understand."

"Yes, of course," said Bryce, dismayed at such unexpected efficiency. "Anybody could get in here otherwise, and read your files."

"Exactly," agreed Hubert.

****

"Hello!" Bryce sounded astonished to see Oskar Hauser sitting on the steps outside his own room while he listened to Beethoven's Fourth Piano Concerto.

"I wondered how long it would be before I saw you again," remarked Oskar.

"I have to annoy people. It's how I earn a living." Bryce tried to appear nonchalant but the young man's self-assurance was unnerving, especially as Oskar seemed amused at Bryce's attempt to be casual, and directness was the only possible retaliation. "Why did you emigrate to Australia?"

"Why did you, or your parents or grandparents?" enquired Oskar. "The reason is probably the same."

"You were fleeing from the police, just like my father?" Bryce hoped that flippancy would hit the target and disconcert a guilty conscience, but Oskar merely smiled.

"This is known as the country for convicts, so your father must have felt very much at home."

"It's also the country where families sent disgraced sons, and where people come to hide from their past."

"So I hear." Oskar looked even more amused, not prepared to help Bryce out.

"Can I ask —?"

"You can most certainly ask anything, but I might choose not to answer."

"People often refuse to talk to me, but I usually get my story in the end." Yet Bryce had to aim at a semblance of professional confidence, aware that things were topsy-turvy. The person questioned should be either hostile or nervous, but Oskar was as relaxed as an experienced politician ready to bluff his way through an interview, something that Bryce found suspicious in a young shop assistant. "How come you decided to leave Vienna?"

"For a change. For a better life. For a chance to see the world. Choose whichever you prefer. Why should my reason for travelling to Watson Valley Migrant Hostel be of any interest to you?"

"Background material," claimed Bryce. "I want my readers to feel that they know you."

"Why?"

"Most of them won't have the least idea what hostel life is like, and I need the details to help them understand."

"What is there for them to misunderstand?" said Oskar. "Migrants live in temporary accommodation while they work and save: an excellent system, straightforward and full of hope. You may quote me."

"It can't be that good a life, stuck in an oven."

"An oven only in summer. During winter, I live inside a refrigerator. When it rains heavily, I inhabit a drum."

"I stand corrected," said Bryce, noting that Oskar had managed to move the questions away from his reason for deserting Vienna. "Did your parents support your decision to emigrate?"

"No parents, and no secret for you to uncover."

"How come you work as a shop assistant when you're so obviously well-educated?"

"Is such a thing obvious?"

"You speak fluent English and listen to classical music." Bryce realized that his answer was ridiculous even as the words were spoken, and he laughed. "OK, for all I know, you had an English mother and worked in a music shop after leaving school without any qualifications."

"Possibly, but I think it will be more intriguing if I remain an enigma to your inquisitive readers."

The final movement of the Piano Concerto thudded to its end, and once again children's voices could be heard, but even they were lethargic in the intensity of that day's heat. The hostel had returned to normal, and neither Clive Leyton nor David Yoxall might ever have lived in Watson Valley at all. It was a fleeting community, accustomed to departures, and no one became irreplaceable. Lives crossed for a short time, and then separated, never to meet again, a metaphor for life itself, but even as Bryce wrote down the thought, he knew that Desmond Hatton would refuse to permit so pretentious a piece of high-flown prose to sully his down-to-earth newspaper. Facts and more facts were mandatory, with adjectives, adverbs, similes, and flowery metaphors surplus to requirement.

"They say that this part of the world will be the last place on earth affected after a nuclear war," Oskar remarked, leaning against the doorframe and looking at Bryce almost patronizingly. "We might be the last human beings ever to live, the very last generation, but if we manage to survive, the future will be ours to create."

"Is that why you chose to come to Victoria?"

"Gaining even a few extra months of life would be a better reason to emigrate than most."

"It didn't work out like that for Clive Leyton or David Yoxall," said Bryce.

"They might have saved their families, if not themselves."

"Do you work in a shop because you think there isn't enough time left to make ambition worthwhile?"

"I have the greatest of ambitions: to live contentedly for as long as possible. What more could anybody want?"

Success, thought Bryce. He wanted to be the famous reporter Bryce Chesney, rather than the nonentity who had married Millicent Hatton. The world might be doomed, but Bryce still hoped for an opportunity to astound Melbourne with a talent yet to reveal itself. If there had been no Millicent and no Hatton father-in-law, perhaps he would be able to sit back like Oskar and await destruction, but Bryce had too much to prove, and a suspicion that he might not have the skills to turn his daydream into reality. Before he met Millicent, Bryce had been happy to meander through life, but she changed everything simply because of her surname.

"It's an odd coincidence that you should be around at the time of both deaths," said Bryce, trying to give the impression that he knew more than he was prepared to disclose.

"Any suspicions you might harbour are groundless. I had the misfortune to find Mr Yoxall, but he was already dead," said Oskar, placidly and aggravatingly unflustered. "Why would I risk being separated from Beethoven and spending what time I have left in prison under a possibly more immediate death sentence? I fear losing even a minute of life."

Bryce's fear was that Oskar Hauser had just told him the truth. "Give me a few further details about the man who was looking for David Yoxall."

"You know all that I know."

"A large man, late twenties, fair hair in a crew cut, jeans, dark shirt," said Bryce, pretending to consult his notebook. "That could be half the men in Melbourne. Was there nothing distinctive about him?"

"Not that I recall, but Mrs Yoxall might have noticed something. She seems a very alert person, and the man was certainly not a match for her."

Bryce had no intention of going anywhere near Irma, but he nodded as though a visit to Mrs Yoxall were imminent. "Would you recognize the man if you saw him again?"

"I am unlikely to get a second chance of seeing him."

"Why do you say that?" asked Bryce, suspecting Oskar of enjoying a private joke.

"The man will know that Mr Yoxall is dead," Oskar pointed out. "The debt is cancelled."

11

It was another dusty, dry, hot morning: a day identical to the previous Watson Valley day and to the one that would follow in a scorching Australian December, but something was due to change. "Start packing up," ordered Inspector Fairfax. "You've finished here."

"We haven't talked to everybody yet," objected Lance, in spite of knowing that any attempted argument against the decision would achieve nothing. "Bryce Chesney's on the front page again this morning with a story linking David Yoxall's death to unlicensed gambling. Chesney's almost certain to have invented the whole thing, especially those thugs who are supposed to roam around the hostel demanding money, but there's a chance that one of the migrants could have spotted something Chesney's deliberately exaggerated."

"Nothing for anybody to spot," declared Wilbur. "And Chesney's got no evidence to back any gossip he might have picked up. We know exactly what happened. Clive Leyton accidentally shot himself, his wife disposed of the gun, and David Yoxall had a fall. Why waste more time here?"

"There's no evidence that Clive Leyton had a gun," said Gilda. "And no evidence against his wife either."

"Oh, we'll probably never prove any of it," agreed Wilbur, untroubled. "But we know what happened."

"I don't. There are other possibilities." But Lance was still not prepared to reveal the Thornthwaite connection, and he merely spoke to contradict Fairfax.

"There are always possibilities," said Wilbur. "I prefer to deal in facts."

"I thought that truth was supposed to be the important thing," remarked Gilda.

"Facts are truth," declared Wilbur, even though the few established facts failed to solve the Leyton case or add up to the whole story, and the Inspector knew it. "Medical evidence indicates that a drunk had a fall. You agree that we can write off Yoxall's death as an accident?"

"It seems a likely explanation," Lance conceded, "but Irma Yoxall did say that her husband was a gambler."

"She also said that he was a drunk. So the Yoxall case is closed. As for Leyton, he had no link to crime, no history of convictions —"

"That only means he never got caught," muttered Lance.

"Clive Leyton didn't make friends on the hostel," said Gilda. "Nobody seems to have liked him."

"If being disliked was a crime, we'd have to arrest a lot more people than we do." Wilbur laughed, conscious that any decision he made outranked whatever opinion Lance and Gilda might have. The scent of promotion was in the air, and should Wilbur Fairfax please those who hoped to smother newspaper interest in Watson Valley Migrant Hostel, he might find himself rewarded for loyal service, and Wilbur was very loyal to those with the power to pull strings. "I'm not saying that the Leyton case is closed, just that there's no need for us to be based here any longer."

"But Watson Valley is where Clive Leyton was shot, and it's where we'll find whoever squeezed that trigger," Lance maintained.

"If Clive Leyton didn't kill himself, then his wife did the job for him and she isn't living in Watson Valley now. I'm not telling either of you to give up, but it's impossible to work at the hostel while we're tripping over journalists all the time. If we leave, they'll leave as well, and we can come back whenever we choose without the press on our heels. The investigation will benefit. I'm sure you agree with that."

"I don't," said Lance. "The hostel's where the deaths occurred, and it's where we'll learn the most."

"There's nothing to stop you going on learning, but without the bother of reporters breathing down your neck, demanding statements and interrogating migrants. It makes sense to give the impression that the work's finished here."

If the police did leave the hostel, press interest was likelier to wane, but the idea that Wilbur could be right annoyed Lance. He wanted the freedom to do his job without being pestered by journalists, but hated having to comply with a strategy that had as its aim the greater glory of Detective Inspector Fairfax. "We'd be letting the press manipulate an inquiry."

"No, it's outwitting the press. If I go and tell those reporters that we're leaving the hostel this afternoon, they should be gone by tomorrow, and we'll be free to work without their constant interference." Wilbur smiled, a public benefactor liberating his downtrodden workforce, and he waved a hand to silence any applause. "Yes, the sooner I tell those hacks, the sooner we won't be hampered in our work. In fact, I'll do it right now."

Wilbur hurried out, eager to seek his audience, and Gilda looked doubtfully at Lance. "A retreat might simplify things, I suppose. It shouldn't make much difference anyway."

"It shouldn't, but it will. If you ask me, the investigation's being shut down."

"I can't believe that. Nobody would dare."

"Oh, wouldn't they?" Lance was always suspicious of Wilbur as well as the Fairfax cronies, and he guessed that further obstacles would be placed in the path of a rapid conclusion to the Leyton case. Millicent Hatton had been right. Somebody in the upper echelons was thinking more about bad publicity for their Ten Pound Pom scheme than either justice or truth, and that Somebody had far-reaching influence.

"I wonder where Bryce picked up his weird tale of gambling gangsters pursuing David Yoxall," said Gilda. "Irma's never mentioned anything along those lines, but I'll go and check with her."

"Better make it soon before we're swamped by work on other cases," Lance commented.

****

"You can't be shutting up shop yet," declared Bryce Chesney. "You're nowhere near finding out who killed Clive Leyton or David Yoxall."

"If you say so." Gilda had been on her way to talk to Irma, but decided to postpone the visit. Life would definitely improve without reporters materializing from behind every hut, and Wilbur Fairfax had not got it wrong when he said that the police would be able to work more effectively after newspapers lost interest in the story.

"Are you leaving the hostel because someone's about to be arrested?" Bryce knew that Gilda was unlikely to tell him, but he could still hope to startle information out of her. "It'll be that gambler who shot Clive Leyton by mistake, obviously."

"What gambler?" queried Gilda, placidly refusing to walk into one of the older journalistic traps. "You're the only person claiming that migrant hostels are gangster-run gambling dens of iniquity."

"I'll trade," offered Bryce.

"But I won't."

"I know that you're being closed down because there's pressure from above."

"Then shouldn't you be working on a story about corruption in high places? Don't waste your time talking to me. I'm but a minion obeying orders." Gilda turned back towards the store-room, realizing that Bryce was determined to follow wherever she went: follow and trade information, but not information that Gilda expected to hear.

"Millicent went out to a restaurant with Jerome Henderson last night."

"Did she? What am I meant to do about it?" asked Gilda. "I cancelled a date with Jerome at short notice, so he might have already booked a table somewhere and wanted a companion. Anyway, I'm not going to investigate or cross-examine either of them. It's your problem, not mine."

"*My* problem? What do you mean by that? Why is it my problem?" Bryce looked taken aback at Gilda's reaction to what he had imagined would be news disconcerting enough to throw her off-balance, and he demanded, "What are you implying? Why should Millicent having a meal with Jerome Henderson be a problem for me?"

239

"I didn't mean problem; I meant that the matter's of more interest to you. I'm not married to Jerome, but you and Millicent — No, I'm making it all sound worse. Take no notice of me. I'm waffling on about nothing." Gilda laughed, but Bryce had difficulty forcing a smile.

"She only met him because Henderson wanted her advice about what sort of engagement ring to buy you."

"As there's no engagement, there's no ring. Millicent must be chasing a story that she doesn't want you to know about. I hope Jerome isn't going to hear a secret recording of himself broadcast on the very next wireless news bulletin. Perhaps you should apply your investigative skills to finding whatever scandal Millicent's uncovered."

"Ask Henderson what it's all about," said Bryce, an order rather than a request.

"None of my business who Jerome dines with," Gilda pointed out, surprised that Bryce should imagine she regarded Jerome Henderson as her own private property. "Interrogate Millicent if you want to know the actual details."

"I did, and she talked about you and engagement rings."

"That's typical press exaggeration. Only one ring would be necessary, but I won't be wearing it. I told Jerome yesterday that we were through."

"Why did you finish with him?" demanded Bryce. "Is it because he's involved with someone else?"

"No, that wasn't the reason."

"Then why would you ditch him?" Bryce appeared to be convinced that Gilda would cling stubbornly to Jerome or to any man unless displaced by a rival, and he probably suspected that

Jerome had actually dumped her in favour of Millicent. The belief came from paranoia, and Gilda knew that there was nothing she could say to persuade him otherwise. Bryce would have to be left to deal with his own delusions.

"I've no intention whatsoever of discussing my private life with a reporter," said Gilda, "especially the reporter who's got a history of doing his best to get Jerome prosecuted."

They had reached the store-room, but Bryce continued walking, so lost in thought that he seemed unaware Gilda was no longer with him, and he vanished around the back of the canteen. There was probably no reason for him to suspect Millicent of betrayal with another man, even if she had lied, but Bryce clearly did not trust her, while Jeffrey Thornthwaite apparently remained oblivious of his wife's extramarital activities.

"Crazy," remarked Gilda.

"Yes, if you mean Bryce Chesney. You were very deep in conversation with him. How come?" asked Lance, disapproving of the answer before he heard it.

"Bryce wanted to trade information, and hinted at a gambler shooting Clive Leyton by mistake: presumably the same gambler who's supposed to have shoved David Yoxall to his doom. At least, that's what I'm assuming after all the sensational garbage Bryce managed to get into the newspaper this morning," replied Gilda, unwilling to speculate about the Chesney marriage with someone whose own marriage was problematic. "I reckon Bryce has developed a convoluted theory about Leyton being shot in error for Yoxall because of a gambling debt. That would mean the bungling assassin made a return visit to the hostel to get the right man, and if Bryce is the next victim, it'll prove he was right and I'll have to resign from the police for not being detective enough to take him and his lopsided ideas seriously."

"If David Yoxall was the original target, he'd probably have been shot as well, not tripped up, and an incompetent hired gun who kills the wrong man ought to refund his paymaster."

"Apart from Irma Yoxall mentioning it, I haven't heard any tales of gambling around here," said Gilda, "possibly indicating that it doesn't happen often."

"What did Irma have to say on the subject?"

"I didn't get as far as her hut to ask because Bryce insisted on tagging along, so I turned back."

"Watson Valley Mafia-type killings exist only in the vivid imagination of a reporter desperate for copy," scoffed Lance. "David Yoxall was a fool who drank, and he didn't have the money for anything but small-time bets. I don't want to admit it, but Wilbur Fairfax was right, and Yoxall's death can be written off as an accident. No one would have given it a second thought if Clive Leyton hadn't been shot the day before."

"I keep thinking that I've missed something obvious about Leyton's death: not asked the right person the right question." Gilda frowned, trying to find words to describe the feeling of blundering around a dark room unable to locate the light switch that had to be there, but Lance merely shrugged.

"You can expect to think that on almost every case at one point or another, unless you're God or Wilbur Fairfax. But none of it matters now because somebody's frightened that all future migrants will be put off Australia by wild newspaper reports of gambling dens and revenge killings on hostels. We'll be given so much extra work that the investigation here will be slowed down to a halt until the newspapers forget anything ever happened in Watson Valley."

"For all we know, there might be a mass-murderer who ought to be stopped before he gets more ambitious," said Gilda. "Isn't anybody worried about that possibility?"

"Not when it interferes with Government policy. But justice has been done in Clive Leyton's case without any need for the law to interfere."

Lance would have denied it indignantly, but he could be very like Wilbur Fairfax at times. Once both men had made up their minds about the solution to an inquiry, supporting evidence became unnecessary. Clive Leyton had deserved summary execution courtesy of Jeffrey Thornthwaite, in Lance's opinion, and nothing would shake that belief.

"So you're saying that we're expected to write off David Yoxall as an accident, and leave Clive Leyton pending until he's stale news?" Gilda asked, unable to credit any of it.

"That's how jobs are kept," said Lance.

****

Gilda's next attempt to visit Irma Yoxall was also hindered by a reporter. "I need a moment of your time," said Millicent, appearing from behind the canteen.

"Inspector Fairfax deals with the press." Gilda had no idea of the blow that she delivered, but Millicent felt as if Victoria's entire police force jeered at her.

"Fairfax is nothing more than a joke," declared Millicent, trying to smile. "I wouldn't waste my breath talking to him. He's just a stooge, a Government puppet."

"Then you ought to be tracking him down, not me. According to you, he's the one with powerful friends, and should you want even more lurid details, talk to Bryce. He's certainly giving the newspaper value for his wages this week, as well as a lot of sensational headlines. Your father must be ecstatic." Gilda had imagined that Bryce Chesney's wife would be pleased at the reminder of her husband's success, but Millicent scowled.

"Bryce must have written his copy after one drink too many during the six o'clock swill. The whole thing's ridiculous, isn't it?"

"No comment," said Gilda.

"I couldn't get away with all that mad speculation. In a radio news bulletin, you have to be concise and accurate, but Bryce fudges everything until the point of whatever he's trying to say gets tangled up in a word jungle."

Breakfast must have been an indigestible meal in the Chesney household that morning, with Millicent brooding on her husband's front-page bylines, and Bryce wondering about his wife's rendezvous with Jerome. "Well, all those Watson Valley headlines are probably at an end," said Gilda, tactfully pretending not to have noticed Millicent's brusqueness. "We're packing up today. End of story."

"End of story!" snapped Millicent. "What do you mean, end of story? And why did you tell Bryce that I went out with Jerome last night? Even though you got dumped, it was still a lousy thing to do."

"Bryce already knew about the restaurant meal when I saw him earlier. He gave me the particulars." Gilda was amused at the face-saving twist in Jerome Henderson's account of their break-up, but nobody would believe that a plain woman in her thirties had thrown away the chance of acquiring a wealthy husband. Even Gilda found it hard to believe, and she had done the throwing away.

"Then who told Bryce about me and Jerome?" Millicent demanded.

"I've no idea. I didn't stake out the restaurant to see who Jerome turned up with."

"Then how did Bryce know I was there?"

"I guess he knew because you and Jerome were together in public, and Desmond Hatton's daughter isn't invisible." A factory worker named Elaine could have given lessons in discretion, but Millicent was a spoilt rich girl under the impression that she was entitled to do whatever she wished, and Gilda felt sorry for Bryce. "If you didn't want to be spotted with Jerome, you should have gone somewhere more private."

"We did, after the meal," snarled Millicent. She was convinced that a jealous Gilda had informed Bryce of his wife's activities, and Millicent clearly thought that snaffling Jerome was an appropriate revenge. Once again, Gilda felt sorry for Bryce.

Millicent stalked away, imagining herself triumphant, and Gilda was glad to see her go. Straightforward Irma Yoxall would be more agreeable company after Millicent's petty world of deceit, and Gilda climbed the steps of Hut 33 knowing that she would be greeted with uncomplicated honesty, apparently one of the rarer human qualities to judge by the past few days.

****

Irma had not long finished a tiring shift in the canteen, but she welcomed Gilda like an old friend, and Gilda was an old friend

245

by Irma's standards as all her friendships dated back to the hours after Dave's death.

"Have you seen any newspapers this morning?" asked Gilda.

"I never bother with them," replied Irma, ready for a chat. "I've got a wireless, although Alan listens to it more than I do. He's over at the Rec helping with a Christmas tree, and then they're going to put up decorations in the canteen as well."

"That sounds nice. About the papers —"

"Do you want to hear the news? I'll switch the wireless on." Irma was keen to be a perfect hostess, happy in the new world that had suddenly opened up for her. Having gone straight from parents to husband, it was the fist time in Irma's life that she had felt in charge of her own destiny, and she rejoiced in the freedom.

"No, I don't want to hear the news," said Gilda, giving up all attempts to lead gently into the subject. "I'd like to ask you about a story in one of the papers this morning. It seems that there might have been an unidentified man hanging around the hostel a few days ago, looking for your husband. Something to do with a gambling debt."

"Yes, a man did come to the hut wanting money, but that was nothing new." The memory appeared to amuse Irma, but she smiled because another part of the past could be exorcised.

"Was this before or after Clive Leyton was shot?"

"Days before: last weekend, I think. I'd almost forgotten about it. I've had years of men hammering at the door and saying that Dave owed them money. It was usually to do with gambling, but not always. If anyone left money unguarded, even for a few seconds, Dave would grab it."

"What happened when the latest man called?"

246

"Nothing much. I told him to get lost, and that he'd have more idea where Dave was than I would."

"Did the man make any threats?"

"No, but I did," admitted Irma, laughing. "I said that he could do what he liked to Dave, but I'd kill him with my bare hands if he went anywhere near Alan, and it was the last I saw of that particular man."

Gilda felt like applauding, but merely asked, "Was he a young man?"

"In his twenties I'd say. He had fair hair in a crew cut. Quite hefty, but the ones sent to collect money always are."

"Would you feel safer on another hostel?"

"When that lot want to find you, they can find you anywhere, but they won't bother as you police are all over Dave's death. In fact, I feel safer now than I have done for years, and nobody's ever going to push me around again. People like that can only get power over you if you give in or let them see you're afraid." It was a good lesson for Irma to have learnt: a lesson that she sounded grimly determined never to forget.

"Do you think your husband's death might be linked to his gambling?"

"More likely something to do with his drinking, if you ask me, but I don't know." Irma shrugged, without apparent interest in either question or answer.

"Have you seen that Bruce again: the man your husband was drinking whisky with?"

"I thought I saw him outside the canteen earlier on this morning after I finished my shift, but I hadn't paid that much attention to him when I found Dave at the whisky, so I might have been wrong. Although, whoever it was by the canteen, he disappeared around the corner pretty sharpish when he noticed me looking at him."

There seemed to be nothing that Irma could add to the investigation, and Gilda closed her notebook. "Will you be staying in Australia?"

"Oh, yes," replied Irma, an enthusiastic Ten Pound Pom advertisement. "Alan will have a better future over here. I don't think that there's any unemployment at all, and he'll be able to choose whatever he wants to do. This country will change his life completely."

Without being aware of it, Irma might have helped change a policewoman's life as much as Australia would alter her son's prospects. Jerome Henderson had been a sidetrack, and from that time onwards, only somebody exceptional could have persuaded Gilda into marriage. Freedom ought never to be lightly thrown away, despite a fear of loneliness, because getting trapped was a far worse fate than being single. No doubt happy marriages existed but not among Gilda's acquaintanceship it seemed, and as she walked back to the store-room, Gilda saw Elaine Thornthwaite hanging clothes on a line to dry in the sun: a totally false picture of domestic tranquillity. Then there was Lance Palmer, who under no circumstances would bother to put on a show of contentment.

"Well? Did a careless gambler shoot Clive in mistake for Dave?" However, even if Gilda had found evidence of Bryce Chesney's creative speculation, Lance would refuse to believe it but, luckily for a harmonious workplace, Gilda had nothing of interest to report.

"A man did call at the hut, asking for both Dave and money, but Irma doesn't know who he was and she sent him packing, presumably with a few well-chosen words, so he couldn't have been much of a desperado. It happened at the end of last week, and as he knew the right hut, he wouldn't have blundered into the Leyton one by mistake on any return visit."

"The whole idea's typical journalist trash," declared Lance. "A drunk tripped over his own feet. No story, so Bryce Chesney had to invent one. Anything to sell a few newspapers and curry favour with his father-in-law. The only mystery here is how David Yoxall managed to convince anyone that he'd be an asset to Australia. Between him and the Leyton pervert, it makes you wonder who's weeding out the migrant applicants in Britain."

"I think Irma and Alan will fit in well, so whoever selected the Yoxall family was only a third wrong."

"Give him a bonus," muttered Lance.

12

"Is Alan here?" Elaine hesitated on the top step outside Hut 33, uncertain of a welcome. Irma had stretched out on the sofa to rest her feet while listening to Norman Swain talk and play records on the wireless, but she sat up at once, happy in the novelty of having a friend drop by for a chat.

"Alan's with the other kids over at the Rec," replied Irma. "No, on second thoughts, they'll be in the canteen by now, putting the Christmas decorations up in there. Why?"

"I want to tell you something, Irma. I have to tell you, and it's going to sound really odd, but listen a minute. Please, listen. I know that it's none of my business —"

"Everything *is* everyone's business on the hostel." laughed Irma, thrilled to be admitted into gossiping circles. "What's going to sound odd?" she added, reaching out to switch off the radio.

"No, leave the wireless on." Elaine pointed to the partition wall to remind Irma that there might be a hidden Kendrick audience listening to the conversation.

"This feels like being in a spy film. Are you going to tell me a secret?"

"Nothing so interesting. It's a bit of advice, that's all, and I did try to warn you about it last night, but I couldn't get you to pay attention." Elaine paused, worried that an irate Irma would start swearing and shouting at her for having the gall to interfere, but someone had to make Irma see sense, and fate had decided that Elaine Thornthwaite was to be the someone. "I noticed that policewoman leaving here just now."

"Yes. She's been really nice, more like a friend than anything," said Irma, marvelling at the sociable world she now inhabited. "I kept forgetting that she was police."

"She didn't say anything then?"

"Anything about what?"

Elaine shrugged, ill-equipped to deal with so delicate a situation. "Did she ask you any questions?"

"Yes, about Dave's drunken mates, but I couldn't tell her much. I always made sure that I never knew any of those good-for-nothing layabouts."

"I'd have done the same." Elaine dithered for a moment, despite having rehearsed the words that she was going to say, and then added in a rush, "Don't ever drink booze again, Irma. Stop completely."

"Why?"

"Because you mustn't taste even a drop of alcohol from now on. It'd be the worst mistake of your life: the worst thing you could possibly do."

"Why?" repeated Irma, intrigued. "I didn't wake up with a hangover this morning, so I couldn't have been smashed out of my head last night."

"You weren't, and I'm not talking about hangovers. You've heard that old saying about there being truth in wine? Well, in your case, it's a fact, and you started to tell me something that I don't need to know. It'd end up hurting Alan the most if you went on drinking and talking the way you did last night. Do you understand what I'm telling you?"

Irma frowned as she attempted to solve the puzzle, and then said, "You're a good friend, Elaine."

"I'm only giving you a piece of advice, health advice, nothing more. Everyone knows that alcohol's bad for you, but feel free to tell an interfering busybody to get lost." Now that Irma had understood, Elaine tried to turn the conversation into a joke. It was what Jeff would have done, and usually she recoiled from being like him in any way, but there seemed no better alternative. "I'm just a nagging big-mouth whose favourite hobby is ordering other people around, and it's a wonder you haven't thrown me down the hut steps by now. Oh, sorry, Irma, sorry. I didn't mean to say that. I always come out with the wrong thing at the wrong time. Jeff says I'm as dense as a London fog."

"He's wrong; he's very wrong," declared Irma. "What did I say last night?"

"Nothing, nothing at all. I don't remember a word, not a single word. But never drink again, Irma, not even a sip at Christmas. Stay in control of everything you say."

"That's good advice, Elaine, and I'll follow it to the letter. No sacrifice, because I don't actually like the taste of drink all that much. I thought alcohol helped when Dave was there, but the booze probably kept me trapped. If I hadn't got drunk, perhaps I wouldn't have put up with him for so long."

"Alcohol's the only enemy you've got now. Nothing else can hurt you or Alan. I hate being a nag, Irma, but booze is risky in your case: risky for your health," Elaine added, her mind picturing Kendrick family members assembled on the other side of the partition wall, listening despite the wireless music. "You're not mad at me, are you?"

"I think you're the best friend I ever had," replied Irma. "I'm glad that you've never needed booze."

"Yes, I'm lucky." Elaine smiled awkwardly at the uncomplicated picture of happy Thornthwaite family life, but she was luckier than Irma. Elaine had the glorious Rodney Fryer as her back-up, not the futility of alcohol, and Rodney believed that she was perfect in every way. He might not go on thinking it as the affair's novelty wore off, but no man ever stayed infatuated for long, although worrying about the future was wasted time when Jeff said that tomorrow could bring a gigantic nuclear blast and the end of the world. So why was she hesitating? Every day that Elaine lingered on the hostel was a day lost from her wonderful new life, but still she dithered.

"I didn't plan to do it," said Irma.

"Of course you didn't."

"It just happened: an accident."

"Of course it was."

"A complete accident." Head thumping in the midst of a hangover, Irma had woken later than usual on her morning of liberation, but a drunken Dave must have thought that she had already left for work because he lumbered his way up the hut steps, and when he saw Irma, he started to swear. He had been swearing at Irma for years, but that time the sight of his bloated red face was suddenly more than she could bear. As Dave swayed unsteadily in the doorway, Irma snatched up the empty whisky bottle that stood on the chest-of-drawers, and hit him over the head with all the hatred of fourteen years behind the blow. Silent for once, Dave toppled backwards down the path, while Irma picked up her handbag and went to work, depositing the whisky bottle in one of the waste bins outside the canteen. "Yes, it was a complete accident."

"Forget the whole thing." Elaine put a finger to her lips in another attempted warning as she turned up the wireless volume even louder.

"I don't want you to think badly of me," said Irma.

"No need to worry about that. I'd have walloped him years ago, if he'd been my husband. I've no idea how you managed to cope for so long, but let's not talk about it." Elaine pointed at the partition wall again, yet she was unable to resist adding, "Everybody's on your side, whatever happens, so don't feel alone."

"Alone? I've never felt more surrounded by friends in my entire life," Irma declared, but she was aware that no friend would ever help her more or give better advice than Elaine had that day. "Will you do something else for me?"

"Anything. Just ask."

"Will you show me how you stop make-up from sliding down your face in this heat? I look like a streaky beetroot before an hour's gone by."

"If there's one thing I know about, it's make-up: make-up in any climate or any temperature," boasted Elaine, glad to feel on secure ground at last. She had been very uncertain how Irma would react to words of warning, and it was a great relief not to be shouted at. It failed to occur to Elaine that the law would disapprove of her having aided a wife avoid responsibility for a husband's death: a wife who had started to brag about her resourcefulness when a few beakers of wine loosened a tongue already far too candid. Dave Yoxall had been a violent drunk who made life insufferable for his family, and the whisky bottle, wielded as a weapon, that sent him crashing down the path might have been used on impulse, as Irma now claimed, or with the deliberate intention of trying to kill him. Yet no philosophical dilemma bothered Elaine's conscience, because she came from a mother who always found fault, whether her daughter had been innocent or guilty, and it meant that getting away with something was the only morality Elaine ever learnt, and Irma would get away with either manslaughter or murder as long as she remained on her guard. As the whisky bottle was unbroken, no fragments of glass would be found embedded in Dave's skin and the fall down a stony slope should disguise the origin of his head wound. Irma was almost certainly safe, as long as she kept quiet, and Elaine merely felt that she had done a second charitable act in assisting a woman protect herself from the danger of getting caught. Elaine's first charitable act had been to remove the whisky bottle from the canteen waste, when on her way to rendezvous with Rodney the previous night, wipe the evidence clean of fingerprints and then transfer it to the pathway behind the station, where Rodney had once said that the local drunks gathered after the bars closed at six in the evening. If Irma kept her mouth firmly shut, all would be well. Elaine had done her good deed for the day, and she relaxed, happy to share her extensive knowledge of make-up and grooming with a pupil grateful for the tuition.

"You should grow your hair long enough to tie back," Elaine advised, head slightly to one side, an artist studying a blank canvas. "A pale foundation, and then a thick dusting of talcum powder to keep it firmly in place. Brush off any loose talc, and add a touch of mascara, not too much though, and lipstick of course. Hold on, I'll get my make-up bag and show you exactly what I mean."

A new face to go with her new life. Irma sighed with contentment.

****

There was nothing to pack up. Gilda put her notebook into a pocket, and she was ready to leave the room that could go back to its original function of storing unwanted hostel files.

"Perhaps I should ask Hubert Webb if he'd keep the table and chairs here in case we need to use the room again to interview someone," suggested Gilda.

"Hope springs eternal," said Lance.

"The Leyton case can't just be shelved."

"But it can be held up until it goes cold. This is a migrant population, and most of them will have scattered across Victoria, across Australia, before it's deemed safe to let us loose again. Some of the migrants might even have gone back home to Europe."

"There's still forensic evidence to come in, and no one can stop that. Reporters like Bryce Chesney would start asking inconvenient questions, and it'd look far too much like a cover-up. In fact, it would be a cover-up."

"The test results will eventually arrive on desks, but after being slowed down because thorough double-checking is utterly essential in this case and so on and so on. Wilbur Fairfax can be very reliable when he wants to please, but for once I don't have a problem with it, as justice has already been done. Thornthwaite's not guilty of murder, not guilty of anything, and he shouldn't be hounded or put on trial."

"Assuming he did shoot Clive Leyton."

"He shot that pervert," declared Lance. "You know it as well as I do."

Did she? Gilda tried to access some sort of detective instinct, but it was mere guesswork, like trying to imagine the end of a film that had broken down half-way through the show, and she envied Lance's absolute certainty. In his scenario, Clive Leyton's death had been good news all round, thanks to Jeffrey Thornthwaite, with only one victim left permanently scarred. "I wonder what will happen to her: to the daughter."

"Which one?" asked Lance, immediately defensive, thinking of his own family.

"I meant Veronica Thornthwaite."

"Well, after what she's been through and with that mother, she doesn't seem to have much going for her, poor kid," said Lance.

13

What happened to Veronica Thornthwaite? It was full circle for Veronica Thornthwaite, but only after an interval of more than twenty-five years.

Veronica's first radio work had been broadcast under a pseudonym, Herodotus 19, and over two decades later, her next radio work was also accompanied by an alias: Olivia Thwaite. As soon as she left school, the hated Vron had been dropped in favour of her second name, and she then trimmed the tediously-long Thornthwaite for playwright purposes to gain what Veronica hoped might be a liberating new identity that would help change a nobody into a somebody.

Australia was in the past, but the country would always remain a part of her, leaving Veronica in a nationality limbo of not being Australian, yet unable to feel English. However, rootlessness brought the superb advantage of freedom from pressure to conform, and any person who had lived contentedly in a Nissen hut could never fall into the trap of believing that an expensive house and fashionable possessions should be the goal of human existence. Back in England, with undemanding part-time jobs to keep her head just above the financial waterline, Veronica got to clean a great many offices and sit behind a variety of superstore checkouts, but she stuck to her Blue Door Theatre dream with an obstinate determination that only dithered each time a script was returned accompanied by yet another rejection slip. There were no substitute ambitions, and no one to tell Veronica that she was frittering life away, so Olivia Thwaite would force herself to recuperate and doggedly send out the next script on its rounds.

Eventually, very eventually, on a glorious November morning when the rest of London saw only dark clouds and murky drizzle, the breakthrough arrived in a plain white envelope that should by rights have been preceded by an orchestral fanfare, because the director of a repertory company wished to arrange a meeting to discuss Olivia Thwaite's script. It was the first step into her future world, a step that led to a stage production of the play, and one performance was seen by a BBC producer who then contacted Veronica about a commission to adapt and record the script for radio, which could mean that more people might hear her play in one hour than during a whole week in Rep. Her dreams were actually coming true, and it proved that miracles did happen.

Brown-haired and tall Olivia Thwaite, playwright, was finally living the life that she had long hoped would be hers. Olivia Thwaite, playwright, was being escorted by a production assistant from the empty church-like foyer of the BBC's Broadcasting House, past two bored-looking security guards, and into a lift that rose to the building's mediocre interior of narrow corridors and small rooms, where the read-through of playwright Olivia Thwaite's script would take place before the team moved into a recording studio.

"Piers was awfully sorry not to be able to direct your play himself." Chatty and cheerful Natalie Prendergast was a young and pretty blonde insider with a debutante's accent, proud of her status as production assistant but quite happy to gossip with a lowly outsider. "He tried ever so hard to fit your script into his schedule, tried for absolute ages, but it simply became impossible

259

after he was asked to take over the Ibsen season, as Piers will have explained to you."

"No, he hasn't written to me for ten months," said Veronica, surprised by such unexpected news. "I'd begun to think that the BBC had forgotten all about my play. The only letter I've had lately was the one from you about the recording dates, and I assumed Piers Cavendish would be the director."

"And I assumed that Piers had let you know what happened, but it was rather an emergency because Giles Mortmorency was suddenly taken ill. Well, not all that sudden as he's been drinking non-stop for absolute years, but anyway Piers ended up with the Ibsen and a chance to nab one of the awards that Giles used to collect on a regular basis. In fact, we strongly suspect Piers of doctoring Giles's brandy at the staff Christmas party. Well, seems a bit iffy that an ambulance had to be called right after he drank it. You wouldn't believe the jealousy and back-stabbing around here. Hamlet and the Scottish play don't even come close."

"I freely admit that my play can't compete with Ibsen," Veronica conceded, hoping to camouflage the sense of having been rejected by Piers Cavendish, so complimentary about her work, and yet so ready to abandon a first-time professional playwright for more distinguished opportunities. "Who's the fall-guy lumbered with my also-ran offering?"

Natalie laughed, but then imitated a vinegary expression as she replied with lips pressed primly together. "Belinda Greville. Grovel to Greville is the motto to keep in mind when dealing with her majesty."

"Then I don't think that I'm going to consider Belinda Greville a close friend."

"You won't be the only one," said Natalie. "Belinda wanted the Ibsen season, and can't figure out why it wasn't given to her. She claims that only a woman can understand Ibsen, which does slightly make you wonder how Henrik managed to write his scripts in the first place."

Veronica tried to smile, but alarm bells were ringing louder and louder at the prospect of facing a director who yearned for the celebrated works of the renowned Henrik Ibsen rather than the mediocre output of the unknown Olivia Thwaite. Getting her play performed was an astounding achievement for Veronica, but she feared that Belinda Greville would fail to appreciate a miracle had taken place, and the sight of a woman in her mid-forties with stiffly-sculptured dark hair and wearing a perfectly-fitting business suit, accessorized by a distinctly sour face, was no comfort whatsoever. Veronica had laboured over her appearance that morning, but such expensive neatness made her feel scruffy as well as an inadequate dramatist.

Turning the pages of a script and looking as though every single word offended her, a frowning Belinda Greville stood bolt upright in an office, but when she glanced up and saw Natalie approach with Veronica, Belinda made a half-hearted attempt to smile. "Our playwright I presume. Welcome. I wish I'd had a chance to develop the script with you, but too late now."

"It's adapted from a stage play," said Veronica, taken aback.

"A little ambitious, aiming at a stage production."

"But my play *has* been staged. Piers Cavendish saw it last year, and that's why I'm here today."

Belinda made no effort to hide her surprise, and Veronica had to fight back panicky laughter at being so firmly put in her place. It seemed that glowering at Greville might come more easily than grovelling to the woman.

"And I've finished a second script for the same rep company," Veronica added, but Belinda's expression implied that she suspected a playwright of lying. "It'll be performed next autumn."

"Your main character's very inconsistent," declared Belinda, dismissing Veronica's fraudulent claim and holding the script aloft as proof. "He says one thing, and then does another."

"Yes, I know," agreed Veronica, bewildered. "That's exactly what he does throughout the play."

Belinda refused to admit that she had failed to understand the character, and she continued in a pretence of not having heard Veronica speak. "The woman's meant to be from Melbourne, but her lines don't read like Australian dialogue in the least."

"Well, I suppose I could throw in a few 'fair dinkums' or 'cobbers' if you like," offered Veronica, now seriously alarmed for the fate of her broadcast play, "although when I was a kid in Victoria, I never once heard those expressions used."

Natalie coughed, either to hide her own amusement or to remind Veronica about the vital importance of grovelling to Greville, but Natalie had never written a play and so could not understand. "I wouldn't have guessed in a million years that you were Australian, Olivia. You sound completely English."

"I am English. My parents emigrated when I was a child."

"Well, the script will have to stay as it is," said Belinda, sighing at the thought of such sub-standard work being transmitted. "Too late now for the alterations I'd have preferred to make, but when I do the editing, I can cut some of the worst defects, and then add music to try and give it a bit of atmosphere at any rate."

However, Belinda's tone inferred that the play was beyond rescue, and Veronica attempted to laugh, a more dignified reaction than bursting into tears. "As long as it isn't *Waltzing Matilda* each time the Australian speaks, in the hope that it'll make her sound more antipodean."

That, presumably, had been the plan forming in Belinda's mind, to judge by her frozen expression as she marched to a desk, and Natalie was unable to stop giggling even as she hauled Veronica out to the corridor in order to deliver a warning. "She'll get you blacklisted if you don't start grovelling. The directors here hate writers and actors with opinions, so it's absolutely essential to kowtow to her, or Belinda will tell everybody you're too difficult to work with, and that'll be the end of your radio career."

"I think it's already ended," said Veronica. "Has Belinda Greville actually read my play all the way through?"

"Oh, she doesn't have to read a play to direct it. Belinda gets me to count the number of characters and summon a few reliable actors, and then she just coasts along on auto-pilot. I'm not joking about the blacklist though, and anybody who doesn't grovel to her gets put on it with a lurid description to scare off other directors. That woman's mean enough to prevent you getting any more work out of BBC radio."

"I'll retaliate by starting my own blacklist with the name Belinda Greville right at the top of it." Veronica aimed at sounding carefree, but the whole experience was spoilt, and three days that she had expected to class among the happiest of her life were reduced to misery. After Veronica's months of work on the stage play and then its adaptation for radio, she had been lumbered with a director who scorned her script, failed to understand the characters and was likely to sabotage the broadcast production by turning it into a Banjo Patterson concert, and there seemed to be nothing a distraught playwright could do to alter the situation. Destiny might harbour worse fates but, at that moment, Veronica was unable to imagine any.

Four actors had arrived, and they gathered around Belinda in her office, chatting, smiling and doubtless grovelling with expertise as well, while Olivia Thwaite, playwright, who had written the script that was the reason for everybody's presence there, felt even more of an outsider as she stood close to the door and watched Natalie arrange chairs in a semi-circle by Belinda's desk. It was then that Veronica realized the seven rôles in her script were to be divided amongst four people.

"The read-through's the actual performance of the play. The recording's all bits and pieces," said Natalie. "Look out, Olivia. You're being summoned by her highness, and for goodness sake, start to grovel."

"This is our playwright, Olivia Thwaite." Belinda was beckoning with imperious authority, and Veronica resisted a childish impulse to stay exactly where she was and ignore the command. "Olivia, our actors, Lynette, Harlan, Terence and Gervase. I'm sure that I don't need to add surnames, as they're all on television so often."

"Not as often as my bank balance would like," said Lynette, but after Belinda's patronizing use of 'playwright,' Veronica was too conscious of being a temp, blundering around in a world of slick professionalism, to do more than force a smile, not daring to look directly at the intimidating group. She was beginning to see the script through Belinda's eyes, and suddenly her ambitions appeared hopelessly futile, her abilities negligible.

"Olivia tells me that there's been an amateur production of her play somewhere in the provinces," remarked Belinda, "and I'm sure that it got a good review in the local paper there. Those provincial am dram societies often have a very loyal following."

"The play was done by a professional rep company," mumbled Veronica, wondering how accidental Belinda's slip of memory had been.

"I saw it," claimed Lynette, "and loved every minute of the production. When the radio script was sent to me, I couldn't believe my luck at getting offered such a fascinating rôle."

Even though fairly certain that Lynette had invented the theatre visit, Veronica was grateful for some moral support and thanked the actress with that in mind, rather than the gushing compliment. Despite being in her mid-thirties at the most, Lynette Adair's television work must have been as extensive as Belinda had said, because there was something familiar about brown-haired Lynette's features, but she was fortunate not to be immediately linked to a specific series or character, so often the end of an actor's career. A little overweight and with a slightly sharp-featured yet blandly attractive face, Lynette would look natural playing a secretary, housewife or shop assistant, the minor rôles that usually brought more work in the long run than the brief few years at the top of many television stars.

"You'll have to be very careful with the accent, Lyn," said Belinda. "It turns out that Olivia's an Australian from Wagga Wagga, and she's ready to criticize every syllable you utter."

"Oh dear, and I've never even left England," said Lynette, smiling ruefully. "In fact, I've hardly ever left London, but I once worked with a girl from Adelaide, and I'm basing my Aussie accent totally on hers so I'll have to rely on you to correct all my mistakes, Olivia."

Belinda frowned, and for a few seconds it seemed likely that the name Lynette Adair might join Olivia Thwaite on the blacklist. There could be no assistant director in a Greville production.

"But even if I'm hopeless, Belinda's brilliant editing will pull me through," declared Lynette, grovelling with effortless grace. "I was dreadful in the last play I did with Belinda, and I owe the good reviews entirely to her skill. She's the supreme wizard. Or should I say wizardess?"

That day's blacklist reverted to a single name, and Belinda condescended to smile again on Lynette. "Then I'll have to work my usual magic during this production."

It would indeed take some powerful magic to rescue the play from Belinda Greville, and Veronica felt close to despair, wishing that she could tear up her contract, return the money, grab all copies of the script and run out of Broadcasting House.

"Don't worry," Natalie whispered. "I chose some really super actors. I've worked with them all before, and they're absolutely reliable." But then Natalie giggled as she added, "And *they'll* have read the script."

"Are you quite sure of that?" asked Veronica, and Natalie laughed again.

"It'll be great fun; you'll see. Sit down and enjoy the read-through. These actors are going to be utterly brilliant, in spite of Belinda."

Veronica moved a chair nearer to the office door, hoping that nobody would spot how nervous she was. All other performances of her play were forgotten, and Veronica felt sick enough to be hearing the words read aloud for the first time. The actors sat down, picked up their scripts and Scene One started, but Veronica was convinced that everybody in the room scorned the dialogue as much as Belinda did. Instead of lines springing into life, they were killed stone dead for Veronica by the sight of the director's rigid face, and it was no good trying to look at the floor because Belinda's expression hypnotized Veronica, and she could not imagine why the mediocre dialogue had seemed worth writing.

Hours passed, days passed, and Veronica could feel herself ageing, but eventually the cast managed to reach the end of the script, and they looked up as though expecting praise for their tenacity in ploughing through so dreary a play, but Belinda merely sighed and then addressed the actors.

"Oh well, we'll just have to go ahead regardless. However, I've got some notes for you that should make a difference." And any difference would be an improvement to judge by the tone of Belinda's voice because the fool who commissioned such a second-rate script had either been drunk or mad, and Veronica thought that she would never again feel so miserable. She was wrong.

Calamity after calamity, closely followed by disaster. Belinda instructed Lynette to overdo an Australian accent as compensation for the weakness of the dialogue. Harlan, a burly and villainous-looking man who had been arrested or shot by every television police officer, was told to ham in falsetto to accompany Lynette's shrillness, and then to add a snigger at the end of each line he uttered. Handsome, clear-spoken Terence was ordered to gabble his way through the three parts he played using French, Italian and Russian accents, while the remaining rôles, tackled by young ex-Etonian Gervase, were reborn as Welsh and American for no obvious reason.

"But all those characters are English," Veronica pointed out in bewilderment. "It says in the play that they're English."

"And that's one of the script's many problems," said Belinda.

"What problem? People who are English and live in England usually speak with English accents."

"Yes, but I have to disguise the play's many faults," declared Belinda.

"If the actors simply spoke their lines in normal voices, perhaps the many faults wouldn't be quite so apparent," suggested Veronica. Natalie shook her head, but it was too late for warnings. Olivia Thwaite's radio career was drawing rapidly to its end, and so Veronica had nothing to lose. "The Lynette and Harlan characters are outsiders in England: strangers in an alien country. If the whole cast's foreign, that aspect's missing, completely lost. Just say the lines. Don't bludgeon them to death," she urged the actors.

"I suppose you think that you know how to direct a radio drama," said Belinda, sneeringly superior.

"I hope I've got an inkling with this particular play, especially after writing the original script, working on it with a theatre company, and then doing the radio adaptation." Veronica managed to get the words out from behind a smile, but she had to fight back an overwhelming desire to aim a punch at Belinda's scornful face. "If you ever write anything, you'll understand what I

268

mean. When the lines are said naturally, the dialogue works. It really does."

The actors might have agreed with Veronica, but Olivia Thwaite was a nobody unable to further their careers, while grovelling to Greville could bring them future BBC employment in an overcrowded profession, and they turned to Belinda for guidance.

****

The recording studio was divided down the middle by a glass wall that separated actors and microphones from the BBC production team as well as Veronica, who felt totally isolated but was still gamely arguing to give her script a chance.

"Take the character that Harlan plays, for example. He's based on a man I knew years ago who certainly didn't feel the need to go into falsetto on any occasion," said Veronica, desperate to save her work from ruin, even though Belinda was tapping fingers and sighing impatiently. "I once heard him tell my father his story. Towards the end of the Second World War, he was found wandering through Vienna as a child, so young that he only knew his first name, but he spoke English better than German, and it was assumed that one of his parents had probably been from England originally, but when a British soldier was asked to place the accent, he thought that there was a hint of Australia or New Zealand in it. They never found out anything more, and eventually he acquired the surname Hauser after Kasper."

"Who's Kasper?" asked Natalie, trying to pretend that Veronica's protests were mere chit-chat.

"He was a boy who turned up in Nuremberg during the early nineteenth century. He knew nothing about himself but his name, and couldn't explain who or where he —"

"So Harlan should speak with a German accent," Belinda concluded. She switched on the studio microphone, and announced, "Harlan, think Conrad Veidt or Anton Walbrook —"

"No!" cried Veronica in alarm.

"What now?" demanded Belinda, sighing again as she switched off the microphone, leaving Harlan to gaze blankly at her through the glass wall as he awaited further instruction.

"A German accent would give the whole plot away. Besides, Oskar Hauser spoke much better English than most of the English do. If anything, Harlan ought to sound like a 1930s wireless announcer."

"A foundling would hardly speak like that," decreed Belinda, seizing on yet another fault in the unworthy script. "And a foundling wouldn't have the education to appreciate Beethoven either. I'll select more appropriate music."

"You don't need education to love Beethoven; you only have to listen to his music. The character relies on Beethoven for courage. It's all explained in the final scene," said Veronica, suspicions confirmed that her play remained an enigma to the woman in charge of its radio production. "Beethoven's got to stay. He's really important."

"What happened to him?" asked Natalie, perhaps hoping to avert an imminent punch-up between playwright and director. "Not Beethoven, but the Vienna orphan. Did he track down his mother and find out his parents' story, the way he does in the play, or did you make that bit up?"

"It's total invention. As far as I know, Oskar Hauser never discovered who his parents had been, and so I wrote an ending for him: invented a fascist-fanatic Australian mother and then moved the story to London, in case Oskar ever heard about the play, realized that the character was based on him, and resented me plundering his life for material."

"Oh, I don't think that there's much chance of him coming across your play," said Belinda, consigning Olivia Thwaite and all her works to drama's dustbin. "Besides, it's not believable that a mother would just walk away from her own child."

"It happens," said Veronica.

****

The ordeal was nearly over, her brilliant radio career had definitely gone bung, and the BBC canteen seemed noisily overcrowded, but Veronica made an attempt to appreciate being there among so many famous voices because she knew that the experience would almost certainly never happen to her again. She was indisputably blacklisted, and it felt an honour for Olivia Thwaite to be included with other playwrights who had objected to Belinda Greville's lackadaisical method of directing radio drama.

"You hate what that woman's doing to your script," remarked Lynette Adair, as she followed Veronica to a free table and put her tray down. "But I'm afraid Belinda's just a bored factory worker, churning out plays on a conveyor belt."

"The dialogue's being beaten to a pulp by all that heavy-handed overacting, and simply because Belinda Greville's too arrogant to admit that she hasn't bothered to sit down, read the

271

script and then think about it," lamented Veronica. "All right, so the play's rubbish, but it's *my* rubbish."

"Piers Cavendish wouldn't have been able to get the script commissioned if it really was rubbish."

"Greville told me that it's full of faults and written in a pretentious literary style," wailed Veronica. "That Queen who said she had the word *Calais* burnt on her heart was lucky. I've got a whole sentence branded on mine."

"Take comfort from the fact that Belinda Greville couldn't write a good play to save her life, and yours is good or we wouldn't be feasting on cheese sandwiches in the BBC canteen now," declared Lynette, smiling at Veronica's tormented anguish. "Belinda makes no secret of despising radio drama, and it says volumes about the woman that she still goes on working here in spite of her contempt for the medium. I've often heard Belinda bragging loudly at parties that she's a director, implying theatre or films and never once mentioning the outdated word *radio*, yet for somebody with such lofty ideals, Belinda Greville's mightily impressed by anyone finding their fifteen minutes of fame in a less-than-exalted television soap."

"She told me that she's leaving the BBC soon to direct a film of *Jude The Obscure*."

"Only in her imagination," scoffed Lynette. "Belinda won't escape radio, and it's simply because she likes the regular pay too much as well as the thought of a fat pension. If Belinda had the guts for independent film-making, she'd have taken the gamble years ago. I bet you've done your share of dead-end part-time jobs while you sent out scripts that got rejected, just as I once toiled as a waitress between auditions, yet Greville's chosen to cushion herself in a safe job that she sneers at, and she'll go on producing slipshod work because Belinda thinks it's beneath her dignity to take radio drama seriously. The woman's jealous of people like you, like me, with the courage to chase their dreams regardless of security, but she ought to realize that nobody who isn't prepared to jump into the water can learn how to swim."

Lynette laughed, and she jerked her head to one side, round eyes and peaked nose reminding Veronica of an inquisitive bird, and twenty-five years vanished.

****

Grade 4. Hot pencil-lines of Australian sunlight forcing their way into the room from the sides of shuttered windows. Listless children wilting at desks in the heat. Mrs Staunton on the dais in front of the wide blackboard. "You've got to jump into the water before you can learn how to swim. Remember that."

"But I don't want to swim," Audrey muttered. "I want to act."

****

"Audrey?" gasped Veronica.

"No. Lynette's the name."

"Yes, of course. Sorry. Something you said made me think of a girl I knew years ago as a kid. I used to write plays for a schoolfriend called Audrey to star in. She wanted to be a Hollywood actress."

"My dreams arrived much later in life." Lynette smiled, the fixed and confident smile that Veronica had been seeing on the faces around her for days. Grade 4 faded away, and the upper-class accents of BBC insiders again filled the canteen. "My thespian hopes might not be inborn, but growing up in London was a big influence with all the theatres around. I was a spoilt only child, so there were plenty of birthday and Christmas outings to fuel my imagination. I'll grovel to Greville to help pay the bills, but I'm not on auto-pilot like her. I've got ambitions that I'll turn into reality by working hard for them."

"I was ten when my parents emigrated to Australia chasing the dream of a better life," said Veronica, studying Lynette's face, but the fleeting glimpse of Audrey was now undetectable behind mature features and an aloof expression. "However, I ended up living on a migrant hostel in Victoria the whole time I was there."

"I thought Belinda said that you were from Wagga Wagga?"

"She did," Veronica confirmed, wondering how many born-and-bred Londoners would know that Wagga Wagga was not to be found in Victoria. "I think she considered it some sort of putdown."

. "Of course, and it's so exactly Belinda." Lynette sounded indifferent to Veronica's information, warmth gone from her tone, but perhaps she only liked the sound of Lynette Adair's voice, and the life and times of Olivia Thwaite held no interest whatsoever. "I can't detect the slightest trace of an Aussie accent."

"That's because I was sixteen when my father decided to go back to England, and I tagged along."

"In order to inhabit the land of William Shakespeare," Lynette proclaimed, as patronizing as Belinda at her most disdainful.

"That was only part of the reason. My mother had waltzed off with a man years before, and Dad found it hard to accept that she'd gone for good." Words so easy to say about an episode so difficult to live through. Elaine had never said goodbye. Veronica returned to the hut after school one day, a day like any other, to find a note on top of the chest-of-drawers: an unfolded piece of paper that merely informed whoever it might concern that Elaine had left Watson Valley and would not be returning. Jeff was stunned by the news, and the man who had seemed so strong, so able to control his life by walking away from any problem without a backward glance, went around in a daze. But many years had passed, and Veronica could now hide behind fluency, even pretend that it had all been a story she once told herself, with Jeff and Elaine practically invented characters waiting for a script. "After my mother took flight, Dad became very dependent on me."

"Perhaps to stop you from running off as well."

"Yes, perhaps, although I'm sure that I'd never manage to leave anyone, no matter what. I dread turning into my mother so I'd force myself to put up with just about anything, and that's probably the reason why I've never dared to get married or have children."

"Oh, I don't know. I'm the product of a rock-solid marriage, parents together for ninety years and all that, anniversary celebrations on a regular basis, yet I've avoided commitment like the plague," declare Lynette, her smile unfalteringly bright. "We're a different generation, so we do things differently. How long did you stay on the hostel?"

On the hostel, Lynette had said, not *in* the hostel or *at* the hostel but 'How long did you stay *on* the hostel?'

"Over six years. I think Dad was waiting for my mother to come back." Something that puzzled Veronica at the time because she had no trouble hating Elaine, and for as long as Jeff's daughter could remember, he had claimed that marriage ruined all chance of a man being happy. However, Jeff finally seemed to realize that he was wasting his life, and going home gradually became an obsession almost as if Jeff imagined that he would find and regain his former overconfident self there. By then, Veronica had become a real little Australian with an exhaustive knowledge of gold-mining, merino sheep, desert irrigation, hydro-electric power and the poems of Henry Lawson. She aimed at University in Melbourne, picturing her whole future in Victoria, but Jeff had made up his mind. Veronica even tried pleading that she must stay in Australia until she earned her Argonaut Golden Fleece, but Jeff was adamant. They were going home. "Anyway, I eventually ended up in London again."

Grey cold London. Grey houses huddled together in grey streets crowded with grey-faced people. A drab world of muted colour, bitter wind and rain. A dreary world in which living was an effort and nobody smiled. It had taken Veronica years to see glimpses of beauty behind London's severity.

"Well, you certainly had a very adventurous childhood, Olivia."

"That's my second name," said Veronica. "When we came back to England, I stopped using the first one. I always hated it."

"Not dramatic enough for you?" Again the supercilious tone.

"Far too dramatic in my opinion. It sounded like a motorbike revving up because I was usually called Vron, and Dad refused to change, claiming that he was too old for such feats of memory."

"Fortunately, Lynette Adair sounded OK for an actress, so there was no need to alter it."

"That was lucky."

"Yes, very. Did your father kick up a fuss about you shortening your surname?"

There was a pause, and Lynette realized the mistake she had made. "You said that you shortened your last name from something," she added smoothly.

"Did I?"

"Yes, you did," stated Lynette. She was wary, but as prepared to stand her ground and argue as ever she had been.

"Well, it doesn't matter now," said Veronica.

"What doesn't matter now?" demanded Lynette.

"I mean, it didn't matter about the surname change, because my father never knew. He was dead by then," explained Veronica. "He'd maintained that the world wouldn't see 1970, but it turned out to be the ending of his own world that Dad foretold. He died a few months before the new decade began, and the earth's still spinning."

"So it is," Lynette agreed, with a ringing laugh that was wholly technique and no heart. "Well, I've had all the lunch I ought to eat because I'm rapidly turning into a barrage balloon, and I really should go and sigh with Harlan about his latest romantic disaster. It's been my duty to commiserate with him since we did a Rep season together years ago."

"I wasn't in the hut that morning," said Veronica.

"Sorry?" Lynette stood up, and waved to a group on the other side of the canteen. "See you later. I'd better rush off and dry poor Harlan's tears. He's forever getting targeted by ambitious twenty-year-olds who think he can provide a short-cut to stardom, and so they swear that it's true love, but the minute he introduces them to a more famous friend, they're off like greased lightning."

"I was actually under the Rec, of all places, at the time."

"I'd love to chat a bit longer, but I've simply got to dash and console Harlan's yet-again shattered heart. Nice to have worked with you, Olivia, and I hope that Belinda doesn't get you permanently blacklisted, but you can probably still save the day after you hear a tape of the recording. Just announce how wrong you were to doubt Belinda Greville's directorial brilliance, and everything will be fine. She likes the repentant, because Belinda thinks that she's got a hold over them for ever after. Don't let one self-important and bitter woman wreck your chances of getting some future money out of Beeb radio."

"I just can't grovel that expertly," said Veronica.

"Then it's lucky you didn't go in for acting."

"Audrey was always the star, not me." But Audrey Leyton would have refused to grovel. Audrey Leyton would have spoken her mind and never compromised. Lynette Adair walked away, and for a few seconds Veronica wished that she too had acquired the worldly commonsense to deal realistically with the Belinda Greville situation. Olivia Thwaite's play was no sacred work of literary genius and would soon be forgotten, however well or badly the radio version was directed. But, all the same, fighting for something you believed in felt better than grovelling ever could.

Audrey Leyton had once been a proud fighter, and Lynette Adair was not even a watered-down version. In fact, Audrey would have scorned Lynette's advice to become a toadying flunkey because of a possible future cheque, and it seemed that Clive Leyton had not been the only person to die on that long-gone Australian morning.

14

Ruby Farrell: a mule-headed, sandy-haired girl aged ten, with more ambition than talent, inclined to bully and threaten, not above telling lies to get an enemy into trouble or to save her own skin. Ruby Farrell: the minor cause of a major event.

Grade 4. Sweltering December. Mrs Staunton was correcting arithmetic papers at her desk on the dais in front of the blackboard that ran the full length of the wall, and Veronica felt very insignificant looking up at her, but Mrs Staunton had said that she was there to listen to problems and that any pupil could tell her anything, anything at all.

"What is it, Veronica?" Mrs Staunton spoke absently, continuing to put a cross or a tick beside each answer on the page with machine-like regularity.

"Please can I sit next to somebody else this afternoon, instead of Ruby Farrell?" Veronica had lingered until the other children left the classroom after eating their lunchtime sandwiches, and the unusual silence made her voice sound too loud, as though she had shouted in a church. A line of sunlight forced its way through the window shutters, and specks of dust danced like fireflies in the brightness, dazzling Veronica's eyes.

"Why don't you want to sit next to Ruby?"

"Because I'll have to write two compositions during the test, and I won't have time to check mine properly."

"What do you mean? Why will you need to write two compositions?" Mrs Staunton moved one page of answers to the pile beside her left elbow, and began correcting the next paper.

"The first composition's for Ruby, so that she can copy it underneath the —"

"Get out!" shrieked Mrs Staunton. Arithmetic papers scattered as she jerked upward to glare in scornful fury at the despicable sneak in front of her. "You're in Australia now, and Australians never tell tales, whatever might have happened in your English school. Get out of my sight at once."

Heart pounding with shock, Veronica ran, and kept running down the passageway to the front door. Then she was outside the school gates, and at the top of the garden-lined hill, far from the gossiping groups in the playground. Veronica knew that she could never go back, never face Mrs Staunton again, never escape the shame. For the rest of her life, Veronica Thornthwaite would be known as the girl who snitched to a teacher about Ruby Farrell's cheating. But it had never felt like cheating, any more than helping Audrey with her homework could be described as lying. Ruby wanted to shine in English the way that she occasionally did in arithmetic, and had threatened and finally blackmailed Veronica into writing two compositions each English lesson: an official Thornthwaite one in the exercise book on top of their desk, and a second for Ruby to copy from another exercise book on Veronica's lap. As two entirely separate pieces of work were involved, it seemed to have no connection at all with cheating, and the system functioned perfectly well for Ruby but meant that Veronica was handing in hastily-done work, far below her usual standard, and she wanted a way out that the vindictive Ruby would not resent. Asking to change desks had appeared the ideal solution, especially as Mrs Staunton had so often declared that anything a pupil told her would remain between them, but

Veronica at last understood how very stupid she had been to imagine that she could talk freely to a teacher or to anybody in authority.

There was only one more day of school left before the long summer gap, but what a day it would be. No lessons, a film called *Gypsy Colt,* prizes handed out, along with ice-cream and lollies according to wild rumour, yet Veronica would have to miss all the excitement. Mrs Staunton was certain to tell the other teachers about the contemptible Veronica Thornthwaite, and Colette, daughter of Grade 5's Mrs Norton, often heard snippets of scandal that she immediately passed on in confidence to her closest friends, who promptly sent the news spiralling around the rest of the school in confidence, until the whole world would be pointing at Veronica Thornthwaite and despising her. Argonauts were supposed to be brave and seek adventure, but some things would daunt Jason himself, and had nuclear war destroyed the planet that particular day, one ten-year-old girl might have regarded it as the greatest piece of luck she ever had.

****

"I feel sick," said Veronica, and it was quite true. She did feel sick at the thought of going to school that day and facing Mrs Staunton, as well as the consequences of an afternoon's truancy and the additional shame of Watson Valley's entire population knowing about the disgraced Veronica Thornthwaite.

Elaine, sitting on the sofa and holding a small mirror in one hand, paused in mid-application of crimson lipstick. "You can't be sick, Vron. Nobody's ill on the last day of term. Go over to the canteen and have some breakfast. You'll feel better then."

281

"No, I'll be sick if I eat anything." Another perfectly true statement.

"She can't be trying to skive off: not on the very last day of school," decreed Jeff, that expert on truants and truancy, looking uncharacteristically tidy in the suit he wore to job interviews and weddings. "The end of term's the only day when going to school can be any fun."

Elaine stood up, and pressed the back of her hand against Veronica's forehead. "She doesn't seem to be running a temperature."

"She can't be really ill. Vron's had every disease in existence, so there won't be a measle or mump able to get past that immune system."

Jeff and Elaine were talking as if Veronica could no longer hear them, but they frequently made the mistake of assuming that their daughter was still too young to understand the conversation of adults. "It can't be anything serious when she hasn't got a temperature. Probably just the heat," Elaine decided, returning to her mirror and lipstick.

"Vron, what's happening at school today?" asked Jeff, recalling that he had a suspect to interrogate.

"A film called *Gypsy Colt* and ice-cream and lollies, but I feel sick thinking about them. Can I go back to bed?"

Even Jeff the sceptical capitulated. "You'll have to stay here with Vron, Elaine. I can't miss the chance of working somewhere else. I'm always being lumbered with the night shifts, and I swear Fryer's doing it deliberately, thinking that I won't notice. He's as thick as a plank of wood."

"Rodney's not stupid," said Elaine.

"That Rodney Fryer's a dim-witted buffoon, and I can't stick him and his warrant-officer mentality any more."

"Then go to your interview, but I can't stay with Vron. I'm doing an extra shift this morning. I promised, and you know that we're short-handed as it is. I'll get Dulcie Leyton to keep an eye on Vron, and you should be back by lunchtime anyway. If Dulcie stays outside the door, she won't pick up any germs to pass on to her girls."

"Perhaps we ought to supply Dulcie with some binoculars, and then she can study Vron through the window," said Jeff. "Not that there'll be any germs involved, if you ask me. It's far more likely Vron's simply got indigestion, as the school apparently feasts on ice-cream and sweets as a matter of routine."

"What did you have to eat yesterday, Vron?" Elaine was hoping to find an excuse not to feel guilty about going out, because a morning in an airless Nissen hut with a miserable child would be unendurable when Rodney was waiting for her. Elaine had once thought that a daughter would be a companion, an extension of herself, but Veronica was an entirely separate person, and often as unfathomable as a stranger. "Did you eat a lot of ice-cream at school?"

"The ice-cream's only for today, but I don't want any." Veronica was so thankful to have escaped the worst ordeal of her life that she could have cried with sheer relief. Late-February and the new school year were months away: in fact, so far off that they might never happen as nuclear destruction was handily imminent. "I don't want lollies either, or anything."

"Then you must be desperately ill indeed," remarked Jeff. "All right, we're convinced. Go back to bed, Vron, but even if you feel better later on, promise that you'll stay inside the hut until I get back from my job interview."

"I promise."

"And remember that's an Argonaut's sacred pledge," said Jeff, derisively solemn.

****

"Audrey!" Veronica said in surprise, looking up from the book that she was reading. Stretched out on top of her bed, an official invalid wearing a nightdress in daytime, Veronica recognized the hand and arm thrust through the window slats to open the door's Yale Lock, and she warned, "You'll be late for school."

"Dad told Mum that she isn't to let us go there today, but I'm not missing that film or the ice-cream," whispered Audrey, as she hurried into the room lugging her schoolbag, the other hand frantically flapping to signal the need for quietness. "I'll hide in here until he goes to work. Your mother told Mum about you being disappointed not to see the film today, and Dad heard. We'd all kept quiet about *Gypsy Colt*, so that he couldn't —"

"Audrey!" Despite musical accompaniment by Beethoven, Clive must have heard Veronica say his daughter's name and then the whispered reply, because a fist hammered on the partition wall. "Come back here at once."

Audrey ran past Veronica, and into Jeff and Elaine's room. The lock on its outer door was turned, and Veronica thought that the fugitive must be fleeing up the road, but then she heard the sofa scrape along the floor. Quick-witted Audrey knew that she was unable to outrun Clive, and wanted him to think she had

284

escaped via the open door, while she actually stayed in the only hiding-place the room offered: behind the sofa-bed.

"Where's Audrey?" Clive appeared in the doorway of Veronica's room, his gaze self-possessed, but his voice menacingly loud, a cold rage that she found more frightening than Jeff and Elaine's occasional flare-ups. "Don't bother telling me a string of your usual lies, Veronica Thornthwaite. I heard Audrey's voice. I know that she's in here."

"She isn't," Veronica said automatically, to give Audrey more time to hide herself.

Clive ignored Veronica, and strode into the next room. The sofa was jerked back and Clive returned, a struggling, shrieking, crimson-faced Audrey, using her schoolbag as a weapon, imprisoned in front of him. "You're a liar, Veronica Thornthwaite," he declared, "and liars burn in hell for all eternity."

Audrey kicked at Clive's ankles, but he forced his daughter past Veronica and out of the door. Terrified that he would come back and shout at her again, Veronica leapt off the bed, pulled skirt over nightdress, shoved feet into sandals, and fled from the hut. Sunlight as heavy as a blanket over her shoulders, she ran across the empty road, threw herself down in front of the Rec and rolled beneath it, heart thudding. The dark clay was comfortingly cool and solid, even though she never liked being under any hut, certain that it would instantly collapse and crush her, but that time Veronica felt safe because, if Clive followed, he was too large to fit himself in the narrow space between earth and floorboards. Hoping that no snakes or funnel-web spiders had made a home in her hiding-place, she peered out through straggles of yellowing grass, but there was no sign of a righteously-angry Clive in

285

pursuit. Echoes of Beethoven had accompanied Veronica over the road, but she could hear no other sound at all, which unnerved her. Normality on the hostel to Veronica meant constant noise, children's voices, radio music, laughter and footsteps, not silence, but even the birds and cicadas seemed to be hushed by fear, and she had never felt so alone in her life.

Clive Leyton was right. She told lies, and would probably tell more to dodge future trouble. Her promise to stay inside the hut had been broken before she even remembered having promised, and Dulcie would soon know that Veronica had gone. An Argonaut's sacred pledge, Jeff said mockingly, and his daughter deserved to have fun made of her.

In a fleeting Beethoven lull, an abrupt blast of sound like a car backfiring made Veronica jump, but then the Ninth Symphony took over again, and the hostel remained motionless until the three Leyton girls suddenly appeared from the back of Hut 34 and ran up the hill with the speed of escaped convicts. Audrey, Thelma and Wendy were getting a better head-start than they could have hoped for, especially as more and more minutes went by without Clive emerging in a fury to hunt them down and end all their fun. He was going to be livid, Veronica thought apprehensively, but at least his daughters might get to watch something of *Gypsy Colt* and have a taste of the fabled ice-cream before he caught up with them.

Sensing rather than seeing movement between Huts 34 and 33, Veronica held her breath until a glimpse of Dulcie, carrying the blue plastic box that she used for laundry, told Veronica it had merely been Mrs Leyton, presumably on her way to do some washing. And still Clive stayed inside the hut.

Such peacefulness was bewildering. Veronica had known Clive for enough time to be certain that he would never accept defeat, and yet his children were being allowed to get away with a rebellion that Clive made no effort to end. To defy him was to defy God, he had informed all three of the girls, but it seemed that Clive Leyton was now content to sit meekly in a hut despite the imminent corruption of his daughters by the Hollywood lies that would permeate *Gypsy Colt*. Baffling.

A few minutes later, a man lurched into view at the side of Hut 33 and Veronica froze until she realized that it was only the drunken Mr Yoxall, staggering slightly as he made his way down the path towards the toilet block. And still no Clive Leyton.

Time had apparently stopped, and Veronica felt that she would never know or do anything more in her life except lie under the Rec looking across an empty road to spy on the inert hostel. It could have been ten minutes or it could have been an hour before Beethoven was silenced and Oskar Hauser appeared, probably on his way to a morning shift at the delicatessen because he crossed the road and strolled past the canteen in the direction of the shops. A woman in a pink party dress came down the hill from the houses and walked by the Rec, yellow curls bouncing on her shoulders with each step, making Veronica think of the traditional golden tresses of a fairy-tale princess, and all was silent again until Veronica caught another glimpse of Mrs Leyton, returning with an empty laundry-box in one hand, but then a few seconds later Dulcie re-emerged, trotting between the huts and over the road, heading toward Mr Webb's office.

Mrs Leyton was going to report that Veronica Thornthwaite had left the hut, in spite of promising that she would stay there until her father's return. Mrs Leyton was going to say that Veronica Thornthwaite had lied to her parents as well as to Mr Leyton, and the result would be an endless stream of trouble. Panicking, Veronica squirmed out from under the Rec, ran across the road, jumped up the steps into Hut 34 and, after a glance back to make sure that nobody had been watching, she locked the door behind her.

Dulcie must have noticed Veronica's empty bed from the window, and once again lies were the only solution. Veronica tore off her skirt and sandals, lay down on the sofa, and hoped she would be able to fool everybody into thinking that she had been in her parents' room the whole time. According to Mr Leyton, liars burnt in hell for all eternity, but Veronica had told so many stories that she was already doomed, and so a couple more no longer mattered.

Mrs Leyton's breathless voice got louder, followed by Mr Webb's chatter as he tried to reassure Dulcie, but instead of going into Veronica's room, they hurried past the window and around to the back of Hut 34.

"It's his heart, isn't it?"

"I don't know, Mrs Leyton, but the doctor should be here soon. I told him that it was an emergency."

The voices came clearly through the partition wall, and Veronica had actually thanked Mrs Staunton's God before recalling her place among the damned. But if Mr Leyton was ill, perhaps the doctor would make him stay in bed, which meant that Audrey, Wendy and Thelma could see all of *Gypsy Colt* while eating ice-cream, and Jeff might never know that his daughter had broken her promise to stay inside the hut. It was better than a

Christmas present. In fact, it was better than Christmas Day itself, and Veronica dared to relax.

First a doctor, then the police arrived, and Veronica could have been listening to the wireless, to one of the Argonaut weekend plays, as nothing was real because death happened to strangers unless nuclear war started and entirely wiped out all human life. She put down her book to pay closer attention, but death could have no connection with an ordinary day and someone who had been shouting at her only an hour earlier. The doctor was wrong, but the police might take Mr Leyton away to a hospital, and at least his temporary absence would mean that Audrey and her sisters had an unexpectedly happier Christmas. Then Veronica heard somebody say *gun*.

It was not that she really thought Audrey had taken Jeff's Luger; it was more to reassure herself that the pistol remained in place and, careful to make as little sound as possible, Veronica eased Jeff's suitcase out from under the sofa-bed. By day, the gun was wrapped in a woollen scarf and kept inside an old tin box that had once held biscuits; only at night did Jeff leave it on the chest-of-drawers, beneath the newspaper that he imagined stopped Veronica knowing of the Luger's existence. The tin was still inside the suitcase, but with its lid open and the scarf uncoiled. The pistol had gone.

****

"It's a secret. You mustn't ever breathe a word," Veronica had said. "Even I'm not supposed to know about the gun."

"I won't tell anyone, cross my heart," Audrey had promised, gazing in awe at the contents of the tin box.

"My Dad was walking down a street in Berlin at the very end of the war, on VE Day itself, when a German Colonel leapt out of the shadows, a pistol aimed right at Dad's heart, ready to kill him. But Dad jumped forward and grabbed the Colonel's arm, fighting like a tiger to get hold of that gun. They struggled for what seemed hours, a life and death struggle, until suddenly there was a loud bang. The Luger had gone off, and my Dad thought for one awful moment that he'd been killed. Then the German crumpled slowly to the ground, dead, shot through the heart by one of his own bullets."

"Gosh!" said Audrey.

"That's what the gun's called: a Luger, and there's always a bullet inside it so Dad can shoot anybody who breaks into the hut and tries to kill us."

"Gosh!" said Audrey.

"If you just point the gun at someone's heart and then press that trigger, you can kill anybody you want to, anybody at all, anybody in the whole world."

"Gosh!" said Audrey.

****

In a way, Clive Leyton had died because of a girl he never knew: Ruby Farrell, the sandy-haired pebble whose actions sent out ripples that turned into the tidal wave engulfing him. If Ruby had not threatened to tell Mrs Staunton a lie about Veronica Thornthwaite cheating in the weekly arithmetic test, and therefore blackmailed her victim into writing extra compositions, Veronica would not have tried to talk to a teacher about the problem and then faked illness the next day to avoid school. Elaine would not have gone to the Leyton side of the hut to ask Dulcie to keep an eye on Veronica, and Clive might not have found out that his daughters were on the brink of being corrupted by an MGM children's film entitled *Gypsy Colt*.

Perhaps now living a blameless life in an Australian suburb among people unaware of the fearsome reputation she acquired in Grade 4, Ruby Farrell would never know what she had unleashed in her efforts to get a supply of ready-written compositions.

Or was it too convenient to put the blame on a ten-year-old bully? Clive Leyton had been quite right in maintaining that Veronica Thornthwaite told lies. If she had had the courage to tell Ruby Farrell to do her worst, Clive might have lived, but Veronica was a coward, and he had died because of it.

Could a coward pass the buck on to Clive Leyton himself, and the egotism that made him believe a voice in his head must belong to none other than a universe's almighty creator in person? Blaming one man's arrogance was the easiest option of all, and that arrogance had alienated a second witness who chose to remain silent. Veronica knew that Oskar Hauser must have heard the Luger shot, despite his claim of a loud-music alibi, but then he would have seen the three Leyton girls running up the hill, and realized that, whatever had happened, they would not desert their mother. Oskar left events to sort themselves out, and as a full account of that morning would certainly implicate Clive Leyton's family in the death, Oskar had deliberately edited his testimony. It seemed fitting that the main character in Olivia Thwaite's first successful script, written lies as Clive Leyton might have termed it, should be based on Oskar Hauser.

15

"We usually go for a drink after a recording, but it's too late now because of all the time-wasting," announced Belinda, with a pointed glance at Veronica so that the actors would know precisely who was responsible for depriving them of a free glass of wine.

"I've got to race off anyway," said Lynette. "I'm chasing the possibility of a fifteen-second appearance and three lines in a drama-docu about Thackeray."

"That's a coincidence," claimed Belinda, not to be outshone. "I'm having dinner with a film producer, but I can't say another word more on the subject. In fact, I've probably said too much already. I'm bound by a Non-Disclosure Agreement."

Whether or not the actors believed her, a cannily grovelling chorus of admiration gathered around Belinda, and followed her down the corridor into the lift. The doors closed behind them, and they were gone without any goodbyes.

"Belinda's actually on her way to a pottery evening class," laughed Natalie. "It was in her diary. Perhaps the film producer will be there as well, throwing clay at a wheel."

It was something of a comfort to know that the haughty Belinda Greville felt obliged to lie in order to impress people, but Veronica was too defeated by events to smile.

"I'm sorry that things didn't work out, Olivia," said Natalie, taking it for granted that she would never see Veronica again. "But if you script a film one day, I'll make a point of letting Belinda know about it, I promise."

And that was that.

Veronica walked out of Broadcasting House, and Olivia Thwaite's career in radio drama ended. Standing by the circular portico of All Souls Church, Lynette Adair was talking to Harlan Dean, but when she caught sight of Veronica, Lynette thrust an arm through his, and hurried him away in the direction of Oxford Street. Audrey had been hurrying away the last time Veronica saw her on the hostel, so many years earlier that it felt more like recalling a film than ever being real life. For a split-second, Veronica was back under the Rec in the heat of an Australian summer morning, and Audrey and her sisters vanished from sight as they ran up the hill, just as Lynette and Harlan vanished into a London crowd.

Did Audrey really believe that Veronica would cause trouble after keeping quiet for so many years? Perhaps Veronica was merely a reminder of an incident that Audrey had managed to push to the back of her mind. Whoever killed Clive Leyton, Audrey was the person who supplied the gun and Audrey the one furiously angry with him, but Audrey had only been ten years old and another ten-year-old covered for her in line with Mrs Staunton's juvenile rules of honourable behaviour: rules that were still in force. Veronica had more in common with the despised Elaine than felt comfortable.

The London around her was cold and dark, but Veronica smiled at the idea of being homesick for a Nissen hut, and the only real regret was that Jeff had not lived long enough to know of his daughter's minor success as a playwright, despite the BBC fiasco. However, rather than cower because of one defeat, Veronica was prepared to fight and work for what she hoped to achieve, and Belinda Greville had no control over the worlds of stage, film or television. An Argonaut had imagined the Golden Fleece to be almost within her grasp, but there was still a lot further to travel.

THE END